# KNOWLEDGEABLE WOMEN

# KNOWLEDGEABLE WOMEN

*Structuralism and the Reproduction of Elites*

Sara Delamont

ROUTLEDGE
London and New York

First published in 1989 by
Routledge
11 New Fetter Lane, London EC4P 4EE
29 West 35th Street, New York NY 10001

© 1989 Sara Delamont

Typeset by LaserScript Limited, Mitcham, Surrey.
Printed in Great Britain by Billings of Worcester

British Library Cataloguing in Publication Data

Delamont, Sara, 1947 -
  Knowledgeable women : structuralism and the reproduction of elites.
  1. Women. Education. Social aspects
  370.19'345

ISBN 0-415-01599-5

Library of Congress Cataloging-in-Publication Data

Delamont, Sara, 1947 -
  Knowledgeable women : structuralism and the reproduction of elites /
  Sara Delamont.
      p.    cm.
  Bibliography: p.
  Includes indexes.

ISBN 0-415-01599-5

  1. Educational sociology. 2. Structuralism. 3. Women—Education.
  4. Elite (Social sciences) I. Title.
  LC191.D445 1989
  370.19—dc19                                    89–19910
                                                    CIP

# Contents

# Contents

# Preface and acknowledgements

My grandmother, Irene Kimber (*née* Hunt) was a pupil at Manchester High School for Girls, and apparently had a gift for languages. She was accepted by Manchester University but her father did not allow her to go. My mother, Lisa Delamont (*née* Kimber) attended the Oxford High School for Girls and won a place at St Anne's College, Oxford to read English. Her father disapproved of 'blue stockings' and refused her permission to take up the place. I went to Fareham Grammar School for Girls, where I was lucky enough to be taught by some intelligent and inspiring women, and got a place at Girton College, Cambridge. This book is dedicated to the memory of Irene Kimber and Lisa Delamont, to Joan Addison, Sybil Hollins, Alice James, Rosemary Cook, and my other teachers at Fareham, and to my father, Dean Delamont, who encouraged me to go to Girton.

I am grateful to Paul Atkinson for the support he has given all my work for the past fifteen years. He is always a tough critic, but equally a believer in the merits of the ideas I am struggling to express. Many of the themes in this book have preoccupied me as long as I have known him, and if I am still illogical or incoherent it is not for want of his advice.

This book was written while on study leave from University College, Cardiff, at the University of Sussex. I am grateful to colleagues at both those universities, and at Leicester University, for intellectual companionship since 1973. In particular Gerry Bernbaum, Tom Whiteside, Tony Coxon, Kevin McCormick, Carol Dyhouse, Barry Cooper, Steve Shapin, Harry Collins and Sydney Holloway helped me clarify my ideas on different themes in this volume.

The material for the book was only gathered with the help of the library staff at University College, Cardiff, especially those of the inter-library loan desk; Roy Kirk and Barbara Barr of the Leicester University School of Education Library, and the library staff at Sussex University.

The book was typed in draft by Joan Ryan, Cynthia Diggins, Lyndsey Nicholas, Elizabeth Renton, Irene Williams, Lillian Lewis, Myrtle Robins and Margaret Ralph. The final version was typed by Myrtle Robins.

# Part I
## Introductory themes

# 1

## Introduction: towards a structuralist sociology of education

There is a set of activities which are prohibited to members of each sex: men are forbidden to wash dishes or laundry, to sew, to sweep the floor; women are forbidden to climb trees and prune vines.... Males are more concerned with what the peasants call... products of the air, that is, the things that grow well above ground level.... Women are generally in charge of... things which grow in or near the soil.... The following adage... points to the difference between the sexes: 'males look up, females look down'. This adage has three distinct meanings: it refers to the differences between male and female genitalia; it refers to the sexual division of labour; and, finally, it refers to a much wider utilization of the dimension opposition above/below as analogically related to oppositions such as heaven/hell, life/death, mind or spirit/body, purity/corruption, socially beneficial/antisocial.

> (Pina-Cabral 1986: 83-4)

Pina-Cabral conducted anthropological research in a remote corner of northern Portugal. The peasants' belief system about sex roles and pollution which he discovered, and which is quoted in summary here, may seem an odd place to start a book about the education of elite women in industrial societies. In fact, as this book will show, similar binary oppositions between male and female, purity and pollution, strength and weakness, underly much of the superficially rational thought and research on the education and training of elite women. We may feel that the peasants of the Alto Minho have quaint superstitions, such as a belief that women must not climb trees while we are free of such notions. Yet the arguments deployed in contemporary industrialized societies to explain the lack of

1

women Nobel prize winners, judges, or headteachers turn out, when analysed, to be grounded in a similar kind of oppositional logic. Sociologists of education have not paid enough attention to the symbolic, underlying, unconscious, and inexpressible oppositional logic that determines our responses to a range of issues about the curriculum, educational structures, and careers. This book argues that studying educational beliefs from a structuralist perspective, akin to the one used by Pina-Cabral on the folklore of Portuguese peasants, will be both revealing in itself and will also revitalize the sociology of education.

This book focuses on the education and professional training of clever, mainly middle- and upper-class women. It does so partly just because they are a valid topic for a book, and any suggestion otherwise is purely made from inverted snobbery. Equally important, though, is the function that this group serves in the sociology of education. It crystallizes, highlights, illuminates, throws into relief, and magnifies flaws or *lacunae* in the existing theories and data collections. In particular the book argues that the literature on cultural reproduction, on professions and professionalization, on social mobility, and on the internal organization of schools and their curricula is flawed by neglecting the reproduction of elites in society, and especially failing to compare the male and female elite systems.

This chapter explains the reasons for offering a structuralist perspective on the sociology of education, then outlines its feminism, and sets out the structure of the remainder of the book. The central argument which underlies the volume is that the sociology of education is desperately in need of a new look. The subject matter and the theories advanced have become stale and familiar, like the recurrent 'crises' in the educational system itself. Familiarity is the biggest hurdle the educational researcher faces, and this book offers a way of challenging the familiarity. Sociology of education has become, to quote Chesterton: 'full of tangled things, and texts, and aching eyes; and gone is all the innocence of anger and surprise'. This volume, attempting to practise what I preached in a controversial attack on my own specialism of school and classroom ethnography (Delamont 1981, 1983d), sets out to make the familiar strange. The analysis offered here, following M.F.D. Young's (1971) injunction that we should 'make' our problems, not 'take' them as presented to us, uses structuralism, gender, and the literature from areas of sociology other than education, to make new problems out of the 'tangled things' which

2

are giving us 'aching eyes'. The use of a structuralist perspective, and the focus upon gender divisions in society, are equally important features of the book; both are employed to challenge our taken-for-granted assumptions and as ideas that are good to think with.

## Why structuralism?

The theoretical perspective of the book is unusual. Structuralism has had little impact on British sociology, compared to anthropology, linguistics and literary studies. It is particularly rare in the sociology of education, as Atkinson (1981a, 1985) has argued. The reason for using it here is simple – it is the theoretical perspective which I find most powerful at the macro-level. For me, there is no other theoretical approach which carries such explanatory power and makes sense of so much. The approach is set out in chapter 2, and the central concepts from structuralism used in the book are explained and exemplified there. There are however other aspects of the use of anthropological structuralism which deserve attention in their introduction.

A great deal of the sociology of education, especially as it is summarized in text books, is dull. The leading introductions to the field do not make it seem exciting or even thought-provoking. Taking a structuralist perspective is intended to revitalize the area by several deliberate tactics. The perspective is intended to lift our 'aching eyes' from the 'tangled things' to enable a fresh insight.

First, structuralism is concerned to 'decentre the subject' – that is to focus our attention upon underlying structures in which the individual person is only one element. Doing this is a useful form of shock treatment: it jolts us into seeing educational phenomena in a new light.

Second, using anthropological theories forces us to think about different aspects of education (myths, rituals, pollution beliefs) and other cultures which are one excellent strategy for making the too, too familiar nature of education strange. This is an argument outlined in Delamont (1981) and developed further during this book.

Third, structuralism offers some ways in which sexual inequalities in previous educational writing can be both exposed and understood.

Fourth, there are some important women theorists whose ideas

3

can be used – something badly lacking in conventional sociology of education and the theoretical knowledge traditionally drawn upon. There is an urgent need for role models who are theorizing women. Mary Douglas and Shirley Ardener deserve a central place in the sociology of education for their ideas, but once enthroned at the new centre of the discourse they will be role models for women students in the sociology of education.

Chapter 2 outlines the version of structuralism used in this book, where anomalous and ambiguous abominations stalk our cosmologies. This introduction now turns to the reasons for focusing on gender in education.

Why gender divisions or 'Why would a man want to read this book'? Shirley Ardener (1985) reports that one of her male colleagues confessed that he wanted to read the collection of papers she edited called *Perceiving Women* but 'couldn't bring himself to'. Men interested in education may wonder why they should steel themselves to read this book, given that its subject matter is women's education. The flippant reply to such doubts must be to appear less of a wimp than that male colleague of Shirley Ardener's! More seriously, the structuralist perspective is novel, and together with a focus on elite women, makes many aspects of education strange.

An important caveat must be made here. Although the empirical focus of this book is elite women (and what I mean by elite is defined below), the women are used to illustrate general themes. The book is not primarily 'about' women as women: it is about how looking at society through women's position makes the familiar strange (Delamont 1981, 1987a). Elite women are a lens for focusing on society in a particular way. Believers in feminist methodology, or in any other separatism in social science, are unlikely to be sympathetic to this way of using women to illuminate the sociology of education.

Evelyn Fox Keller (1985:3) reports how a former professor of hers heard she had been doing research on women and science. He asked what she had learnt about women. She replied 'It's not women I am learning about so much as men. Even more, it is science.' She continued: 'The widespread assumption that a study of gender and science could only be a study of women still amazes me.' For Keller 'science' is socially constructed just as 'male' and 'female' are – and all three social constructs should be subjected to scrutiny. The perspective is the same in this book – though about women and education it tells us more about education than women. Fox Keller hoped that men interested in science would find her analysis illuminating. The purpose of this text is to encourage men and women to think about both structuralism and gender in a novel way.

## The empirical focus: women's education

This book is a contribution to the sociology and social history of education, as well as to women's studies. It addresses central topics in the sociology of education – class, knowledge, power and cultural reproduction – via key problems in the education of women. It is written in the belief that good social science is non-sexist, but good feminist scholarship can only be built on solid theoretical foundations, sound empirical material, and analyses that male social scientists can see to be appropriate.

Essentially this book focuses on women in education both because they are an interesting topic on which much remains to be written and because, when gender divisions are highlighted, many hitherto taken-for-granted features of society are made anthropologically strange. Using the insights of that strangeness we can proceed to novel accounts of educational issues.

It might appear that everything which could be written about women and education has been produced, for since the rise of the new feminist movement in the late 1960s there has been a rapid growth in research on 'women's studies'. In educational research there is now an American bibliography with 1,134 items (Wilkins 1979) and ample material to fill a *World Yearbook of Education* (Acker *et al.* 1984). While the research activity captured in such yearbooks and bibliographies has been refreshing in the new perspectives it has opened up on all stages of education (from pre-school through to graduate school) and has raised interesting issues about schooling, there are also weaknesses in its product. Many topics have not been adequately investigated – including the education of elite women – and the new research on women has been poorly integrated with the rest of the subject. The fifteen years of research have produced a ghetto called 'women's studies' rather than any change in mainstream educational research. Thus while Kay Wilkins's (1979:x) introduction to her bibliography *Women's Education in the United States* claims that 'The impact of the women's liberation movement on educational research has been very strong' her evidence for this claim is minimal. Appendix 1 (p.269) shows the impact of the new feminist scholarship on textbook authors in the sociology of education, and on the field of adolescent cultures. The material in that appendix contradicts Wilkins's statement. Both the introductory textbooks and the publications on adolescence show little sign of the impact of the women's movement.

Banks (1976) in a review of thirty years research in the sociology of education highlights recent work on sex inequalities as one of the field's achievements. It is, however, an achievement which is not yet fully realized. One of the ways in which the work on women has been limited is by its emphasis on working-class girls in education, a bias which this book attempts to redress. The next section explains why this volume focuses on elite women and outlines how the term elite is used in it.

## Why elites? Some background to the argument

In so far as this book uses historical material on the education of clever elite women, it builds on my earlier work on the history of education for ladies (Delamont 1978a, 1978b). The contemporary analyses it contains build on my ethnographic work at St Luke's – a public school for girls in a Scottish city – where I did my Ph.D fieldwork. The research, consisting of participant observation of fourteen- and fifteen-year olds, has been described elsewhere (Delamont 1973, 1976a, 1976b, 1983d, 1984a, 1984b, 1984c) and is not recapitulated here. However there is a lesson about the sociology of education in the reception of the findings. For a variety of reasons detailed elsewhere (Delamont 1984a) the thesis was never published as a monograph such as Hargreaves (1967), Lacey (1970), Ball (1981) or Nash (1973). While it would be *hubris* to speculate that a monograph would have had a status in the sociology of education approaching that of Sharp and Green (1975) or Willis (1977), the data are interesting. In practice, commentators who do refer to the study frequently reject it as 'abnormal' and 'irrelevant' to mainstream sociology because it is about an elite girls' school. For example, Rosemary Deem (1978: 40) dismisses the whole ethnography (without citing the thesis) by saying that 'in any case the girls studied are a quite atypical group in class terms' as if that made them unworthy of research attention.

The sociology of education and feminist scholarship on

education have suffered from this form of inverted snobbery. Authors in both are more interested in studying groups less privileged than themselves, and therefore neglect elites. This point has been made by Dell Hymes and the contributors to *Reinventing Anthropology* such as Laura Nader (1974), and by Connell *et al.* (1982). Nader argues that anthropologists have focused far too much on the poor and dispossessed, and those who are powerless. She points out that the powerful and wealthy are not only interesting and valid objects for study in themselves but that 'studying "up" as well as "down" would lead us to ask many "commonsense" questions in reverse'. Connell and his team conducted research in both working-class high schools with high drop-out rates and elite private secondary schools preparing wealthy pupils for university. As Connell *et al.* (1982: 26-7) argue:

> Notoriously, sociologists look 'down' and not 'up'. A good deal of research was done on what was going wrong with Rockwell High and the Roberts, very little on what was going right with Auburn College and the Phelans.

Connell and his co-authors show that understanding why an elite school like Auburn College is able to engage its girls in an active relationship with academic knowledge is just as important as grasping why so many pupils at state comprehensives fail to become involved with their curriculum. This book is grounded in an agreement with that view. It is an attempt to use data from two unacceptable sources, elite groups and women, to revitalize the whole subject.

Connell and his colleagues studied three elite girls' schools, and their findings are strikingly similar to mine from St Luke's. In both studies the education of girls who are both clever and upper-middle class is treated seriously. This volume is concerned with elite women in that double sense: women and girls who are both clever and either born into the professional class or rise into it. It is about women doctors and doctors' daughters; women professors and professors' wives; and female scientists and scientists' womenfriends.

There are other elites in Britain which are not discussed in the book. Heath (1981) divides the top social class in Britain into three sectors: owners of capital and entrepreneurs; top managers in large bureaucracies; and manipulators of knowledge (the traditional 'professionals'). All three sectors should be subject to sociological analysis; women's roles in all three are a neglected research area. In Thatcher's Biitain the first two sectors are in the ascendency, and sociologists ought to be examining them. This book is almost entirely about the third sector: the new middle class, or professional intelligentsia. There are three reasons for this focus. First, it is this sector that those most successful in the education system entered (at least until the mid-1970s) as their first choice of occupation. Consequently these occupations are of particular interest to the sociologist of education. Second, this group have been the most enthusiastic proponents of women's education : they began it, they developed it, and their daughters do best in it. Third, the goal of the pioneers of women's education was entry to that sector of the top social stratum; a goal which after 150 years of struggle is now being achieved.

Women in business and finance are important, so too are the attitudes of senior managers and owners of capital towards women's education. Neither features in this book because it is about the new middle class, not the old.

## The structure of the book

The book is divided into four sections: introductory material, historical material, contemporary dilemmas in women's schooling and adult lives, and conclusions about current debates. The central concern of the volume is cultural and social reproduction, epitomized in the work of Pierre Bourdieu and Basil Bernstein, set in their proper intellectual context as structuralist anthropologists like Mary Douglas (see Atkinson 1981a and 1985 for a parallel argument). The structuralism used throughout the book is explained and exemplified in chapter 2, so readers familiar with Mary Douglas, the Ardeners, Bernstein and Bourdieu may wish to skip that chapter. Chapter 3 illustrates the notion of women's role in cultural reproduction with the empirical examples of Connell *et al.* (1981) and my own St Luke's material.

The second section of the book, containing three chapters (4, 5 and 6), follows. These chapters demonstrate the analytic power of the structuralist programme by applying it to themes in the history of elite women's education from 1850-1945.

The third section, containing chapters 7, 8, 9 and 10, uses the same structuralist focus to examine the contemporary ideology which constrains the schooling of elite girls, the careers of women teachers in contemporary society, the education and careers of women in elite occupations, and women's role in the cultural reproduction of Britain's elite. The final section concludes the book by examining how contemporary educational policy issues are illuminated by the structuralist perspective. The structuralist ideas will be applied to the findings of the existing literature on elite social mobility, career success in science and medicine, and women's role in creating and reproducing cultural capital. Each of the topics re-examined in this volume is a familiar one, so that the reader's appreciation of the arguments is not impeded by unfamiliar content. As all the topics focus on aspects of elite women's education in Britain, the USA or Australasia since 1850 the book can be read simply as a contribution to the growing (but still small) body of material on that subject. However, the arguments are more far-reaching than the empirical topics to which they are applied in this volume, and I hope no one reads it purely as a book on women's education.

Mary Douglas (1973:11) has written of the 'heavy social load that is carried by apparently innocent-looking taxonomic systems'. The chapters which follow will show how seemingly trivial issues – such as the prohibition on trousers in the English ladies cricket team, and on women in the Alto Minho region of Portugal pruning vines – are elements in taxonomic systems which carry the enormously heavy load of cultural reproduction in the education system.

# 2

## Cultural capital and muted groups:
## the theoretical perspective of the volume

When the proverb says: 'Man is the lamp of the outside and woman the lamp of the inside,' it is to be understood that man is the true light, that of the day, and woman the light of the darkness, the dark light; moreover she is, of course, to the moon what man is to the sun....One is not justified in saying that the woman is locked up in the house unless one also observes that the man is kept out of it, at least during the day. As soon as the sun has risen he must...be in the fields or at the assembly house....The man who stays too long in the house during the day is either suspect or ridiculous.

(Bourdieu 1971)

In this extract from Pierre Bourdieu's analysis of the Berber house (and world view) lies the theme of this chapter. Bourdieu's anthropological research in Algeria does not usually figure in British sociology of education books, and the prominence it is given here is an essential aspect of this book's unusual slant on some familiar material. Central to the analysis used in the volume is the work of Mary Douglas, Shirley and Edwin Ardener, Edmund Leach, and, in so far as they have all drawn on his work, Lévi-Strauss. The educational theories of Pierre Bourdieu and Basil Bernstein are located, unusually for a British book, squarely in that tradition, and not in their more usual place at the head of a motley crew of curriculum theorists. This volume is, therefore, a structuralist analysis of certain key topics in the sociology of education.

There have recently (Gibson 1984; Sarup 1983) been two introductory books on structuralism and education. They differ from this one in two main ways: neither credits Douglas, Leach and

10

the Ardeners with anything interesting to say about education; and, even more oddly, neither analyses the work of Bernstein and Bourdieu within the intellectual tradition they are outlining. In both books the latter two theorists are dismissed in short sections and made to seem marginal to any structuralist analysis of educational institutions or practices in contemporary Britain. Both authors appear to see more analytic potential in the work of Roland Barthes. This volume, in contrast, places Bernstein and Bourdieu at the centre of a structuralist sociology of education. In this endeavour it follows, and can be seen as parasitic upon, the exegesis of Basil Bernstein performed by Paul Atkinson. Paul Atkinson (1981a, 1985) has recently interpreted the work of Basil Bernstein in a new way by placing him squarely into that continental tradition of structuralist analyses of social phenomena.

This chapter outlines the central concepts from each of the key theorists (Douglas, the Ardeners, Bourdieu, Bernstein) whose work is drawn on in this book, with an example from current educational issues to illustrate the potential of the ideas. Before plunging into this, however, it is worth examining Lemert's (1981) explanation for the relative ignorance about, coupled with hostility to, French ideas in Anglo-Saxon discourse. Lemert argues that, apart from the language barrier (and few Anglo-Saxons scholars read French well), there is a cultural gap between the Anglo-Saxon and Francophone worlds inhabited by scholars. He claims that the small, Paris-based intellectual community shares a common culture and therefore fails to make explicit much of what its work is about. He writes:

> French writing is.... very often shaped in and by a literary space unknown to most foreigners. This is the space between the surface of the published text and the social deep structure of the *tout Paris* debates which exert their pressure on the author. This is why.... many of us are frustrated by that large portion of French writing in the human sciences which makes constant – though often uncited – reference to what others are saying.... We search for frequently non-existent footnotes.... The Parisian author... often finds documentation superfluous because 'everyone knows' that the reference is to Sartre.... or to Aron, or whoever. (p.5)

Lemert goes on to explain many of the features of Francophone (Parisian) intellectual life which are baffling to the outsider. He

11

warns that isolating Bourdieu from his field, his territory, is an invitation to be confused by his work. Accordingly Lemert urges his reader to work through all the papers he has gathered together, rather than treat them as an *hors d'oeuvres* tray. In this volume the work of Bourdieu is wrenched away from Parisian debate but, because it is juxtaposed with ideas from other authors working in the same Francophone, Durkheimian tradition (Bernstein, Douglas, Ardener, Leach and Lévi-Strauss), the theories make more sense than they do when contrasted with British Fabianism (e.g. Halsey, Heath and Ridge 1980).

The reader may feel that all the scholars whose theories are drawn upon in this volume are either unknown in the sociology of education, or incomprehensible, or rendered infuriating by conflicting interpretations, or indeed all three. My intention is that by the end of the volume the explanatory power of the theoretical ideas will have been made clear. In this chapter the theoretical perspective of the book is set out, but before the exposition begins, a *caveat* must be issued.

Precisely because the ideas used in this book are opaque and difficult, I make no claim to providing an authoritative, definitive, or indeed accurate account of the authors' theories. The perspective offered is my own interpretation of structuralist theory: of cultural capital, of cultural reproduction, of muted groups, and of *habitus* and symbolic violence. Bourdieu, Bernstein, Douglas and the Ardeners will probably not recognize their ideas, and they must bear no responsibility for them as I have transmitted them.

## The Durkheimian tradition

The theoretical approach used in this book derives from Emile Durkheim (1858-1917). The ideas of Durkheim's which have dominated Anglo-Saxon sociologists' work have been popularized via Radcliffe-Brown , a founder of structural functionalism. These ideas influenced the American sociologist Talcott Parsons and dominated the sociology of education taught to a complete generation of British social scientists who studied at the London School of Economics (LSE). In France, Durkheim's nephew, Marcel Mauss, popularized a different aspect of his work which came into Anglo-Saxon scholarship via Lévi-Strauss (1908–). Thompson (1982) and Giddens (1978) both make this point clearly.

Lévi-Strauss, latterly Professor of Social Anthropology at the College de France, is the most controversial and thought-provoking anthropologist in the world. Bourdieu belongs in the French tradition, as Lemert (1981) has shown, drawing on the structuralist legacy of Marx and Durkheim.

Edmund Leach (1954, 1961, 1970, 1976) popularized these structuralist ideas in Britain, becoming a controversial figure himself in the process. Mary Douglas (1966, 1970, 1973, 1975, 1980, 1982a, 1982b) has continued a parallel task within social anthropology, and it is in this Durkheimian tradition that Shirley and Edwin Ardener work (E. Ardener 1972, 1975; S. Ardener 1975, 1978, 1985).

Leach, Douglas, Bourdieu and the Ardeners are all recognizably anthropologists who have conducted foreign fieldwork and are at home in exotic cultures. Bernstein may seem a strange companion for these seasoned fieldworkers, having spent his whole career in central London. He is undeniably a Durkheimian, as he admitted in his much quoted remark: 'I have yet to find *any* social theorist whose ideas are such a source (at least to me) of understanding what the term *social* entails' (1977a: 17).

It is usually assumed that Bernstein is talking here about his period at LSE, and referring to the Anglo-Saxon Durkheim. In fact, as Paul Atkinson (1981a, 1985) has demonstrated, much of Bernstein's work makes more sense as a contribution to the French, structuralist tradition in social science, deriving from the Durkheimian via Mauss and Lévi-Strauss. It is precisely because Bernstein's work is related to the French structuralists that it can be allied to the theories of Mary Douglas (1966). And, while Bernstein makes no references to the Ardeners' work, nor they to his, there is an important congruence between the two bodies of theory.

In the following sections the ideas used in this book which have been adapted from each branch of structuralism are illustrated in turn. The sections are called 'Central ideas adapted from X' because no claim is made that the scholar's ideas are accurately reproduced, that all a scholar's ideas are covered, or that the concepts are seen as central by the scholars themselves.

My first theoretical approach is that of Shirley and Edwin Ardener (1975) and this is perhaps the least known branch of structuralism in the sociology of education. Yet, as I hope to show by the end of this volume, their ideas on 'muted groups' are a potentially powerful explanatory device in education.

## The central ideas from Shirley and Edwin Ardener

The central idea used in this book which has been adapted from the work of Shirley and Edwin Ardener is that of dominant and muted groups. This idea was put forward in Ardener, E. (1972) and further developed in Ardener, S. (1975). They have subsequently inspired a set of volumes emanating from a series of women's studies seminars in Oxford, published as Ardener (1975, 1978, 1981), Burman (1979), Jacobus (1979), Hutter and Williams (1981), Holden (1983), Callan and Ardener (1984), Hirschon (1984) and Caplan (1987). Shirley Ardener (1985) has written a brief reflection on the decade of publications from this group. The idea of dominant and muted groups was used by Delamont and Duffin (1978: 11-14) to illuminate material on nineteenth-century feminist campaigns, and is used in this chapter to focus particularly on teenage girls and their world view.

The factor which attracted me to the use of anthropological work as a source of illumination for historical data is the subtlety of the Ardeners' use of dominant and muted groups, rather than a simple model of male oppression, as an explanatory device. This argument can be used with profit to analyse aspects of Victorian female experience, as chapters 3, 4 and 5 show, and data on contemporary scientific and professional work, as chapter 9 reveals.

Shirley Ardener has expressed the idea of dominant and muted groups in the following way. Every group in a society generates and shares common models of society and of sections of society so that, for example, Victorian bourgeois women shared a model of bourgeois society and a model of middle-class women, plus models of servants' worlds, proper schools, and so on. However, Victorian males of the middle classes also had their models of these things, and because of the way society was structured, it was the men's models which, if any discrepancies existed, were sure to predominate. As Ardener, S. (1975) argues:

> a society may be dominated or overdetermined by the model (or models) generated by one dominant group within the system. This dominant model may impede the free expression of alternative models of their world which subdominant groups may possess, and perhaps may even inhibit the very generation of such models. Groups dominated in this sense find it necessary to structure their world through the model (or models) of the

dominant group, transforming their own models as best they can in terms of the received ones.

The Ardeners have suggested that women typically form such a muted, inarticulate group, but there may be others, formed or defined by criteria other than sex. Gypsies, deviants and the young may be seen as good examples of such muted groups. The argument so far has considerable similarities with ideas about the 'marginality' of female adolescents (Powell and Clarke 1976) and Kraditor's (1968) discussion of 'spheres', but we argue that it has more potential for depth and subtlety. The concept of the model as used by Ward (1965), Douglas and the Ardeners is capable of great sophistication.

Thus, models are said to exist at different levels of consciousness and generality. The Ardeners suggest that while both dominant and muted groups probably generate ideas of social reality at deep levels, the ideas of the dominant group so blanket the surface of everyday life that the muted group is likely to find its generation of surface ideas inhibited by the blanket coverage. It is not clear quite how muted groups adjust to the dislocation between their deep models and the surface models of the dominant group, but it is argued that they will learn to express their own deepest ideas in terms of the dominant group's surface ideas. Thus a muted group transforms 'their own unconscious perceptions into such conscious ideas as will accord with those generated by the dominant group'. Such transformations may require the investment of 'a great deal of disciplined mental energy'. This expenditure of energy may well explain the conservative nature of many muted groups' world views: their attachment to models which leave them at a disadvantage. For as Shirley Ardener argues, it is not surprising if people cling to a dearly-won accommodation and fear the prospect of a fresh start.

Ardener argues that studies of the position of women frequently illustrate how women are placed in an inferior category in the predominant system of a given society compared to the men of the society. However, even after the relative position of women in the structure has been documented and established, there is another fruitful area for research. This is the whole topic of the unclear, vague, and probably repressed alternative theories which women have about the world and, perhaps even more interesting, about themselves. It is these, and the relationships between them and the dominant ideologies, which form one topic for this book.

The utility of this idea can be well demonstrated using the material on differences of opinion between male and female adolescents on friendship patterns and sexuality. The dominant teenage voice in the sociology of education literature, like that in 'deviance' and 'urban studies', is that of an urban, working-class, anti-social male. In a series of vivid studies from Thrasher (1927) through Parker (1974) and Patrick (1972) to Willis (1977) and Robins and Cohen (1978) we have heard these young men tell us how school success is only for 'cissies', how they spend their time with a group of other males, and how the females they know can be simplistically divided into 'slags' who will have intercourse with everyone, and 'respectable' girls who can be taken home to meet mother. These young men are the dominant group in adolescent society, and their voice has been collected and recorded by generations of eager researchers. Too often, it has swamped all the other voices: the muted groups.

One such muted group is the adolescent girls who know these boys. It appears, from the work of the few people who have taken the time to listen, that on at least two issues they see the world rather differently. However, they also accept that it is the male definition of the situation that has power behind it; that they are a muted group. There is evidence that this difference of perspective applies both to friendship groups and to sexual activity, and that some researchers have failed to notice it when their own data exemplify it.

Murdock and Phelps (1973) are a prime example of this. Buried in their data on adolescents and the media is a wonderful example of adolescent males and females seeing the world in different ways. All the fourteen-year olds sampled were asked whether they spent their leisure time with a group of the same sex, a group of both sexes, a special friend of the same sex or a special friend of the opposite sex. Boys reported spending their time in a single-sex group, girls in a mixed group. In other words the two sexes differed in their conceptualization of group membership, friendship, use of time and so on. Murdock and Phelps, however, fall into a trap common to researchers and accept the boys' account as 'true' or 'real', arguing that the girls are deluded, not real members and so on. In so doing they ignore what could be seen as the most fascinating insight into adolescent friendships ever collected: that boys and girls see them differently, that membership has different meanings, that girls have a different understanding of groups and so on.

16

Lesley Smith (1978) studying skinheads in Bristol found a similar divergence of opinion between the boys and girls. The boys saw the girls as peripheral appendages to the real, all-male, gang, attached only as the possessions of individual boys. The girls themselves felt that they were members in their own right, with duties and responsibilities, and therefore understood the gangs as mixed. They had a distinct perspective on the whole topic of adolescent groups which, while muted, was there to be collected by a researcher interested enough to listen for it.

A similar disparity is apparent when sexual activity is considered. Adolescent males studied by researchers appear to operate with the classic double standard. Nice girls are either virgins or faithful to the one important man in their life, while 'tarts' are promiscuous. Such a simplistic picture of women was recorded by, for example, Paul Willis (1977: 43-6) who stressed how sexist were the beliefs of the 'lads' he studied in Hammertown about women. They operated a double standard between the steady girlfriend (virtuous and sexually faithful) and the 'easy lay' (cheap and promiscuous). One of his informants claimed that 'once they've had it, they want it all the time, no matter who it's with' so that the 'easy lay' is damned by the whole group for her sexual desire. Willis suggests that girls have no scope to be assertive or sexual, and are forced into romantic silliness. However, he apparently did not enquire whether the girls held the same double standard about themselves and other girls. There is evidence that girls, realizing that is how boys think, organize their lives by the distinction between slags and virgins but are not necessarily convinced by it in their own minds. This double standard was clearly recognized by the girls studied by Deirdre Wilson (1978) and Lesley Smith (1978). Wilson's sample of girls between 13 and 15 in a city in northern England divided them into virgins – 'nice' girls who only had sex when in love with a steady, responsible boy – and 'lays' who would go with anyone. Nice girls avoided friendships with 'lays' because association with a bad girl could tarnish their own reputations. Lesley Smith's sample of 14 and 16 year olds in Bristol held similar views, even when they doubted the justice of them. For example:

> Liz: Look I don't believe there should be one standard for a boy and another for a girl. *But there just is round here and there's not much you can do about it.* A chap's going to look for someone who hasn't had it off with every bloke. So as

17

soon as you let them put a leg over you, you've got a bad name. (emphasis mine)

Here again we can see the teenage girls as a 'muted group'. They know that life is not actually a simple matter where sexual activity means a person is easily classifiable as a virgin, a nice girl, or an easy lay, but they also know that the males in their world believe that, and that the male belief is more powerful, so they go along with it. Lees (1986) offers a further exemplification of this point, with an ethnography of London schoolgirls.

This may seem a matter of purely academic, or feminist, interest. Yet, as I have argued elsewhere (Delamont 1984d) there are policy implications. Part of the male double standard is the idea that only 'slags' use contraceptives. Consequently exhorting girls to use contraception is frequently pointless. While in their own world view girls may accept that it would be prudent, they also know that all the males in the neighbourhood will regard them as sluts if they do. Health education needs to be aimed at boys to instill the ideas that 'real men' take the responsibility or that 'nice girls' are the ones who use contraceptives (while 'slags' are too stupid to, or do not bother, or are trying to trap you). Listening to a muted group can not only be disconcerting, but also have important policy implications.

One of the things revealed by the brief excursion into adolescent beliefs about sexuality is the prevalence of ideas of contagion (once a girl has experienced sex she cannot manage without it: 'only slags are friends with slags'). This material therefore takes us neatly on to the second theorist, Mary Douglas, whose most famous work is an analysis of pollution beliefs. While Bernstein admits an intellectual debt to Mary Douglas, her work has had little impact and is not widely understood in the sociology of education. Douglas's *Purity and Danger* and *Natural Symbols* do not appear in the bibliographies or recommended reading of such sociology of education texts as Banks (1968, 1976), Musgrave (1965, 1972, 1979), Robinson (1981), Shaw (1981), Morrish (1972) and Reid (1978). Indeed, structuralism is not a theoretical perspective addressed by these authors. Yet Douglas's 1973 anthology contains a seminal paper on Bernstein, and a later one (1982) a review of work by Bourdieu. One task of this volume its to introduce Douglas to a sociological audience.

## Central ideas from Mary Douglas

Mary Douglas has published four books and two collections of her own papers (1966, 1970, 1975, 1982a, 1986, 1987) which offer her work on human cognitive systems in general (as opposed to the reports of her fieldwork in Africa). She has also edited several volumes of papers by other scholars who share her perspective (1973, 1982b, 1984), and written with collaborators (Douglas and Isherwood 1978; Douglas and Wildavsky 1982). Her complete output is impressive and all the work is an attempt to come to terms with the subtleties and ambiguities of human belief systems, especially the relationships between the sacred and the profane, the battle of the sexes, and the nature of religious and secular belief systems. Her work is fascinating and perplexing, particularly for the non-anthropologist, but the insights make it worth the effort involved in 'mistressing' her material. The main ideas used in this book come from Douglas (1966, 1970, 1975, 1982a, 1982b) and are those of purity and danger, and group and grid.

The main argument of Douglas's most important book is summarized in her contention that 'dirt is essentially disorder' and 'dirt offends against order. Eliminating it is not a negative movement, but a positive effort to organize the environment.' This effort consists of attempts, practical and ritualistic, to organize the environment and eliminate all forms of dirt – moral and religious as well as physical. In other words, we classify as dirt, as pollution, everything which is out of place. Shoes are not themselves dirty, but they are unhygienic on the table; cigarette ash is alright in the ash tray but not suspended in the teatime jelly; nail varnish is pretty on nails but a stain on your best skirt and so forth. As with the physical world, so too with the moral order. A harmless fornication becomes a heinous crime if the partners are later discovered to be siblings; a simple fight becomes parricide if the participants are father and son. It is not the act *itself* which has absolute value, but the social classification of it.

Douglas goes on to develop the basic ideas of order and disorder into a more complex theory about the multitude of ways in which humans impose order on the essential chaos of human and animal life. The world is a complex mass of events and processes which would overwhelm us if we did not divide it up, organize it, catalogue and classify it. The classification – or labelling, or naming – of the many significant aspects of the world enables us, in part, to control it. Things and people which we cannot name,

19

label, pigeonhole, or catalogue are frightening, threatening, disturbing, nasty. Labelling a phenomenon also gives us a basis for predicting what will happen when we face it; how it can be expected to behave, how it will affect us.

This basic idea, the centrality of classification as a source of personal stability, makes sense of many apparently bizarre customs reported from foreign parts. It also makes sense of many features of life in western industrialized societies. The hostility expressed by older people who claim that long hair makes it impossible to tell boys from girls is a good example. At one level it is silly, because the anonymous figure in the street is a stranger, and the sex of strangers does not matter. At another level, we can understand the anger because sex is one of the first classifications we impose on the human universe, and we cannot begin the cataloguing process until the sex label is firmly assigned. A creature which is neither male nor female is an anomaly – a danger – and a teenager who cannot be labelled is therefore anomalous, matter out of place. For the Portuguese peasants whose cosmology was summarized in chapter 1 a woman who climbed trees to prune the vines was violating a central value of the society because the classification 'woman' implies 'close to the earth'. Similarly for the Berbers studied by Bourdieu (1971) a man who stayed indoors 'is either suspect or ridiculous' because the classification 'man' implies 'leaving the house', being 'outside'. In both these cultures assigning an individual to a sex is the first step on the way to knowing whether that individual can climb a tree, or stay indoors. In contemporary Britain, the norms for men and women are less clear cut but still exist, and unisex clothing disturbs those people who would prefer them to be more sharply defined and differentiated than they are.

Anything which muddles our classification system or weakens the boundaries between important categories is dirty, dangerous, unnatural, sinful and threatening. Of course different groups of people in one society, and different societies, have very different classification systems and worry about different infringements of the cataloguing. In modern Britain the issue of women clergy is a good example of differential boundaries. Some people find the two categories 'woman' and 'vicar' quite complementary, while others react violently against the idea of the woman as priest and foresee terrible consequences. For opponents of the ordination of women some important boundaries are being shifted, and two clearly distinct categories have been mixed where they should be rigorously separated. Una Kroll (1975) has written sensitively about the distress caused to both sides of this controversy by the deep emotions aroused in each's opponents. She describes how she gradually became aware that for some Anglican men, women were aliens who contaminated and polluted the church. Women can be tolerated as worshippers in the pews but, for these men, any other role would contaminate the faith and the building itself. Kroll writes that she became aware of these deep feelings in 1963 when:

> I was scarcely aware that sexism existed....I was married, and pregnant with my fourth child. One day, I noticed a small item in a newspaper which reported the speech of a priest who said that the sight of a pregnant woman in the sanctuary of a church would be indecent, and a blasphemy. (1975; 71)

Subsequently her campaign to enter the priesthood brought intense hostility down upon her, and she was called, among other things, a witch and a prostitute by her opponents. These are both, of course, well-known terms with which to abuse women who challenge the dominant male category system!

If such conceptual gaps can exist within one society, then much wider gulfs can be found between different cultures as the materials of social anthropology have shown. What is clear is that in all cultures the mixing of categories can have terrible consequences. However, no system of classification can adequately organize the complexities of the real world, and all systems have ambiguities and anomalies, and ways have to be found to handle these potentially dangerous – and highly sacred – 'monsters'. Douglas suggests five solutions which can be found, often in the same culture, to the problem of the anomaly:

1. One may firmly place it into one category and deny its other attributes. The Nuer define badly malformed babies as hippopotamus young, and so place them in the Nile, their true home. A monstrous birth is redefined as an animal.
2. Physical control can be used to remove the anomaly. Widows were an anomaly in high caste Hindu society, and the custom of suttee removed them from the social world.
3. Anomalies can be rigorously avoided as abhorrent. Thus Douglas explains the abominations of Leviticus by arguing that they are the anomalous and ambiguous products of a complex classification of the animal world.

21

4. Anomalies may also be seen as highly dangerous things. By labelling an anomaly as a social danger, conformity can be enforced by insisting that peril will result from association. The pollution beliefs discussed later follow this principle.
5. Finally, ambiguous symbols can be used in poetry, mythology, and ritual to enrich meanings and call attention to other planes of existence. By using such symbols evil and death can be reunited to life and goodness into a single pattern.

The *tour de force* of Douglas's book is her explanation of the abominations of Leviticus, culminating in the ambiguous and anomalous status of pork in the Middle East. Indeed pollution and beliefs about it formed the central part of *Purity and Danger*, with a particular focus upon three varieties of pollution belief:

(i) those about the dangers of bodily emissions and invasions;
(ii) those which reinforce social boundaries (such as incest prohibitions and pollution arising from breaking them);
(iii) those which arise from conflicting aims in the same culture.

All three types are to be found in contemporary education institutions, just as they were identified in Victorian Britain (Delamont and Duffin 1978: 22-3). The threat of bodily invasion and dangers of bodily emissions can be seen in adolescent boys' fears of homosexual teachers (Measor and Woods 1984: 23) and in adolescent girls' beliefs about menstruation; and most vividly in teachers' and parents' fears about children carrying the AIDS virus. The second category of pollution beliefs is explained by Douglas as follows:

> people...think of their own social environment as consisting of other people joined or separated by lines which must be respected. Some of the lines are protected by physical sanctions....But wherever the lines are precarious we find pollution ideas come to their support. Physical crossing of the social barrier is treated as a dangerous pollution...the pollution becomes a doubly wicked object of reprobation, first because he crossed the line and second because he endangered others. (1966: 138-9)

Douglas uses this argument to analyse beliefs about adultery and incest pollution in a variety of primitive cultures, but the model applies equally well to complaints about 'scruffy' teachers (who break the lines between adults and teenagers), parents who try to challenge school knowledge, or teachers who seduce pupils.

The third category of pollution beliefs concerns the area of sexual relations, and involves exaggerated avoidance. Here we find ideas about cosmic powers which include sexual energy as a dangerous and valuable force. Douglas mentions New Guinea tribes where men are believed to be dangerous to women, and vice versa, and 'each sex approaches the other with deliberate control', and tribes where men fear women as 'strength sappers'. The latter is particularly apposite when applied to Willis's (1977) Hammertown adolescent society, and the description of a tribe called the Mae Enga could be applied immediately to the Boy Scouts:

> There is a strongly held belief that contacts with women weaken male strength...from early boyhood...[they] are taught to shun female company, and they go into periodic seclusion to purify themselves from female contact. The two dominant beliefs...are superiority of the male principle and its vulnerability to female influence. (1966: 147)

Douglas suggests that belief in male superiority will not result in pollution beliefs even when the system is contradictory if women can be physically controlled, and have no protection, but adds that:

> When the principle of male dominance is applied to the ordering of social life but is contradicted by other principles such as that of female independence, or the inherent right of women as the weaker sex to be more protected from violence than men, then sex pollution is likely to flourish. (1966: 142)

Douglas goes on to analyse some primitive social systems which are at war with themselves. She suggests that while all social systems are probably 'built on contradictions', it is sometimes possible for 'the structure to be self-defeating'. When this is the case, Douglas says, the social institutions concerned with sex and sexual relations will express rigid separation and violent antagonisms. It is in these conditions that complex beliefs about sex pollution flourish. This book argues that several educational issues, both in historical periods (chapters 4–6) and in the present day, can be best understood by seeing the social system containing them as 'at war with itself' in Douglas's terms.

Douglas's ideas about pollution and boundary maintenance are better known than her subsequent elaborations of them into a set of propositions about group membership and social control: her work on group and grid. Although Bernstein (1977) has maintained that he is unable to comprehend these concepts they are, in essence, 'the same' as his ideas of classification and framing. Consequently they are discussed in this chapter after the more familiar concepts of classification and framing, and visible and invisible pedagogies.

Leaving Douglas for the moment, the idea of a system 'at war with itself' affords a way into some of the key ideas used in this book which have been drawn from Pierre Bourdieu, especially that of symbolic violence. There are several Anglo-Saxon attempts to grapple with the work of Pierre Bourdieu (e.g. Kennett 1974; Lakomski 1984) whose work appears peculiarly Gallic to the British researcher.

## Central ideas from Bourdieu

This section is deliberately called 'Central ideas *from* Bourdieu' because as outlined above, I am making no claim that what follows is an accurate resumé of Bourdieu's ideas – merely what my interpretation of his ideas is. That is, I have taken some of Bourdieu's ideas for use in this volume, and these ideas are explained in this section to help the reader understand what I take their meaning to be.

The ideas I have purloined from Bourdieu are:

(i) cultural capital
(ii) symbolic violence
(iii) *habitus*

Lemert (1981: 20) points out that Bourdieu has a 'prodigious' list of publications, having published thirteen books between 1962 and 1975. Only Giddens in Britain comes anywhere near such a massive output which is far greater than Douglas, Bernstein or either Shirley or Edwin Ardener. Many of Bourdieu's books are not available in English translation, and the educational sociologists who refer to him typically draw on a few papers and two or three of the books. For example Blackledge and Hunt (1985) cite one book translated in 1977 and three papers all translated in the early 1970s. The work of Bourdieu's to which I feel greatest affinity, the anthropological studies of the Berber (Kabyle) peoples of Algeria, is never cited in the educational literature. Yet not only is this work beautifully written, and a marvellous example of structuralism at its best, but it leads the way forward into seeing educational institutions as places where *symbolism* is crucially important. The quote at the head of this chapter is one extract from Bourdieu's discussion of the spatial symbolisms of the Berber house, divided into an everlasting and kaleidoscopic series of oppositions. The sheer beauty of the following passage continues the oppositions:

> The dark and nocturnal, lower part of the house, place of objects that are moist, green or raw – jars of water [...] wood and green fodder – natural place also of beings – oxen and cows, donkeys and mules – and place of natural activities – sleep, the sexual act, giving birth – and the place also of death, is opposed, as nature is to culture, to the light-filled, noble, upper part of the house: this is the place of fire and of objects created by fire – lamp, kitchen utensils, rifle – [...] and it is also the place of the two specifically cultural activities that are carried out in the space of the house: cooking and weaving. (Bourdieu 1971)

With an analysis of this complexity as our goal, the first idea adapted from Bourdieu, cultural capital, is explained.

## Cultural capital

This crucial term in Bourdieu's theories of education and social reproduction deserves some attention. Mary Douglas argues (1982a: 125) that it derives from the American notion of human capital which Bourdieu expands to separate four types of (intangible) 'wealth'. These are: cultural capital, social capital, symbolic capital, and honorific capital.

*Honorific capital* is civic recognition of a successful life in the top echelons of society; in Britain such things as being elected an FRS (Fellow of the Royal Society) or being given a CBE or better. Such honours carry little direct financial reward and do not necessarily produce actual power over subordinates, but they are valued as a symbol of civic recognition. C.P. Snow's novels *The Masters* (1951) and *The Affair* (1960) contain good material on the passionate feelings evoked by the failure of certain scientists to be elected as an FRS. Anyone unfamiliar with the emotional charge carried by such honorific capital should skim pages 39, 107-10 of *The Masters*. Such honorific capital is also important in state socialist societies (e.g. The Order of Lenin).

*Symbolic capital* is, for Bourdieu, the power of creative artists – novelists, playwrights, artists, film producers, poets and songwriters – to challenge and criticize the society. Their actual power to change society is minimal or non-existent, but they have symbolic significance. Thus one might see Salman Rushdie's novels as a powerful, symbolic, attack on post-colonial racism in Britain, but his actual power to change anything is negligible.

*Cultural capital* is for Bourdieu something inherited by children from their families, as they are socialized. Just as some inherit real capital (land, a house, stocks and shares) so some are privileged enough to inherit the rich culture of the elite: e.g. the language and style of French 'high culture'. Others inherit only devalued regional or lower-class cultures. So while the daughter of a full professor in Paris grows up, not only in a flat at a good city address and in a cottage on the Loire, but also with an appreciation of, and familiarity with, the paintings in the Louvre, the operas of Rossini, the novels of Flaubert and the plays of Racine; the daughter of a Breton fisherman gets a bed in a tiny cottage, a smattering of Breton, and a few folktales. When they start school, the Parisian professor's daughter has many intangible advantages. Her home is, in Bourdieu's terms, well endowed with *social capital*.

It is very important to realize that Bourdieu is arguing that these are not aspects of life that we are *conscious* of. The professorial family does not get up every morning and announce that the little girl must, as it is Thursday, learn the names of two Rossini operas. The power of these forms of cultural capital lies in their being taken for granted by those who have them, and transmitted effortlessly and unconsciously. The little girl is told she is to spend the night at her aunt's because her parents are going to the opera to see *The Barber*. She learns that there is an opera house, that many operas exist, that there are composers, conductors, singers. No one ever teaches her, or explains that opera is a culturally-valued high-status art form in France. There is an outstanding evocation of the homes of intellectual Americans and their cultural capital in Cochran-Smith (1984) which displays both how pervasive a shared literacy is, and how unconscious the parents are of its transmission.

The second important thing to realize about the ideas underlying cultural capital is that Bourdieu is convinced that the particular form of any culture is arbitrary. He argues that the 'da

Vinci/Rossini/Flaubert/Racine' scenario I have outlined has no inherent superiority to Breton language and folklore. The status that is given the former in France (and the educational success which later accompanies its acquisition) is derived from its associations with the dominant (powerful, ruling) class. Thus Rossini is not inherently superior to a Breton sea shanty; it is superior in modern France because the ruling classes value it more. All aspects of culture can be ranked (music, literature, food, dress, sexual activities, toys, sports, and modes of transport) because of their association with particular classes. However, only perceptive observers such as Bourdieu and you, the reader, can see that the rankings are not natural, god-given, pre-ordained or inherent but are cultural products based on power. The French professor and her family do not realize that Rossini is not inherently superior to a Breton folk tune, but merely achieves superiority in France because people like her value it more highly.

Food is a good example of something which is culturally ranked, in an arbitrary way which comes to be seen as natural, taken-for-granted – even normal – or unchallengable. Imagine two menus for a main meal.

Menu one

Tomato soup
Roast beef, Yorkshire pudding, roast and boiled potatoes, brussel sprouts, gravy
Sherry trifle

Menu two

Smoked salmon
Roast venison with redcurrant jelly, game chips, pureed celeriac and gravy
Stilton cheese and Bath Olivers
Fresh fruit

Both menus are equally nutritious; if properly cooked, both equally nice to eat. Yet the second menu is, to any British person, 'higher' class. It is not only more expensive, it is 'posher'. The food items are those associated with richer, 'posher' families over several hundred years. Yet it was not always so: Robin Hood and his merry men poached wild deer to feed the Sherwood peasants who would hardly ever have seen beef, had never met the tomato or tasted sherry. The second menu is seen as 'classier' today because it is currently elite food; in another century it may not be , and will have lost status accordingly.

While the status accorded any item, whether Rossini's operas or roast venison, is arbitrary in Bourdieu's scheme, and while this arbitrariness is hidden from all but a few intellectuals, the social fact of an item's status has to be recognized. We may know that inherently *The Barber of Seville* is not superior to *A Chorus Line* or *Cats*, but we also have to recognize that in contemporary Britain it is believed to be, treated as such by all powerful people and organizations, and its superiority is a social fact we have to live with. Pointing out that such rankings are arbitrary is one of the ways that social scientists make themselves unpopular.

The power of such hierarchies leads us on to the second concept that is borrowed from Bourdieu for this volume: symbolic violence.

## Symbolic violence

For Bourdieu the imposition of ranking systems on cultural items (food, clothing, music, visual arts, sport, etc.) is a form of symbolic violence. Because the class and power basis of such rankings is unrecognized, and the rankings are accepted as 'natural' or 'inherent', their imposition on all of us is a form of symbolic violence. This is why Bourdieu says that 'culture classifies – and classifies the classifiers'. Humans have created systems of thought and are then constrained by them.

Education is a particular form of symbolic violence, because it is through the education system that we are taught the ranking systems in our society as if they were neutral, true, scientific, objective – whereas they are actually arbitrary hierarchies reflecting the power structure of our society. Some of the ranking systems are actually taught explicitly (undergraduates studying English taught the Leavisite gospel for example), others are implicitly conveyed by the structure of the school (physics is higher status than woodwork), others are transmitted to us as invisibly as the air we breathe (like the food example above).

To sum up these complex ideas so far, Bourdieu suggests that education is marked by a system of violence – not the open, palpable violence which the term normally connotes, but symbolic violence. This operates through the imposition of meanings and definitions such that the real relations of power and interest are hidden. Education promotes a consensual view of the legitimacy of certain varieties of knowledge, while masking the social differences it serves to promote and reproduce. For Bourdieu 'cultural reproduction' does not refer simply to the functionalists' copying of the taken-for-granted social order. Cultural reproduction serves to preserve the appearance of neutrality while legitimating sectional interests. Hence the social organization and transmission of educational knowledge furnishes a cultural code whereby the social structure is reproduced. Through the educational system what Bourdieu calls 'cultural capital' is differentially distributed, in a manner which parallels capital of a material sort. A key here is Bourdieu's notion of *habitus*.

## Habitus

An elusive concept, this refers to the distinctive 'modes of perception, of thinking, of appreciation and of action' associated with any given collectivity. The *habitus* thus defines the 'taste' of a group – its characteristic, taken-for-granted view of the world. In the world of education the *habitus* which defines successful schooling remains implicit, Bourdieu argues. The education system assumes that its pupils are possessed of the necessary cultural competence, the character of which is never made manifest. The qualities pupils need for success are never clearly defined, but the upper-middle or middle-class child appears 'naturally' gifted because she is already versed in the mysteries. Thus what is really a social distribution of cultural capital appears to be a natural distribution of individual gifts.

The idea of the *habitus* has been used to illustrate socialization processes into medicine by Atkinson (1981b, 1983) and teaching (Atkinson and Delamont 1985a). In both areas it has been argued there is a strong element of what Jamous and Peloille (1970) call 'indeterminacy': of tacit, undescribable competencies. 'Success' in clinical training and on teaching practice both depend on knowledge and on 'performance', that is on technicality and indeterminacy. Atkinson and I (1985a) argue that

> 'indeterminacy' and appeals to it are not *the* habitus of professional education. Professional training is characterized by great tensions over the balance between indeterminacy and technicality; between the tacit and the scientific. Jamous and

Peloille show this for French medical education, and similar debates characterize socialization into other occupations in higher education.

Bourdieu's habitus, then, cannot be understood in any simple all-embracing sense for any given education setting. Indeed, it is its very investigation of professional process and conflict. The issue of 'indeterminate' knowledge in professional education does, however, illustrate rather nicely Bourdieu's contention that the habitus may remain implicit, while its mastery is treated as the realization of natural talent. Competence as the tacit knowledge of, say, classroom discipline, is, as Jamous and Peloille put it, regarded as a personal 'virtuality' of practitioners – and hence of successful recruits. Hence the widespread belief that successful teaching is an 'art', and/or a function of personality rather than drawing upon technical skills.

Bourdieu himself sees habitus as a sufficient explanation of the differential outcomes from the French educational system. When professional training is our focus, we are dealing with segmentation within the occupation, *and* with the ways in which the occupation maintains its exclusivity and its public face as a 'community'. Both these can be illuminated via the concept of *habitus*. This may, in part at least, account for the notorious propensity of such occupational groups to self recruit: there is a sort of 'mythological charter' that such candidates have already assimilated much of the profession's oral tradition and habitus – though it is not expressed overtly in such terms of course.

Since completing that article Brian Simon's (1985) paper on the failure of England to develop a concept of pedagogy has been published. He speculates that one reason why educational theory in England has remained 'amateurish' and 'highly pragmatic' is the attitude of the universities and boys' public schools to education. He points out that the boys' schools 'have until recently contemptuously rejected the idea that a professional training is in any sense relevant to the job of a public school master' (p.79). Teaching in a boys' public school was something that any gentleman 'having the appropriate social origins including a degree at Oxford or Cambridge, could learn, through experience, on the job. Certainly no special training was necessary' (p.79).

This belief is beautifully captured in a novel by Angela Thirkell (1937) in which Colin Keith, newly graduated from Oxford, proposes to teach for a term before going to London to read for the bar. His sister asks

'Do you think you can teach, Colin?'
'I don't know. I never really thought about that. How do you learn to teach?'
'I think they go to training colleges', said Kate. (p.34)

At this point Colin remembers that at his public school they had once had a substitute master 'from somewhere where they taught teaching' and 'even the drawing master could keep order better than he could'. Simon (1985) locates the attitude of the Headmasters' Conference to teacher training in the nineteenth century, when their schools 'played a major role in the symbiosis of aristocracy and bourgeoisie' by socializing their sons. This socialization 'involved little emphasis on intellectual (or cognitive) development. More important...was the formation of character, specifically of the qualities embodied in the concept of "manliness"' (p.80).

Simon uses Bourdieu to argue that the staff and boys at the public schools shared a 'common culture' and similar homes, interests and language:

The teacher's pastoral responsibility – in terms of upbringing – was as important, or more so than his intellectual (teaching) responsibility. In this situation upper middle class culture and attitudes were 'naturally' assimilated and reinforced – the process did not require the application of specifically 'pedagogical' means. (1985: 80-1)

Simon excepts Sanderson at Oundle and Thring at Uppingham from this, because they were concerned to innovate. Any kind of training for teaching boys at public schools in the majority of Headmasters' Conference schools 'simply did not appear as relevant to the schoolmaster's profession' (1985: 81). Simon does not mention that the great girls' schools to which the daughters of the same classes went took a different view, and this is something well worth exploring. He goes on to link the boys' schools to Oxbridge, pointing out that these universities have not 'contributed to any serious extent to the study of education or to the development of educational theory and practice' (p.81). Oxford still has no Chair of education; Cambridge founded one in 1949 when women finally received degrees. Simon therefore sees Bourdieu's ideas of cultural capital and *habitus* as powerful explanatory devices for the lack of any scientific pedagogy in England.

This extended example of teacher training has offered one way in which Bourdieu's ideas can be illuminating about the history and sociology of British education. The three related concepts (cultural capital, symbolic violence, and habitus) are used in such ways particularly in chapters 8-10. Interwoven with the central ideas taken from Bernstein, outlined next, they also appear in parts II and III of the book.

Turning from Bourdieu to Basil Bernstein we come to probably the most difficult theorist of all to utilize, not because his ideas are any harder to grasp than those of Mary Douglas but because Bernstein's work is seen in Britain through a distorting glass which makes it almost impossible to grasp its real nature.

Rex Gibson (1984: 125) has complained that 'Bernstein's writing, like European structuralism, has become impenetrable to the layman' and so in the following explanation of the central ideas borrowed from Bernstein for this book, my understanding may not be widely shared. Certainly Gibson is not alone in having little patience or understanding, for Blackledge and Hunt (1985: 60) calmly announce that 'Bernstein has adopted the worst aspects of Durkheim and neglected the best.' However, their discussion of his work neglects the paper by Atkinson (1981a) which locates Bernstein as a structuralist, and shows that they have failed to grasp many of his central concepts. Such failures and misrepresentations are a common feature of British discussions of Bernstein. This point is made at some length in Atkinson (1985a: chapter 8 on the fate of the text), and is not recapitulated here. Suffice it to say that Bernstein has been almost alone in British sociology of education in his recognition of the role played by women in class formation and reproduction, and the symbolic importance of knowledge, and it is these ideas which have been purloined from his work for this volume.

## Ideas from Bernstein

The central ideas used in this volume which come from Bernstein are as follows: classification and framing; visible and invisible pedagogy; the 'new' middle class.

I have discussed the concepts of classification and framing elsewhere (Delamont 1983d) and will not dwell on them here as they have become widely known since their original publication. Classification was the term offered by Bernstein (1971) to describe the strength of the boundaries that are maintained between areas of knowledge. Thus strong classification characterizes a medical school where anatomy, physiology, and biochemistry are taught quite separately (i) from each other (i.e. at different times, in different labs and lecture halls, by different staff, for separate exams, from different textbooks) and (ii) from the clinical work on living patients (Armstrong 1980). A medical school with weaker classification mixes 'clinical' and 'preclinical' subjects, uses live patients from the outset, and stresses the links between surgery, anatomy, physiology and internal medicine.

An example from my own biography also illustrates boundary strength between content areas. At Cambridge in the 1960s the Tripos in Archaeology and Anthropology had a Part 1 of Social Anthropology, Physical Anthropology and Archaeology. Some of the subject matter of the syllabuses of the latter two subjects was 'the same': human evolution in the Pleistocene. Each group of staff taught the material in their own way, however, and they *disagreed* about the length of the Pleistocene, the place of the Mousterian, and the fate of Neanderthal Man. In Archaeology we were told the Pleistocene lasted two million years, in Physical Anthropology five million, and so on. As well-socialized British students we made different notes, read different authors, and cynically wrote essays and exam papers in which we reported the conventional wisdom taught in each subject. We treated the two courses as separate, and never asked, publically, for any *rapprochement* or explanation.

Classification, then, is strong or weak, and means the strength of the boundaries that are established and maintained between subjects. A curriculum with strong frames has separate subjects kept apart, one with weak frames has integrated subjects mixed up.

Framing can also be strong or weak. It refers, however, to the control over the pacing of work, and its selection, organization and timing which is exercised by teachers and pupils. A perfect example of strong framing is programmed learning, or many 'educational' computer games, where material is laid out before the student/player in a predetermined sequence over which she has no control. A textbook is more weakly framed; you can flip over dull bits, look at the back cover, turn back to the acknowledgements. Several curricular innovations – such as IGE (Individually Guided

Education) in the USA (Popkewitz, Tabachnick and Wehlage 1982) are strongly framed; and a worksheet system can be strongly framed if the pupil has no choice over what sheet they do next.

Bernstein was interested in those national education systems where classification and framing are both strong, and those where both are weak. He later (1973a) coined the terms visible pedagogy (for strong classification and framing) and invisible pedagogy (for weak classification and framing). The best example, in terms of familiarity, for students is the contrast between a taught course leading to an exam, and a student dissertation. A taught course leading to an exam is an example of a visible pedagogy because it is strongly classified and framed. For example, I teach a course in the Sociology of Mediterranean Societies. This is strongly classified: it is sociology, not literature, or economics, or law or politics or history or geography; and strongly framed: students have to come to a particular room at a particular time every week, take notes, write essays on topics I have chosen to be handed in on dates I set, and inexorably a three-hour examination looms at the end. In contrast the same students may choose to do a dissertation. This is weakly framed: they have three years to do it in, and can choose when to work on it; and weakly classified: it can be a mixture of literature, geography and politics if they choose.

The spread of invisible pedagogies is closely related, by Bernstein, to the emergence of a *new* middle class alongside the traditional one.

## Bernstein's theory of the 'new' middle class

Bernstein's main concern in his paper on 'visible' and 'invisible' pedagogies (1973a) is the clash of two ideologies within education – the debate about traditional versus progressive schooling – as revealed in the Black Papers, the Tyndale Enquiry (Auld 1976) and the controversy over Bennett (1976). Bernstein is interested in the origin, function and expression of these opposed educational philosophies. Arguing that disputes over the form and content of education are middle-class debates (because the working class does not hold effective control over the education system), Bernstein holds that the debate on primary schooling can only be understood as a clash of competing ideologies held by different sectors of the middle class.

Bernstein locates the adherents of the visible ('traditional') pedagogy within the 'old middle class' and the supporters of the invisible ('progressive') pedagogy within the 'new middle class'. However, in passing, Bernstein sketches in the beginnings of a fundamental reworking of Durkheim's concept of organic solidarity which carries potential for an analysis of the interrelationships of class, sex and education as a means of cultural reproduction. The ideas on organic solidarity are confusing, opaque and unsupported by empirical evidence. However, they do provide a tantalizing glimpse of a theoretical framework for understanding divisions within the middle class and their ideologies. Bernstein argues that in the traditional primary school, the social control and control over knowledge are visible and explicit; while in the 'progressive' primary school, the control system is invisible and implicit – though no less powerful. The idea that different sectors of the middle class espouse different pedagogies goes with the idea that these sectors have different family lives ('positional' and 'personal') which socialize the children for different adult roles. The support for different early schooling systems is partly a desire to recapitulate the home environment and its socialization style, and partly a derivation from very different philosophies of life and human nature. Thus, Bernstein argues, the 'new' middle class believes in the adaptability and plasticity of human nature, the importance of nurture, and the principle of meritocracy.

Bernstein offers no historical or sociological evidence for his postulated division of the middle class, commenting that it is a 'matter of empirical research to identify specifically which groups, concerned with what symbolic controls,... are active representatives'. Elsewhere he suggests that the 'new' middle class is represented among the new agents of symbolic control – 'the major and minor professional class, concerned with the servicing of persons', but at the same time he admits that not all members of these occupations are members of the 'new' middle class. It is clear that Bernstein's central idea is that members of the 'new' middle class are controllers of others by virtue of their manipulation of *symbols* rather than by the ownership and management of property. The old middle class controls the means of production while the new controls the symbolic systems in the society. Thus, the 'new' middle class is recruited from teachers, social workers, architects, planners, psychiatrists, and those working in design, fashion and the mass media – the creators of the symbolic ordering in society.

Bernstein locates his ideas on the emergence of these two sectors within the middle class in relation to Durkheim's organic solidarity.

He argues that Durkheim foresaw only one type of adulthood under organic solidarity – individualism – whereas his theory allows Bernstein to postulate a parallel form – personalized organic solidarity, unforeseen by Durkheim. The individualism predicted by Durkheim grows out of an increasingly complex division of labour in the productive sphere, whereas Bernstein's alternative arises from increasing complexity in the division of labour in the cultural or symbolic sphere. The old middle class has occupied the productive sphere and the new the cultural or symbolic.

The two different spheres of organic solidarity – individualized and personalized – and the different bases of economic power and prestige – productive and cultural – demand different socialization to produce different adults. The visible pedagogy socializes the middle-class children into adults with unambiguous individual identities and an inflexible role performance. The new middle class is socialized, in part, via the invisible pedagogy to have ambiguous personal identities and flexible role performances. That is, Bernstein is arguing that socialization in the old middle class is designed to reduce variety and ensure cultural reproduction, while in the new middle class the goals are increased variety and cultural interruption. (Bernstein has borrowed this latter term from physical science – deriving it from an interrupter system – but its meaning in class terms is undeveloped and unclear.)

Bernstein points out that many of the ideas espoused by the new middle class are at variance with its objective class position, and so its ideology is riven with ambivalences. For example, this group believes in meritocracy, yet wishes to ensure that its children enter middle-class occupations. Then again, it supports the use of the invisible pedagogy in schools, yet its children need to succeed in conventional, high-status education if they are to enter suitable careers, and high-status education is characterized by a visible pedagogy. Bernstein suggests that this second paradox can be resolved by socializing children via the invisible pedagogy at home and at primary school, shifting them into conventional schooling for public examinations.

There are clear links between these ideas of Bernstein's and those of Douglas and Bourdieu already outlined. In particular, Bernstein's opposition between the visible and the invisible pedagogy is closely related to Mary Douglas's theory of group and grid.

## Group and grid

Mary Douglas's ideas about group and grid have affinities with Bernstein's notions of classification and framing, and hence share their explanatory potential and empirical problems. Douglas's (1982a) most coherent account of group and grid is found in the introduction to a collection of papers by sociologists of science who use the concepts to examine a variety of knowledge domains. That account is followed here.

*Group* – in Douglas's theory – is all about membership, and allegiances. A society, sub-culture or organization which is characterized by strong grouping is hard to enter, relatively exclusive, and demands high levels of commitment and loyalty from those who do gain admittance. Thus it is relatively easy to join the RSPCA (Royal Society for the Prevention of Cruelty to Animals), the National Trust or the Church of England (low group) but difficult to enter the Athenaeum, the Royal Society or the Royal Institute of British Architects (RIBA) (high group). Being a member of the RSPCA does not demand great loyalty or sacrifice or commitment, while being a Fellow of the Royal Society involves adherence to a set of standards concerning scientific behaviour, and commitment to an historic British institution.

*Grid* – which can also be strong or weak – is Douglas's term for the degree of social control or regulation that is exercised over the membership or participants in any society, organization or event. When grid is strong – maximum regulation – behaviour is prescribed and the timetabling is rigid. When grid is weak – minimum regulation – people's lives are free, unrestrained, unregulated. Douglas can, she argues, locate any society, subculture or organization somewhere in the two-dimensional space made up of weak and strong group and grid; as shown in figure 2.1.

*Figure 2.1 Douglas's group and grid system*

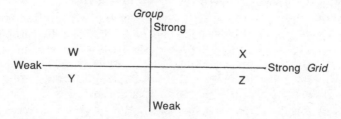

37

Goffman's (1961) 'total institutions' are institutions with strong grid. In quartile X we will find total institutions to which members are loyal and committed: monasteries, nunneries, elite public schools and the Krisna temple (Daner 1974). In quartile Z are total institutions where the inmates' lives are regulated, yet they have little or no loyalty or commitment to the organization: such as prisons, mental hospitals, sanatoria and so forth. In quartile Y we can locate any society characterized by individualism – where autonomous actors negotiate and build alliances. Finally quartile W – weak grid and strong group – is characterized by Douglas as 'a form of society in which only the external group boundary is clear: by definition all other statuses are ambiguous and open to negotiation' (1982: 4). This would include any culture or sub-culture which has an obvious demarcation line round it, but does not control its members with multifarious rules and rigid timetabling. In modern Britain members of the 'learned professions' will be liable to be found in this quartile: a barrister is marked off from other workers, but her everyday life is not subjected to detailed regulation. Douglas (1982: 4) labels the four quartiles as shown in figure 2.2.

*Figure 2.2 Douglas's names for the four social systems*

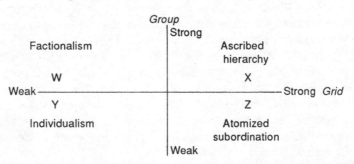

Intrinsic to Douglas's argument is that when a whole society or sub-culture can be located in one of the quartiles, it will have a world view, a cosmology, which characterizes that quartile's position (e.g. strong grid and group) as 'natural', normal, desirable, and moral. In a complex society, many different organizations, sub-cultures and occupations will co-exist each located in a different quartile. Thus for example, different religious organizations classified into each quartile can be easily found in every town and city. In a simpler society, where all citizens share

*Figure 2.3 Four styles of religious life*

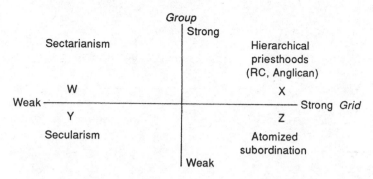

one belief system, the whole social system would be located in one quartile. Figure 2.3 shows four styles of religious life found in contemporary Britain located in Douglas's system.

Douglas sees the main benefits of her analytic schemes as enabling us to stand back from, and make problematic, things we normally see and experience as 'natural' and therefore taken for granted and incontrovertible. She argues that her analysis 'can expose the normally invisible screen through which culture lets options be perceived. It means that most values and beliefs can be analysed as part of society...' (1982: 7). Any set of people who operate in the same quartile share a cosmology, and

> There is nothing natural about the perception of nature; nature is heavily loaded with political bias. In so far as there is a consensus about the best kind of society to live in, there is agreement too about the kind of cosmos that the society is found in and consensus about the good life and right behaviour. (p.7)

Douglas is particularly interested in what happens to dissenters in any quartile, and in the pollution beliefs which are held by the members of any particular type of sub-culture or organization. As Douglas puts it: 'Each inhabitable part of the grid/group diagram has got its own miseries and compensations. The theory predicts or explains which intellectual strategies are useful for survival in a particular pattern of social relations' (p.7).

Douglas offers a classification system to display four different types of worker in any learned discipline, shown in figure 2.4. In quartile X (strong group and grid) are found the 'Grand Old Men' of any discipline, those who award the honours, legitimate new

*Figure 2.4 Styles within a learned discipline*

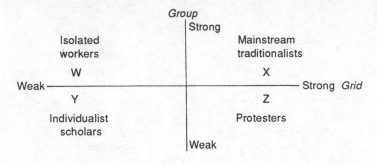

knowledge, award grants, act as gatekeepers for publishers, jobs and journals, and so on. Sometimes new insights invigorate a discipline, and these will come from quartile Y, where Kuhn's paradigm changes are to be found. In square W are found the mass of anonymous workers in any discipline who receive no public recognition or honours, and make no contribution to pushing out the frontiers of the subject. Finally in quartile Z, are found the few protestors who challenge and/or are excluded from the award system and 'invisible colleges' of the discipline, and remain rebels on the margins of the subject. This analysis will be used in chapters 6 and 8 to examine data on women in elite/learned occupations and professions. Before moving on to compare Douglas's idea that her schema allows one to 'see' the normally invisible screens which come between us and the natural world with the work of Bourdieu, the pollution beliefs associated with each quartile of her schema need discussion.

Michael Thompson (1982) has developed the Douglas schema, and argues that each quartile of her group and grid model has its own type of pollution beliefs. These are shown in figure 2.5. These pollution beliefs (or their absence) will be used to analyse material on the curriculum and knowledge in chapters 4 and 5, and on school rules and regulations in chapters 3, 6 and 7.

The use of Douglas's group and grid has been most pronounced in the sociology of science rather than in educational sociology. This has been educational researchers' loss, and is partially remedied in this collection. My use of this schema is *not* uncritical, and as the problems which are associated with its use are equivalent to those of Bernstein's classification and framing, the difficulties of both systems are discussed now, before the end of the chapter.

Figure 2.5 *Pollution beliefs in different organizations and societies*

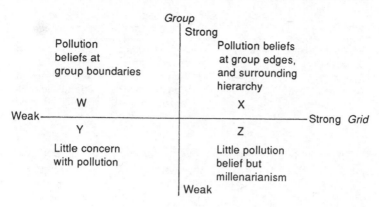

## Two caveats about the continua

Both Bernstein's continua of classification and framing, and Douglas's of group and grid share some disadvantages which need to be rehearsed before this chapter can be concluded. The two problems which arise most frequently when either set of constructs is used concern (i) the level of analysis, (ii) the vantage point for analysis. Each of these is briefly explained below.

The level of analysis problem can usually be solved once it is recognized but, if left, can render any account meaningless. Briefly, if a social scientist is to use either classification and framing, or group and grid, to focus upon any specific social or educational issue it is essential that she specifies the level of analysis at which she is working. Both Bernstein and Douglas are frequently cavalier about this, so that they sometimes classify whole cultures (the American and French education systems, or the Lugbara and the Tallensi) and sometimes individuals or single families are contrasted (as in Bloor and Bloor's (1982) study of scientists or Bernstein's (1971: 153-6) appendix on lavatories). I argued elsewhere (Delamont 1983d) that when applying classification and framing to educational issues it was essential to specify the level of analysis because the same phenomenon may be differentially located at different levels of generality. As figure 2.6 shows, using the English literature teaching at St Luke's, there are differences in the strength of the framing of English at classroom, subject department, school and national levels, *and* variations between the hidden and the manifest curriculum.

*Figure 2.6 The framing of English literature at St Luke's*

|  | Manifest curriculum | Hidden curriculum |
|---|---|---|
| National (Scottish) Level | Weakly framed | Strongly framed |
| School Level | Weakly framed | Strongly framed |
| Department Level | Weakly framed | Strongly framed |
| Teacher's Level | Weakly framed | Strongly framed |
| Pupil's Level | Strongly framed | Strongly framed |

In Scotland, the national examination board did not specify particular titles (of novels, plays and poetry) to be studied, but ostensibly left the schools free to choose whether to read *Persuasion, King Lear,* and *The Prelude* or *The Golden Notebook, A Taste of Honey* and Sylvia Plath. In practice, schools like St Luke's chose novels from the 'great tradition', Shakespeare, and Chaucer, Burns and Dunbar, because they felt obliged to teach material they were familiar with, had copies of in stock, and which the universities would expect pupils to know. Individual teachers were constrained by their school, and their head of department, or not, depending on the regime of their institution. Thus what was at national level, in the manifest curriculum, weakly framed for the teachers, could be experienced by the girls in Miss Keats's lessons as very strongly framed indeed. In the hidden curriculum the tenets of the 'great tradition' produced strong framing: certain authors were possible (Austen, Eliot, Brontë, Conrad, Hardy) others were not (Woolf, Durrell, Pinter, Wesker). In the manifest curriculum the individual teacher chose what to teach, but the pupils had no choice, and so experienced both covert and overt strong frames.

There are many other examples which show that classification and framing are powerful, analytic tools, but *only* if the level of analysis is carefully specified. The same issue applies to group and grid. An organization may be officially low group at national level, but in practice a local branch may operate with exclusive standards and demand high commitment. Similarly an institution may officially have a high grid – tight specification of behaviour and timetabling – but in practice segments may operate with low grid. For example, Janet Finch's (1984) work on pre-school playgroups in a working-class area could be an example of both the level and the overt or hidden agenda differing on the group dimension, as shown in figure 2.7. Similarly work on hospitals and prisons, both

*Figure 2.7 The strength of group in pre-school playgroups*

|  | Official policy | Practice |
|---|---|---|
| National (PPA) level | Weak group | N/A |
| Local playgroup | Weak group | Strong group |

in theory high-grid institutions, reveals that at ward level they frequently operate as low-grid ones.

These variations are not a problem for the social scientist as long as the level of analysis is specified before the phenomenon is located on the continuum. The same is true for the second caveat, which concerns the vantage point for analysis.

The issue here is basically that, when a social situation or institution is to be located according to the dimensions of classification and framing, or group and grid, it is important to specify whose perspective is being adopted. In particular it is important to decide, and communicate to the audience, whether the location of a phenomenon – as, for example, high grid, low group – is based on the outsider/research perspective *or* that of the participants in the action. So, as a social scientist I stated (p. 37) that it is 'relatively easy to join the RSPCA...but difficult to enter the Athenaeum'. That was a generalization made by an outsider, drawing on demographic facts about British society, such as sex (the Athenaeum is men-only, the RSPCA open to both sexes), wealth (the annual subscription to the former is £313, that of the RSPCA is £8) and entrance procedures (nomination by two members is a necessary first step for the Athenaeum, a coupon for the RSPCA is regularly printed in the *Radio Times*) and so on. It is important to realize, however, that there will be those who find joining the RSPCA difficult (illiterates, the very poor, those with no English) and others who find joining the Athenaeum quite unproblematic (a wealthy, Oxford graduate, white, male, old Etonian, Anglican bishop whose father, uncles and godfathers are already members, for example). Thus if the concepts are to be useful, the vantage point of the analysis needs to be specified.

The paper by Bloor and Bloor (1982) shows industrial scientists are a good example. The authors draw on interviews with twenty scientists employed in industry, and then use group and grid *both* as outsiders, to locate their respondents, and *then* as insiders, when they set out how the respondents themselves see their research work

*Figure 2.8 Dominant group's mapping of adolescent girls and sexuality*

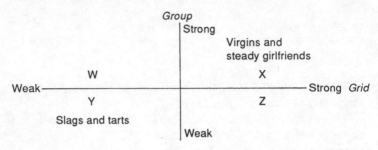

in terms of group and grid. Differentiating between the observer's standpoint and that of the informants is particularly important when one of the topics under examination is the social role of any muted group, because it is likely that a muted group will experience the 'same' situation rather differently. Thus the material on teenage sexuality outlined on pp.16-18 suggests a different mapping of the social world of teenage girls along the group and grid dimensions when viewed by the dominant group (boys) and by the muted group (girls). The boys' view is shown in figure 2.8 and the girls' in figure 2.9. In the boys' model, which is very simple, all teenage girls are of two, opposed, kinds. 'Virgins and faithful girlfriends' is a difficult category to enter and remain in (high group) and one where rules about time and behaviour are strict (high grid). Thus 'nice girls' have to dress in particular styles, avoid certain locations and people, must not get drunk, do not use contraceptives and so on. 'Bad' girls is an easy category to fall into, and once there, there are few rules.

Adolescent girls, however, see their social world in a more complex way, as shown in figure 2.9. For girls, the X quartile is occupied by girls who are, as yet, too childlike to be involved with boys, are kept at home, and therefore are 'good' through no effort of their own. All girls who date boys are located in a confusing, and complex world where group is weak, and only the strength of the behavioural rules (the grid) serves to demarcate four types of girl. These are the virgins, the nice girls who only have sexual relations with one boy to whom they are attached (by love or a ring, or both), 'unlucky' girls who were nice girls whose relationships have proved fragile, and lays. Unfortunately for the girls, they are sure that boys do not recognize these fine gradations in the low group

*Figure 2.9 Muted group's mapping of adolescent girls and sexuality*

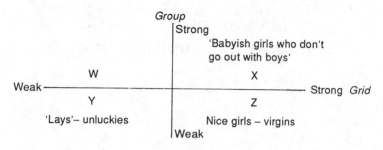

half of the world, and so the muted group used the boys' model to organize much of their own lives.

Some commentators on Bernstein (and on Douglas but to a lesser extent) have found the necessity of specifying levels and vantage points of analysis before using these continua, and Bernstein's frequent failure to do so himself, so disconcerting that they reject the whole conceptual apparatus. This is a great mistake because the conceptual power of the two continua is considerable. Throughout this volume classification and framing have been used when knowledge is the centre of the analysis (as in chapter 5) while group and grid are operationalized when organizations and societies are discussed.

The themes from the Ardeners, Bernstein, Douglas and Bourdieu are illustrated in the next chapter with a case study of elite education for girls.

# 3

# Lessons from St Luke's:
# women and cultural reproduction

Whereas the old middle class could reproduce itself through strongly classified and framed (education) systems, the new middle class reproduces itself through cultural systems characterized by much weaker boundaries. One of the key cultural elements of the new middle class...is the role of women as agents of cultural reproduction.

(Atkinson 1985a: 160)

The feminist education pioneers, whether or not they realized it, were creating a new kind of woman who had two novel roles to take: as members of elite professions including teaching and/or as mothers in the new middle class. These educated ladies were crucial agents in cultural reproduction. Amanda Cross's (1976) novel *The Question of Max*, based loosely on Winifred Holtby, Vera Brittain and Dorothy Sayers, focuses on how these women and their contemporaries created new lifestyles. In the novel a contemporary man asks, when it appears that he might be the son of one of these pioneers, 'who would want, for a mother, however goddesslike, a feminist, a free thinker, a socialist, and a pacifist?' (Cross 1976: 161). The male character rejects a whole way of life: the degree, the novels, the peace campaigning, the socialism and the feminism. However, the answer to his question is actually: the new middle class, and/or the intelligentsia. Women such as Vera Brittain, Naomi Mitchison and Edith Summerskill, who married and had children, were reproducing a new kind of cultural capital, needed by a new sector of the upper middle class.

Mary Douglas defines cultural and social capital in the following way: 'Cultural capital is based upon educational qualifications but it includes subsequent self-education in various ways. Social capital is the advantage that comes to a child from a home well-endowed with cultural capital' (Douglas 1982a: 129). The aim of this chapter is to examine the role played by women in reproducing cultural capital. As Atkinson (1985a: 160-6) has pointed out, the 'significance of women in the cultural reproduction of the middle classes', though mentioned in passing by Bernstein (1973a) has been left undeveloped in his sociology of education. Atkinson continues that Bernstein's observations do *not* merely 'recapitulate' the one way in which women have always been visible in the sociology of education: as mothers. Instead Bernstein's views on the role women play in cultural reproduction is only one aspect of his conception of the relationships between the moral order and the gender order of society. It is this relationship which forms the subject of this chapter.

The chapter begins with a brief description of the relationships between sex roles and elite reproduction in one girls' public school. It then builds on this case study to explore further how the themes it raises are fundamental to understanding how the education system of contemporary Britain works. Readers who have read about cultural reproduction at St Luke's may wish to skip over the first half of the chapter. The data presented here have been published before (Delamont 1984b, 1984c). The data were collected between 1969-75, they are Scottish, and the sample was small. I wish there were larger, more recent, studies from other countries such as England and Canada which could be used to illustrate cultural reproduction, but the problem has not received sufficient research attention since 1969. Compared to the data bases used by Bourdieu (1973) and Bernstein (1973a) the St Luke's study needs no apology. Bourdieu's data are not data at all in any sense that Anglo-Saxon sociologists can recognize, and Bernstein's theories in the last decade have not been based on any data. The St Luke's study is limited, but the subsequent Australian research by Connell *et al.* (1981) in several schools are entirely compatible with it. Connell *et al.* conducted an interview-based project, in several Australian cities, which reinforces my arguments about elite women and cultural reproduction.

## St Luke's: a case study of cultural reproduction

St Luke's is the pseudonym of an elite girls' school – a member of the organization of girls' public schools – in a Scottish city. An ethnography conducted there in 1970 has been fully described elsewhere (Delamont 1973). The focus was a pair of parallel forms of 14- and 15-year old girls containing forty-four girls. Observational data were supplemented by interviews, questionnaires, and other paper and pencil tests. The material gathered allows an analysis of how two different sectors of the upper-middle class in Scotland were both using the school to reproduce themselves. This analysis, published originally in Delamont (1976a), has subsequently been elaborated in the light of additional data in Delamont (1983a, 1984a, 1984b). It concerns the relationships between sex roles, maternal occupations and qualifications, father's employment, clique membership, academic achievement and interests, and the social position of St Luke's.

St Luke's is an expensive school. In 1984 the fees were £520 per term for a senior school day girl. It is also socially and academically selective – as it is oversubscribed the school takes only clever girls, and ones from elite homes. Pupils who attend St Luke's meet other girls from upper-middle-class homes, and therefore mix with appropriate age-mates. Just as John Finlay Scott (1980) argues for the American College Sorority, one of the functions served by St Luke's is social selection. However, since Scott's work on dating and marriage rules among sorority members plays down the academic aspects of the elite American women's colleges, that is a lop-sided account of them. The Seven Sisters, like St Luke's, provides both an outstanding education and a social network of a class-based kind. Connell *et al.* (1981) have made a similar point in their analysis of Jamieson College, an 'old established private secondary school for girls' in an Australian city. Jamieson College offers parents and pupils: (i) a moral order (Protestant and protective); (ii) high academic success; (iii) an 'all-round' education (cultural, musical, sporting); and (iv) social exclusiveness and a social network. St Luke's could be said to deliver the same things to the Scottish parents whose daughters I observed receiving them.

However, where my analysis differs from that of Connell and his colleagues is that St Luke's (and I suspect Jamieson College, too) was being regarded differently by two distinct groups of girls who co-existed in the same classrooms but took away from the school quite different 'packages' of experience.

St Luke's, situated in a wealthy area in the East of Scotland, has an intake which is highly selected, both socially and academically. The school is one of the most expensive in Scotland, and all the girls come from homes in the highest social class, many fathers being managers of national or multi-national companies, or owners of Scottish-based small firms of the type discussed by Scott and Hughes (1980). Others are senior staff in higher education, members of the traditional professions – doctors, lawyers, dentists, architects and so forth, or senior government employees. St Luke's was founded in the nineteenth century by feminist pioneers to educate the daughters of the upper strata and to prepare them for entry to university, the professions and 'semi-professions'. The staff, all female, are highly qualified: the academic secondary teachers will have honours degrees, and three have Ph.Ds.

There were forty-four girls in the third year studied, a quarter of whom were boarders. They had been at school together for some years before my research: a quarter had been at St Luke's since they were 5, and the mean length of their time at the school was 6.2 years. The girls were divided into two parallel forms for administrative purposes but were taught in 'sets' for each subject. This meant that there was none of the polarization caused by streaming or tracking. The forty-four girls formed themselves into five cliques or friendship groups – voluntary associations of pupils which would gather in break (recess) and at lunch, and sometimes met outside school, plus some detached isolates. Clique 1 was made up of ten boarders who were thrown together by the organization of St Luke's rather than common interests. Cliques 3 and 4 had four members each and were doing relatively badly academically. The two large groups, 2 and 5, are the central concern of this chapter, exemplifying two distinct types of cultural reproduction in one classroom. The forty-four girls who appear in the sociometry of the third year were not all attending St Luke's during my observation period. Una was on a ski-ing course and Isabelle away ill. Table 3.1 shows how the girls were divided into six cliques, plus three isolates; each clique has been given a nickname as a mnemonic.

Group 1 – 'the boarders' – consisted of the ten third-year girls who lived together in the boarding house. It was relatively self-contained with only four choices crossing its boundary. All the third-year boarders were included in the clique. The boarders were relatively successful academically, and many of them were active in school sports, providing the backbone of several teams. Group 2 was the largest group with twelve members and had a clearly distinguishable lifestyle. They called themselves 'grown up' and were self-consciously involved in an adolescent lifestyle. They dressed fashionably, drank coffee (and perhaps alcohol), smoked

*Table 3.1 Friendship groups at St Luke's*

| Group no. | Name | Composition |
|---|---|---|
| 1 | The boarders | Alexandra, Jackie, Barbara, Fleur, Eleanor, Janice, Esther, Hazel and Mary |
| 2 | 'Debs and dollies' | Vanessa, Nancy, Katherine, Lorraine, Yvonne, Gale, Louise, Tessa, Zoe, Monica, Caitlin and Olivia |
| 3 | 'Little women' | Belinda, Cheryl, Lorna and Geraldine |
| 4 | 'Proud riders' | Rosalind, Sharon and Frances (Isabelle) |
| 5 | 'Swots and weeds' | Jill, Charmian, Philippa, Evelyn, Henrietta, Penny and Michelle (Mandy) |
| 6 | 'Intermediates' | Angela, Selina and Clare |
| | Isolates | Wendy, Una and Deborah |

cigarettes (and perhaps pot), wore make-up and went around with a crowd of boys. This was demonstrated during the research when a large number of this group arrived for their interviews (which were taking place in the school holidays in a flat in the city centre) with a group of boys. They had all been thrown out of a coffee bar which was later raided by the drug squad. Vanessa was eventually expelled from the school. However, many of the group were academically ambitious, and were doing well at schoolwork. This group, along with the boarders, was the mainstay of the sports teams.

Cliques 3 and 4 were both small. Belinda, Geraldine, Cheryl and Lorna made up group 3. These girls were keen on the Guides and spent their leisure time in family and church-based activities. Group 4 – Rosalind, Frances, Sharon and Isabelle (an absentee) – were similar but could be distinguished by a love of riding. These two groups were not involved in school sport, were doing relatively poorly at their schoolwork, and were not academically ambitious. However, they were not badly behaved and worked hard, so were no trouble to staff.

Group 5 had seven members and called themselves 'the clever ones'. Henrietta even said, 'We're the academic set – the intellectuals.' They were hostile to school games, and had more intellectual leisure pursuits than any other group. Group 2 girls called group 5 'the swots and the weeds'. This, though rude, does capture two of their main characteristics – hatred of team games and a devotion to reading and other solitary, intellectual pastimes – archaeology, computing, origami, *petit point*, psychology and music. Equally apt was Henrietta's nickname for group 2, 'the debs and the dollies'. Group 2 girls were either involved in the lifestyle chronicled in the Scottish *Tatler* (hunt balls and grouse shooting) or in a more teenage lifestyle centred on disco dancing. Very few of the group 2 girls enjoyed reading, few played an instrument and none belonged to the Guides. Group 6 had only three girls, Clare, Selina and Angela, who scored higher academically than any group but 5. These girls were relatively colourless, and had no distinguishing hobbies or lifestyle. Additionally, there were three relatively isolated pupils – Wendy, Una and Deborah.

Delamont (1973, 1984b) contains the detailed material on academic achievement, leisure activities, amount of non-school reading, and other measures used to distinguish these six cliques. In 1973, I used Punch's (1970) distinction between intelligentsia and bourgeoisie to throw light on the differences in family style which lay behind cliques 2 and 5. Punch, like Bernstein (1973a), highlighted the paradox whereby the intelligentsia are 'objectively' placed by 'their economic and market situation' firmly in the 'privileged strata'. But many manifestations and symbols of that class position are utterly despised by them – organized religion, xenophobic patriotism, repressive conformity, class materialism, philistinism. Punch goes on to argue that:

> children crystallize the intellectual's dilemma because there may well emerge an incipient conflict between his ideology and his children's perceived interests....He may, too, have socialized his children out of an orthodox educational environment which can find it hard to accommodate the precocious, outspoken, capricious, imperious, sensitive child of intellectual parents, who have probably transmitted their distaste for uniforms, corporal punishment, compulsory religion, authority and so on, to their progeny...

The academic set came from the intelligentsia. They combined a distaste for some of the authoritarian and moral aspects of the school regime with an eager acceptance of its academic offerings. Apart from their dislike of team games and religion, these girls were not rebels – and they saw the school as a desirable scholarly environment which tolerated intellectual diversity. The girls in the academic set came from homes with a parent employed in higher education, had a graduate mother with a career of her own, or both. Indeed, three girls had two parents with careers in higher education, while another's were both practising doctors. In this, they formed a contrast to the 'debs and dollies', where none of the girls had a graduate mother with a career, and no parent was employed in higher education or the 'liberal professions'. In the academic set, the girls showed various attitudes related to their 'dual-career family' background. They were more likely than others in their classes to see their futures outside the East of Scotland – attending Oxbridge rather than the local university, and following careers rather than jobs, which stretched beyond undergraduate work into research. They were also more likely to see themselves as individuals rather than just wives and mothers – a finding which is supported in research on Scottish college and university students by Galloway (1973). She found that girls with working mothers held significantly more 'liberated' attitudes on woman's role than their peers with non-working mothers.

The 'progressive' ideology of the intelligentsia was reflected in the girls' perspectives on life inside and outside school. One girl in clique 5 wanted to be a Marxist MP, and all of them had political views to the left of their peers. Interestingly, in the light of Punch and Bernstein's ideas, girls in the academic set were likely to regard their very presence at St Luke's as anomalous. That is, they were the only girls who felt it necessary to explain and justify their attendance at St Luke's as if it were something *not* to be taken for granted. Other girls never mentioned their presence: St Luke's was the right sort of school. All clique 5 had been to another school before coming to St Luke's for their academic secondary education, and these former schools were either progressive state primaries, a Parents' National Education Union (PNEU) school or a Steiner. All were able to reproduce their parents' justifications for transferring them to St Luke's. These form a fascinating collection of liberal vacillation attempting to reconcile the contradictions Bernstein outlines.

The 'debs and dollies' were not failing academically. They were a mixed group in terms of success in school. Some were doing 'intellectual' courses in school, and had high ambitions. However, many of the girls in this group were hoping to enter the 'feminised semi-professions' – the paramedical occupations, social work, teaching small children and so on. It is tempting to argue that this was associated with their early adoption of a 'girlfriend' role in their leisure time – feminine jobs for feminine girls. However, none of them said that they thought these jobs suitable for women, or that they combined well with marriage. Rather they claimed to be motivated by social consciences and to like working with people. As one girl put it:

> I think I've always wanted to do something like – primary or infant teaching – I – well I wouldn't like to do it in a private school – I'd like to teach in a Corporation school because the kids – if you got them doing something it would give them great satisfaction 'cos they're deprived.

Another characteristic of this clique was their hostility to the school rules, which they regarded as 'petty', 'stupid' and 'nothing to do with school work' especially rules about dress, talking and deportment. Their attitudes were captured best by an incident which Vanessa recounted. A senior teacher had found her putting up a poster and selling tickets for a dance and confiscated both. Vanessa complained that the dance was 'nothing to do with my French, but she told me off next lesson too'. This clique perceived that some staff disapproved of their leisure activities and their manifestations in school, and they believed that staff allowed their disapproval unfairly to influence their school behaviour *vis-à-vis* the girls.

The major part of the research at St Luke's was focused upon teacher-pupil interaction in the classroom, and especially on a search for differences in pupils' patterns of verbal contributions to classroom discourse. The hypothesis was that individual differences in attitudes to schoolwork, and in study habits, would be reflected in their contributions to classroom talk; and that there might be sub-groups of pupils who shared common attitudes to schooling and common patterns of contribution.

Classrooms at St Luke's were quiet, orderly and academic places. Most lessons were teacher dominated. The typical forty-minute lesson at St Luke's contained twenty-five minutes of teacher talk and eight of pupil talk. Very little silence occurred, and little time was lost in confusion (about four minutes in forty). I have collected a detailed breakdown of the eight minutes in each lesson when a girl was talking. In an average lesson, there were twenty-four pupil contributions, approximately fifteen directly related to the academic content of the lesson and nine tangential to it. These findings accord well with other research done in academic secondary classrooms, such as Barnes (1971), Bellack *et al.* (1966) and Smith and Meux (1970). Teachers varied in number and type of pupil contributions they received, and pupils varied in the amount and type of contributions offered. For example, the senior classics teacher Miss Iliad, received hardly any tangential contributions while a popular English teacher, Mrs Milton, received many. Similarly, some girls (such as Wendy and Geraldine) hardly ever spoke in class, while others (such as Henrietta and Cheryl) took an active role in the discourse. There are no published studies of this type on pupil contributions, so it is not possible to relate the St Luke's girls to other pupils. It would be interesting to know if the boys studied by Bullivant (1978) in a very academic Jewish school, and the students observed by Larkin (1979) and Lightfoot (1983) in elite American high schools had similarly varied contribution patterns. Connell *et al.* (1981) did not do any observational research, so it is not possible to find out whether Jamieson College and the other elite girls' schools they studied in Australia also included pupils with such varied classroom styles.

Nearly all pupils made more content-oriented contributions than tangential ones, but there were large differences between the pattern of different girls' contributions as well as their volume. There were relationships between the amount of speaking each girl did and her perceptions of what school was for, as well as between the nature of her speech and these perceptions. There were also marked variations in the classroom speech patterns of the different cliques. Most pupil talk was centred on content – over two-thirds of all pupil talk – and all pupils made many contributions of this type. Attempts to broaden the focus were rare, but those that did occur were significantly likely to come from the 'academic set'. Those girls made their fair share of ordinary contributions, but they also queried the teacher's definition of knowledge. Mostly, this was just intellectual curiosity, but occasionally they issued a more threatening challenge. These girls had families with access to knowledge. Their parents and siblings took learned journals and some were working in academic institutions. This gave the girls access to sources of knowledge more potent than their teacher. They could, and did, challenge teachers – 'My father says no-one holds that theory any more,' 'Mother says this week's *Nature* has an article on that,' or even 'Daddy's disproved that.' Only girls in clique 5 had this type of cultural capital, and only they used it to commit a form of symbolic violence on their staff.

Group 2, the daughters of managers and owners of businesses, were heavily involved in adolescent culture. Outside school, they went around in large, mixed groups; while inside, they resented the institutional control system, and had an instrumental attitude to the academic work. These girls did not challenge the teacher's definition of knowledge, even when they disagreed with her. One girl, Olivia, told me that popular girls with the staff 'Always say yes to them – always agree with them.' She continued her interview by complaining about the left-wing views of the staff and their attitude to pupils: 'They don't like to think that we're old enough to dispute what they say.... You can't obviously disagree with facts, but disapproving of rules, petty, stupid unnecessary rules.' Inside school group 2 never engaged the teachers in intellectual dialogue or tried negotiating knowledge.

These two groups can be seen as both recapitulating their family lifestyles in their own adolescence, and using the school to prepare for their own adult lifestyles. Both cliques wanted to pass public exams and enter further education or training, and St Luke's provided this service for both. In addition, it provided a socially exclusive atmosphere in which the future wives of the next generation of Scottish capitalists could meet and form networks, while for the future manipulators of culture, it provided an arena in which they could practise symbolic negotiation with highly qualified staff. It is, however, likely that this second group have been prepared for learning through active negotiation with staff not by St Luke's, but by their previous educational experience outside, in the invisible pedagogy of progressive schooling.

The different lifestyles of the six groups which were apparent at 14 were maintained throughout the rest of their school careers. The girls who stayed at school until 18-19 (predominantly from groups 1, 2 and 5) showed the same divergence in school involvement as they had in the third year. Academic success was achieved by girls from all groups. The results obtained by my sample, who had taken O-grades in 1971, H-grade in 1972, and further H-grades and/or A-levels in 1973, are shown, by clique in table 3.2. Only Belinda from group 3, and Frances and Isabelle from group 4 were still at school after Highers, and all group 6 had left. Most of the boarders, all group 5 and about half of group 2 were still in school at 18-19. The average number of passes at O-grade, H-grade, and at A-grade obtained by girls remaining from those three cliques and from the rest, is shown in the table. As expected, group 5 obtained the most exam passes at all levels, but the other girls achieved considerable

*Table 3.2 Public examination results of cliques (of girls staying till age 18)*

|  | Average no. of passes per member | | |
|  | (1971)<br>O-grades | (1972)<br>Highers | (1973)<br>A-levels |
| --- | --- | --- | --- |
| Group 5 (swots and weeds) | 9.3 | 5.4 | 2.6 |
| Group 1 (boarders) | 8.6 | 5.2 | 1.6 |
| Group 2 (debs and dollies) | 8.4 | 5.1 | 1.0 |
| Rest of sixth year | 8.4 | 5.0 | 1.0 |

success. Thus while the groups differed in their involvement with school activities, they all had successful academic careers.

The continuation of different types of involvement in the life of St Luke's can be seen from the school awards, offices and distinctions they achieved. School awards and distinctions can be divided into school offices (prefect, house captain, head girl, etc); sporting honours (captains and vice-captains of school teams); intellectual offices (president of the school history society, captain of the choir); and awards for social responsibility (running charities, the Duke of Edinburgh's Gold Award). The number of each type of award or office held by girls in each clique is shown in table 3.3. This reveals that group 5 dominated the intellectual activities, while groups 1 and 2 divided the sporting ones. The boarders (group 1) held many school offices, but all groups were involved in that sphere. The predominance of girls from groups 1

*Table 3.3 Table of school honours at St Luke's, 1973*

|  | Group 5 | Group 2 | The rest | Group 1 |
| --- | --- | --- | --- | --- |
| School officers<br>(e.g. house captain) | 5 | 3 | 3 | 12 |
| Sports honours<br>(e.g. squash captain) | 0 | 4 | 0 | 6 |
| Intellectual officers<br>(e.g. president of the<br>school history society) | 7 | 0 | 2 | 2 |
| Social responsibility awards<br>(e.g. Duke of Edinburgh Award) | 2 | 5 | 5 | 1 |

*Table 3.4 Membership of school first teams by clique, 1973*

| | SPORTS | | | | |
| | Lacrosse (1st XII) | Hockey (1st XI) | Tennis (1st VI) | Badminton and squash | Fencing |
| --- | --- | --- | --- | --- | --- |
| Group 1 | Hazel<br>Fleur<br>Mary<br>Jackie<br>Alexandra | Fleur<br>Mary<br>Jackie<br>Alexandra | Fleur<br>Mary<br>Alexandra | Mary<br>Esther | |
| Group 2 | Tessa<br>Monica | Tessa<br>Monica | Tessa | | Monica<br>Gale<br>Lorraine |

Note: Girls' names by cliques

and 2 in sport is evident from team membership as well as captaincy. The sixth-year girls who were members of St Luke's first teams are shown in table 3.4 with their group membership. Responsibility as house captains and vice-captains was equally divided among the groups.

To summarize the argument thus far: St Luke's contained in 1969-70 among its 14- and 15-year olds at least two distinct sub-cultures each using the school to reproduce itself. These two family/class sub-cultures – one based on dual career families with cultural-intellectual capital, the other based on single earner entrepreneurial/managerial fathers with financial wealth – both valued St Luke's, but for rather different reasons. Classroom contributions, leisure activities, career aspirations, and attitudes to what learning involved, were measurably different between the two groups, and these differences continued for the next four years till the pupils left the school.

Groups 1 and 2 (boarders, debs and dollies) held an essentially passive view of learning. They believed that pupils should listen, and accept the information they were given. For example, Hazel (a boarder) saw learning as an essentially passive process. Teachers have knowledge, and the pupil's task was to listen to them. Hazel told me cheerfully that she spoke very little in class, and made few contributions in any category. Another boarder, Alexandra, described her outlook as follows: 'I mean, I'm quite content to take facts,' and she too spoke very little. In contrast, most of the girls in group 5 had an active view of schooling. In response to my enquiry about what type of pupil teachers like, Charmian told me:

C  Popular with teachers? – well – the bright ones to start with
   – it's awfully difficult to think of what a teacher would like
   – they're always telling you not to quibble. It depends on the
   teacher – Mrs Flodden likes it. If you can produce things
   about the period you're in – like I once took something in
   Greek that I wanted translated to Miss Iliad and she –
   positively beamed at me. A great occasion. It depends – I
   think perhaps enthusiasm's probably the most important
   thing.

SD  And girls who are unpopular?

C  People who never put up their hands and even try to answer
   a question.

This active orientation is carried over into behaviour. The girls in
group 5 spoke more than their classmates, and made more
independent contributions than pupils in any other group. My
argument is that they saw the creation of school knowledge as a
shared activity, in which they had a role to play, and not as a fixed
body of material which they merely had to learn, passively. One or
two other pupils had similar contribution problems, but no other
group consisted entirely of pupils with a high participation level
and many independent contributions. These differences in
classroom style at 14 clearly paid off in terms of public exam
success, in that group 5 girls were the outstanding performers in
their cohort.
   Any explanation of this success is inevitably somewhat
speculative. However I wish to argue that group 5 contained those
girls who came from the intelligentsia rather than the
entrepreneurial upper-middle class, and that they were the
possessors of what Bourdieu has called 'cultural capital'. As I have
argued elsewhere (Delamont 1976a), group 2 girls – the debs and
dollies – were from entrepreneurial homes (the old middle class in
Bernstein's (1973a) terms), and St Luke's was preparing them to
take their places in that sector of the Scottish elite. The swots and
weeds (group 5) were representatives of Bernstein's 'new' middle
class, and were preparing to enter the intellectual elite of the
country. Evidence from the girls' family backgrounds supports this.
Girls in group 5 had parents in higher education or the 'liberal'
professions or the civil service; both mothers and fathers were
graduates, and all the mothers had careers. Group 2 had no graduate
mothers, no parents in higher education or the liberal professions,

and most fathers were in industry or were self-employed. For example, both Michelle's parents were university lecturers, while Monica's father manufactured sports equipment and her mother was not employed. Group 1 (the boarders) was an intermediate clique, in that many of the fathers were in 'the professions', but the mothers were not employed. The 'typical' boarder was Barbara whose father was a doctor in a rural area of Scotland.

The three large groups of girls could be seen to bring differing amounts of cultural capital to the school. St Luke's can be used as a test of the sociology of Pierre Bourdieu. Such a test is badly needed in Britain. Halsey *et al.* (1980) attempted to test some of Bourdieu's ideas on their sample of 10,000 adult males in England and Wales. Hammersley (1981) criticized this attempt, and a debate ensued (Heath *et al.* 1982; Hammersley 1982). All parties appear to agree that

> A sensitive ethnographer might well get a much better sense of a family's cultural capital than we (Halsey, Heath and Ridge) could ever get from our survey research. But even the ethnographer has to know what to look for. (Heath *et al.* 1982: 88)

The difficulties arise because 'Bourdieu's theory is couched in obscure, ill-defined language. He does not specify what would constitute an acceptable operationalization of his concepts' (Heath *et al.* 1982: 88). Halsey *et al.* (1980) were concerned with gross differences between sectors of male secondary education (secondary modern, grammar, direct grant, and public schools) and argued that differences in cultural capital between families did not seem to have much importance once selection for male secondary education has taken place. For these authors, economic capital – wealth – was more significant in enabling school fees to be paid. Their conclusion rests on a crude operationalization of cultural capital (parental education) and has been attacked by Hammersley (1981).

My own position is that, just as Atkinson (1983) has argued against the application of Bourdieu's work 'in any simple all-embracing sense for any given educational setting', it is too simple to see St Luke's girls as being equally endowed with cultural capital. Rather the group 5 girls have a much larger cultural legacy than their peers, deriving from *both* parents. Nowhere in the debates has the issue of girls' education been examined, but my contention is that the professional careers of the group 5 mothers meant that the group 5 girls saw women as active negotiators of knowledge in a different way from other pupils. Unfortunately I did not arrange to interview the girls' mothers, not did I gather sufficient data on their perceptions of sex roles (Delamont 1984b), so this has to remain a speculation. It is, however, a speculation supported by the 'swots and weeds', as the following material on Charmian shows. Typical of the 'academic set', Charmian wants to be both intellectual and original in all spheres of her life, including her hobbies. These are predominantly musical – playing two instruments and singing – but she also belongs to the Girl Guide Movement, where her attitude is intellectual and idiosyncratic: 'I don't like doing things like Child Nurse and Homemaker – far more interesting to do the interesting things like Speaker, and Singer – Local History.' (These are also, of course, the awards which have no particular feminine or domestic qualities). These qualities come through particularly in science lessons where Charmian and her friends in group 5 adapted better than any other to the pupil-centred, guided-discovery science. This issue has been discussed elsewhere (Delamont 1976, 1984; Atkinson and Delamont 1976).

The staffroom saw this divide rather differently. Group 5 girls were seen as coming from the 'right' kinds of family – one with books, and one which supported the school. Henrietta, for example, explained how both Dr Michaels and Mrs Flodden were family friends, as one of her parents is an historian, and they 'came to our bonfire party, and all knew each other at Oxford and Cambridge'. In contrast, many of the families of girls in group 2 were seen as 'inadequate' – plenty of material goods, but uncultured. One teacher summarized this view by dismissing a group 2 father with 'he made all his money in scrap metal'. This type of judgement is a perfect example of Bourdieu's (1977) arguments about the school testing things which are not taught there.

At St Luke's the 'debs and dollies' lacked some element of cultural competence which prevented them becoming active manipulators of knowledge. Compared with most Scottish adolescents, of course, they were enormously privileged and achieved academic success. However, in the context of St Luke's, they had failed to grasp the opportunity to become active manipulators, users and eventually producers of knowledge, and remained mere consumers of it.

## The wider implications

The work of Connell *et al.* (1981) and the St Luke's study are the only pieces of empirical work which focus on how elite families use schools to reproduce cultural capital. The central issue of how elite social groups who rely on cultural capital for their reproduction manage to transmit it to their children has been left under-researched. Little has been done on elite schools in general, and on childrearing in upper-middle-class families (Cohen 1981 being an exception). The lives of upper-middle-class girls at home and school are probably the least researched topic in the whole of sociology of education, despite being the group who have been, over the last century, the most influential group in rearing and marrying the men who are the most successful products of the British education system. Connell and his colleagues found that parents paying for an expensive elite education for daughters envisaged them entering the professions, but *not* commerce and business.

One hundred years ago parents in similar class positions supported elite girls' schools to educate their daughters but did not expect them to work for wages all their lives. Today the intelligentsia plans for its daughters to work in its own sector of the elite, but not enter the entrepreneurial elite or that of bureaucratic management. Ironically, as more women enter medicine, law and similar occupations, they are losing their power, influence, and relative earning power to the financial and entrepreneurial sector, as the concluding chapter argues.

Bourdieu (1986:80) points out that 'the same educational qualifications may guarantee quite different relations to culture' but that in the higher strata of the educational system 'more value comes to be set on ways of using knowledge and less on merely knowing'. It is precisely because the 'swots and weeds' placed value on ways of using knowledge that, as they grew older, they were more successful in educational achievement than any other group. At least two young women from group 5 are now active academic researchers themselves; not one person from any other clique is.

## Four implications / questions for further study

The St Luke's study was small, and could certainly have been done

61

better. It does, however, raise four issues which deserve research attention from sociologists, and my conviction that these topics need to be pursued is reinforced by the conclusions of the handful of subsequent studies which explicitly show families with cultural capital using the schools to reproduce that capital and enhance it (Connell *et al.* 1981; Cochran-Smith 1984). Each of these sociological issues can best be illuminated by structuralist theory of the kind displayed in the previous chapter, and it is that structuralist illumination which occupies the rest of this volume. Structuralism is the appropriate theoretical perspective because each topic is grounded less in the material world than in the cosmological and symbolic one where deeply-felt convictions about what is 'natural' operate, rather than rationality and reliance on evidence. These four issues are:

1 How did elite (girls') schools come to exist in their present form?
2 What are the occupations in the 'intelligentsia' section of the elite like for women who enter them?
3 What does studying women's experiences in those occupations tell us about those occupations as a whole?
4 What can we learn from the reproduction of cultural capital in these elite families about (a) the relationship between the home and the school in general, and about (b) family background and educational success.

These themes or questions are the focus of the rest of the book. In part II the rise and development of the elite girls' schools and colleges in Britain, the USA and Australasia is examined in terms of Douglas's theories of pollution control. Part III then focuses on the occupations that make up the 'professional' sector of social class one, and on the relationship between family background and educational success, using Bernstein and Bourdieu. Each section has an introduction, which the reader familiar with the basic issues may wish to skip over.

# Part II:
The mountains of inertia and prejudice:
A structuralist discussion of the period
1845 - 1944

# Introduction and background

Strenuous efforts were made by a band of pioneer women to improve the education of girls, whose interests had been allowed for so long to lag behind those of their brothers. The present generation, which has benefited by the many good schools now to be found all over the country, can have no conception of the mountains of inertia and prejudice which had to be removed before they could be brought into existence, or what it involved for the devoted women concerned and a number of enlightened men who backed them up.

(Sturge 1932: 9)

## Introduction

The three chapters which follow discuss the struggle to shift the mountains of inertia and prejudice to obtain for middle- and upper-class women three goals: academic secondary education, entry to higher education and membership of the 'liberal professions' of medicine, law and so forth. These chapters do not provide a detailed history of women's entry to these three spheres, but offer a theoretical commentary upon it. A reader completely unfamiliar with the historical record may wish to read Dyhouse (1981), Bryant (1979), Turner (1974), Vicinus (1985), Fletcher (1980), Kamm (1958, 1965) or Borer (1976) on the UK and/or Woody (1929), Farello (1970), Stock (1978), Horowitz (1984) or Soloman (1985) on the USA. However a knowledge of the campaigns to gain ladies an education and an occupation is not necessary, and what follows can be read by the uninitiated. Sturge (1932: 9) offers a useful summary of the dilemma which faced the pioneers of women's education. She praises the headmistresses — the group Glenday and Price (1974) have called *Reluctant Revolutionaries* — as follows:

There were a number of women able to organize and carry on the new institutions. Some of them deserve to rank with the great headmasters who did so much for the boys. It required an unusual combination of qualities, for they had to work out their own methods, and form their own traditions, and to do this without alienating timid parents still fearful of too much change.

The pioneers were setting out to create a revolution, but they had to do it 'without alienating timid parents'. This introductory section discusses briefly what the problems were, and the solution adopted, before chapters 3, 4 and 5 analyse the struggle with the ideas of the Ardeners, Douglas, Bernstein and Bourdieu.

## The background

For the first fifty years of the nineteenth century the daughters of the upper and middle classes (except for a few exceptional nonconformist and intellectual families) received an education which was specifically designed to be useless. They were carefully brought up to be ornamental and not to have any vocation, while male education was designed to fit men for occupations and professions, or for the male version of a life of leisure as a country gentleman. After about 1850 a movement grew up to change female education in the middle- and upper-classes which opened up male subjects, especially maths and classics, to middle-class women although at a price, as we shall see. The movement for the education of ladies had two stages. The first consisted of founding good, academic schools and offering lectures and classes to adult women given by distinguished male scholars. The second stage was the provision of university education for women, and the opening of the 'liberal professions'.

The pioneers of ladies' education inevitably became tangled in a web of conflicting demands and directives. They were trying to please several disparate groups and risking pleasing no one. Solving any one problem produced a host more, and the enemies and critics of women's education held so many different, and often contradictory, views that they could only be countered by running schools and colleges along paths which look odd in the twentieth century. Chapters 3, 4 and 5 look at the contradictions which surrounded the pioneers, how they resolved them, those they failed to resolve, and analyses these events and strategies in terms of women as a 'muted group'.

Until the 1850s the education of middle- and upper-class girls was essentially a private affair. Girls were educated at home, by mother, governess, father or siblings, or in small private schools. Peterson (1972) has written an intriguing analysis of the governess in Victorian Britain, highlighting the anomalies of her position. Pedersen (1975) has drawn our attention to the essentially private nature of the schools which the feminist campaigners deplored. Peterson (1972) summarizes the contradictions of the governess's position as follows. The governess was a lady fallen on hard times, and as such had no education except in the 'useless' accomplishments herself. She was rarely a teacher by choice, had no training for the work, and her unmarried state was a living testimony to her failure in the only contest open to the lady, husband-hunting. She was, therefore, unlikely to be regarded as skilful at man-trapping, and had little else to impart. Her role in the families which employed her was highly ambiguous and hence filled with tension, as Peterson (1972) has demonstrated.

Peterson starts from the oddity of so much attention being paid to the governess and her plight in Victorian periodicals when there were far fewer governesses than other servants (in 1851, there were 25,000 governesses and 750,000 servants) and when 'the suffering of the governess seems pale and singularly undramatic when compared with that of women in factories and mines'. Certainly governesses did not engage in any political agitation, and were not a potentially revolutionary group, seeking as they did 'genteel obscurity'. Peterson sees the symbolic importance of the governess in her status incongruity: the ambiguity of being a lady and wage-earner, living in the home but neither a servant nor a member of the family. The governess was a form of conspicuous consumption for the middle- and upper-class family because she was a symbol of the wife/mother's emancipation from the last type of work – teaching children – and her adoption of a totally ornamental role. The governess had to be a lady to live in the family, yet ladies did not earn money so all governesses were people whose father or brother had failed to support them. Becoming a governess was the only possible occupation for a destitute lady, yet it was only a precarious form of gentility. The salary was so low that there was no margin for illness or unemployment. The lady who had been reared to ornament her father's drawing-room had to sell herself to display her employer's prestige and the resulting tension could be great. Part of the 'failure' of the governess was that she had to leave her home, and enter someone else's. The lady's sphere was a private one, as Pedersen's (1975) work emphasizes: 'Ladies who kept private schools attended by young ladies are familiar figures in Regency and Victorian novels (who) fit comfortably in the framework of the domestic drama.'

Pedersen demonstrates how deep the divide was between the ladies who ran small private schools in their homes and the new breed of public figures: the heads of the big, public girls' schools. The available sources for studying the ladies who kept schools (schoolmistresses as Pedersen terms them) and the pioneering headmistresses are themselves different. A large literature exists on the headmistresses (see appendix 2), very little on the lady schoolkeepers. Pedersen argues:

> The disparity in the sources that survive for studying the two types of teachers reflects the different roles they sought to play. Whereas the private schoolmistress aspired to a leisured, amateur role in a secluded, quasi-domestic setting, the public school heads aimed rather to secure professional recognition and sought distinction in the public sphere.

Like the governess, ladies who kept private schools were 'members of that anomalous social category – poor ladies obliged to work for pay. The social position of such women was ambiguous...'

One such woman, driven to schoolkeeping, was Mrs Lawrence Ottley, mother of Alice Ottley the founding headmistress of Worcester High School for Girls. Canon Lawrence Ottley died and

> Mrs Ottley was confronted with the problem of providing, with a very limited income, for the education of her seven sons....From the first she made up her mind that they should have those opportunities in life which only a first-rate education can give. Accordingly she took a house in Hampstead, intending to receive into her family a few girls, to be educated with her own two youngest daughters.

Alice Ottley learnt to teach in her mother's private school. The lady schoolmistresses aimed at seclusion, a domestic arrangement with a small number of pupils, ideally boarders. The Taunton Commissioners were told that the aim was not 'to have large schools. They aimed rather to attract a small number of pupils of high social rank whom they could charge high fees.' Twenty was the maximum for a really genteel establishment, and the privacy was fiercely guarded. As Pedersen (1975) points out, these schools were based on ascribed status (homogeneous in social class terms) and ties of kinship and patronage were important in recruiting and holding pupils. The growth of the large, public girls' schools was a shift from privacy, ascription and patronage towards a system of girls' education based on openness, achievement, and competition. The two systems, however, remained alongside one another for at least a century. Some upper- and middle-class girls were still being educated by governesses at home or in tiny private schools run by impoverished ladies at least until the 1944 Education Act. The pioneers were successful but they did not destroy the opposition for many years.

The pioneers of academic secondary education, higher education and professions for women were scornful of the quality of the teaching and of the curriculum and facilities offered by governesses and private schools. Sturge (1932: 8) is typical:

> There were private schools for girls also, some of them so poorly taught and equipped as hardly to deserve the name, while even in those with more pretension, little provision was made for serious study, accomplishments being then the order of the day for girls....

Her family were influential in establishing the Redland High School for Girls in Bristol to replace this despised type of education.

The feminist educational pioneers objected to these schools on several grounds: poor buildings, teachers who had been forced to the task by poverty, the nature of the curriculum, and their domestic, private, secret nature. The debates in the USA and Australasia were essentially similar, except that governesses were rare, and poor seminaries or academies were seen as the source of the shallow accomplishments. The evidence on the seminaries and contemporary condemnation of them in the USA can be found in Woody (1929), Goodsell (1931), Thompson (1947) and Curti (1959). The pioneers of women's education in New Zealand (Wallis 1972) and Australia (Anon 1953; Fitzpatrick 1975) had similar motivations. In all three continents there were several contributory causes which produced the new type of girls' school. The nonconformist religious groups, especially the Quakers, were already giving girls academic instruction, and they were totally opposed to the frivolity of accomplishments. Then, as the idea of public elementary schools to civilize the lower classes caught on, the demand for teachers grew more acute and with it the notion that women could teach in these new schools if they were better educated themselves. This movement is portrayed vividly in the collection *Women's True Profession* edited by Hoffman (1981).

In all three continents the problems faced by the pioneers were the same, because the beliefs and practices they were challenging were essentially similar.

## Climbing the mountains

To scale the mountains of inertia and prejudice, the campaigners for women's education had to deal with three equally pressing problems. They had to find money to open and run schools and to start colleges and universities for women, and they had to prove that females were physically and mentally capable of learning Latin, Greek, Algebra and Chemistry in their teens; of reading classics and mathematics at university; and of mastering law and medicine and building a professional practice. The medical orthodoxy of the period was that women's bodies and brains could not stand the strains of education (Atkinson 1978, 1987; Burstyn 1980) without mental and physical collapse. Delirium and death were threatened, and few people believed that the female brain was capable of scholarship. So the pioneers had to show that girls and women could do the same intellectual work as boys and men, and that doing it would not destroy them. Allied to these 'biological' prejudices it was also widely accepted that educated females were *socially* handicapped – that men would not marry such women.

The fears about biological frailty and social handicap were directly related to the financial problems faced by the educational pioneers. Such negative views had to be challenged if any parents were going to pay for their daughters to go to schools, colleges and into professional training. Many boys' schools, and the existing university colleges, had endowments, and were not totally dependent on fees from parents. The pioneers had no such wealth behind them.

Two consequences followed the lack of finance for women's education. First, there was a sustained campaign, chronicled by Sheila Fletcher (1980) to rescue the girls' share of ancient endowments which had been left for educating children but were largely diverted to boys' schooling by the mid-nineteenth century. Second, the pioneers became adept at a kind of deception, disguising revolutionary activity behind a rhetoric of ladylike conformity to reassure their paying customers.

The financial problems which beset the campaigners for academic schooling for young ladies are detailed in all the institutional histories (e.g. Atkinson 1980 on the Northgate Grammar School for Girls in Ipswich; Fitzpatrick 1975 on the Presbyterian Ladies College in Melbourne; and Keep, R., 1946 on Mills College in the USA). The lack of secure, permanent funding meant that the committees and individuals who ran the early institutions were peculiarly dependent on the goodwill of their clients, so they had to provide something parents would buy, or close down. Kamm (1958: 55-6) tells us how parents reacted to serious academic subjects for girls at Cheltenham Ladies' College under Miss Beale in the 1850s and 1860s:

> The very name 'College' had an intimidating sound to parents, who were fearful that their girls 'would be turned into boys'. Then the curriculum, simple as it was, was considered too advanced and complicated. A mother who removed her daughter at the end of one quarter, complained bitterly that it was all very well for the girl to read Shakespeare, 'but don't you think it is more important for her to be able to sit down at the piano and entertain her friends?' Meanwhile the teaching of arithmetic was suspect. 'My dear lady', a father grumbled, 'if my daughters were going to be bankers, it would be very well to teach arithmetic as you do, but really there is no need'. He sent his daughters to another school.

This man died, leaving his daughters a fortune which they were too ignorant to manage and they fell into what Miss Beale termed 'pecuniary difficulties'.

The financial dependence on parents' whims could be overcome or circumvented, and the pioneers were often devious. One strategy adopted was to lie about the content of the curriculum; for example sciences could be hidden behind domestic labels, or disguised as geography, a subject not done by boys. (Miss Beale did this at Cheltenham Ladies College.) However, the best way to reassure parents was to emphasize how ladylike the school would make their daughters. Many Victorians believed that scholarship and ladylike behaviour were incompatible, so the schools and colleges set out to prove them wrong, as I have discussed elsewhere (Delamont 1978a). Basically, very strict standards of behaviour were applied

71

by the pioneers to their own conduct and enforced on the students and staff of the schools and colleges they founded. No whisper of impropriety was allowed to sully the occupants of educational institutions, or the whole cause could be lost. The early schools were very careful to keep girls away from boys, and 'masculine' pursuits were strictly controlled and often hidden. I have called this the 'double conformity' strategy, because the pioneers behaved like ladies and obeyed all the rules governing male scholarship as well. Double conformity was a strategy for achieving a revolution, but it can also become a trap.

The three chapters in this section focus in some detail, using theoretical ideas, on how the pioneers, a 'muted group', managed to create a revolution while publicly upholding traditional values. Ideas of purity and pollution, of cultural capital and of visible and invisible pedagogies are mobilized to illuminate themes from the campaign to scale the mountains of inertia and prejudice. The sources used for these chapters are discussed in appendix 2, with a critical note on the existing histories of education and their neglect of these issues.

# 4

## Chaperons, gloves, and cycling in skirts: strategies against pollution in women's education

Among the places out of bounds [to girls at Cheltenham Ladies College] were not unreasonably the race course, the polo ground, and the boys' college football ground.

(Benson 1934: 42)

Benson was at Cheltenham Ladies College in 1914. This chapter and the two following cover a period from about 1850 up to about 1945, with particular emphasis on the 1870-1918 era. The pioneers of academic education for ladies in America, Australasia and Britain were establishing schools and colleges where the rules and conventions which applied to the students (and staff) were strict, limiting, and to modern eyes, ridiculous. This chapter examines these rules and conventions, but it is important to stress at the outset that the pioneers adhered to them consciously and gladly, as a small price to pay to obtain an education. C.L. Maynard, at Girton in the 1870s and later the founder of Westfield College, London, wrote about these early days:

When nearly every elderly lady pretended to be shocked and grieved at the unfeminine nature of our proceedings, and nearly every old gentleman murmured something about the colour of stockings or asked if we had a boat on the river, and when girls of our own age tended to stand aloof, it was indeed time to be careful, and very careful we were. It was a time to be careful with regard to the strictures of our adversaries....The conventionalities of the age...were the best possible shelter for the new aspirations, and firmly we kept to them...and the very least deviation, whether in dress or manner, from the ordinary rules of society was laid down in unwritten law to be avoided. (1910: 189-90)

Douglas's (1966) theories about pollution beliefs have been outlined in chapter 2 (pp.19-24). While all the types Douglas proposes can be found in Victorian society, this chapter deals with those pollution beliefs which reinforce important boundaries within the social system. It also relies on Douglas's argument that if the 'social structure is strictly articulated' it will impinge strongly on male-female relationships, and the researcher can expect to find pollution beliefs enlisted to bind men and women to their ordained roles. The chapter focuses upon the ways in which the feminist pioneers reinforced the boundaries between themselves and their charges (ladies) and a variety of potentially dangerous pollutants. The same ideas can be applied to many other areas of Victorian society, as in the work of Davidoff (1973) on the etiquette (which is a version of pollution avoidance behaviour) in the highest circles of the London season. The third type of pollution belief is also characteristic of a society where the doctrine of separate spheres operated (Kraditor 1968) and will also be apparent in this chapter.

The pioneers whose strategies concerning the organization of education are the focus of this chapter (its content is the subject of chapter 5) were a muted group who were trying to change the important boundaries of female behaviour that the dominant group held. Changing the model of society is a perilous enterprise, and the educational pioneers had to be very careful not to infringe the rules of ladylike behaviour. A lady who had lost her reputation was not only herself polluted, but would corrupt others: the adulterous wife must never see her daughters again, the girl who wore bloomers would be condemned as an atheist suffragette. The woman attending one of the new schools, or a college, was seen as particularly vulnerable to pollution, and so her behaviour, dress, activities, and companions were hedged round with a complex system of rules and prohibitions. This chapter examines the rules and procedures introduced in the schools and colleges to protect the staff and students from pollution by men, the public gaze, games, bicycling, acting, other social classes, and other denominations. The chief strategies used by the pioneers were chaperonage, conduct codes and dress codes, physical barriers to maintain institutional privacy, and social barriers to prevent 'mingling'. These are described in turn, starting with chaperonage.

## Protection against men: chaperonage

The social world inhabited by the ladies who were the potential
pupils of the new schools and colleges had the strictly articulated
social structure which strongly impinged on male-female
relationships described by Douglas (1966). Pollution beliefs were
therefore found to reinforce important boundaries, such as that
separating men and women. The schools and colleges relied on two
strategies for ensuring that pupils and students did not become
contaminated by men: enforcing the presence of a chaperon and
making rules which prevented male-female contact. Both are here
called 'chaperonage' and evidence of both can be found in the
Australasian, American, and British schools and colleges.

The history of the King Edward VI School for Girls in
Birmingham (Vardy 1928: 24), which was founded in 1883 sharing
the boys' school building, tells us how 'the doors into the girls'
part' were 'kept carefully locked'. Two small girls once followed a
caretaker into the boys' building and were caught. This was 'a most
dire offence, the true heinousness of which did not dawn on them
till long afterwards'. Similarly, when Bedford got a girls' high
school in 1881 it 'began at 9.15 so that boys and girls should not
throng the streets at the same time' (Westaway 1932: 23). The new
school had a music room with glass partitions so 'A mistress sitting
at a table in the space outside correcting her exercise books would
be able to chaperone several masters at once' (p.35). This was not,
apparently, practical for Hutchins and Godber (1982: 146) say
'Where sound could not get out, air could not get in, and the first
time Mr Bond-Andrews saw the glass cubicle he dragged his piano
out of it and refused to be suffocated. And that was the end of it.'

However the symbolic force of the chaperonage was no doubt
reassuring. By 1920 Bedford did not have an 'explicit rule against
speaking to boys in the town; parents were assumed to exert some
influence...and girls were 'on their honour' to behave properly. The
propriety would be judged by the standards of the day' (Godber and
Hutchins 1982: 52). A pupil at the Oxford Girls' High School
between 1892 and 1907 remembered:

> an older girl being reproached for walking down the High Street
> with a boy with no chaperon – and when she protested 'but Miss
> Soulsby, it was my *brother*', the retort was – 'Remember –
> everyone does not know it is your brother. Do not let it occur
> again!' (Stack 1963: 59)

The Americans were equally careful about chaperonage. When Abbot Academy was being planned in New Hampshire in the 1820s, the mothers of potential pupils objected to the girls' school being built on the main street because the boys from Phillips Academy and the theological students thronged there (Lloyd 1979: 24-6). In the 1850s and 1860s the pupils were allowed to receive boy callers if they were known to the girls' parents (pp. 120-6). By 1913 there was a school dance, where meetings with boys were chaperoned, but free association was still ruled out. The head 'moved fast to block the routes out into the countryside or down the road to the Orchard Street ice-cream parlour' (p.218) because the boys from Phillips were there, and specified twenty-three 'approved' walks. Short walks could be taken with one other girl, longer ones had to be chaperoned by an adult. The school was vigilant, and 'The two Boston Symphony tickets became three, one for a chaperon paid for by the two student ticket holders, when an alert Andover neighbour reported the two Abbot seats empty one afternoon' (p.218).

Chaperonage was equally strict in the universities. As late as 1908, when the middle-aged headmistress of Laurel Bank School, Glasgow, visited Newnham she ran into the strict rules:

> On the night of my arrival Miss Corner asked me if there were any friends in Cambridge whom I would like to see. I mentioned the names of a friend of my young brother and of another very young man. Imagine the surprise of a headmistress when Miss Corner, saying that this could easily be arranged, added that it would give pleasure to one of the Fellows to be my chaperon! (Hannam Watson 1953: 13)

Miss Watson was over 30, and the headmistress of a pioneering girls' school, but the rules still had to be obeyed. As Stephen (1927: 203) writes 'Young women were not in the habit of going about the world unchaperoned – and any breach of this rule would appear even more conspicuous in a university town than anywhere else.' This insistence on chaperons in Cambridge was not only to regulate association between the young ladies and men, but also to distinguish the female students from the prostitutes who thronged university towns.

When Eleanor Lord (1938), an American, came to Britain to work on her Ph.D in the 1890s, she spent some time at Newnham: 'I was nonplussed at the rigidity of the Newnham regulations' (p.116), but when Mary Paley Marshall gave a lecture on the history of the college, Lord understood the reasons. The rules included: 'No Newnham student should appear to take any notice of a university undergraduate at lectures, or on the street, even if he were her own brother' (p.117). Lord found that 'neither sex looked the other in the eye under ordinary circumstances'. She had tea in Sidney Sussex College, chaperoned, and discovered going to religious services in Trinity needed a chaperon but because the services in Kings were open to the public, women could go unchaperoned. Marshall's talk would have recalled the 1870s, when Girton and Newnham were very new, and their survival uncertain. Girton was very strict. The girls lived outside Cambridge itself, well away from both the male students and the prostitutes they frequented. They were carefully chaperoned in lectures and on social occasions. Sara Burstall, a student at Girton in the early days, writes: 'The social rules for us women students were very strict in these days, we could be chaperoned to men's college parties only by some lady we knew at home, independently of Cambridge' (Burstall 1933: 86).

The same care was taken in Oxford, and Bailey, describing the early days of Lady Margaret Hall (LMH) says:

> It is curious to look back now and see how necessary the chaperon was. In 1890 girls had hardly begun to walk much about Oxford alone. Many did, of course, but others might be seen accompanied by a maid, and Oxford was particularly ready to remark on any advanced behaviour on the part of a woman student. (Bailey 1923: 71)

The LMH students were not allowed out alone, so 'even a dash into town to buy a cake involved the search for a companion' (Bailey 1923: 61). Dalglish, an Oxford undergraduate during the First World War describes how 'as a fresher' she 'had to slink into Magdalen with a chaperon because no other women students were attending certain lectures' (Dalglish 1938: 84). Outside Oxford and Cambridge, women students were equally sheltered. At Manchester, the first female students in the 1880s could not use the library:

> It would have been the height of impropriety to enter the library and demand a book in the hardened manner now usual. No, we

had to 'fill up a voucher', and a dear little maid-of-all-work, aged about 13 went to the library with it. (Tylecote 1941: 13)

The class difference here is particularly interesting, in that a working-class child could go to the library, where young ladies could not. Louisa Martindale, the distinguished surgeon, was at Royal Holloway College, London in the 1890s and could only go to a political meeting with friends 'on condition we took a cab and a chaperon!' (1951: 27). Crow summarizes the British scene in the early days of women's higher education:

> to share lectures with men students would have been unladylike – a hazard that may seem laughable today but one which was of crucial importance....To be considered unladylike was to court the outer darkness – and often to reach it! (1972: 53)

The American pioneers had to proceed with equal care and circumspection when founding colleges for women. Newcomer (1959) discusses the importance of good conduct, and the American use of chaperonage. Plum and Dowell (1961: 9) report that when Vassar opened in 1865 there was a rule that 'no one will be allowed to receive calls from gentlemen, excepting their fathers, without a letter of introduction from their parents to Miss Lyman', and one woman who was found to have passed off a stranger as a cousin was instantly dismissed from college. Histories of Bryn Mawr, like those of other colleges, show the same attention to the proprieties:

> Not going off the campus after dark in parties of less than three was a rule stringently enforced....The receiving of men in a student's study called for curious degrees of chaperonage, depending on the degree of relationship, whether brother, cousin, father or great uncle. (Meigs 1956: 57)

The early colleges for women in the USA were in the East, in places where social rules were strict. As women were admitted to colleges in less 'civilized' places, such as California and the mid-West, the pioneers imposed the standards of the Eastern seaboard.

Marion Talbot (1936: 59) was the first Dean of Women at Chicago known (in 1892) more for the stock yards than for its genteel social life. Talbot says: 'It was necessary to formulate the essential principles of good social form and to decide what social conventions had lost their meaning and could be discarded.' Some

women graduates went to a dance in a public hall, which was a
social error, and it got written up in the papers. Later a male student
told her that 'He was very glad, in case he had a sister who wanted
to enter the university, to know that some degree of social
protection would be given her and social standards set before her'
(Talbot 1936: 63).

In 1910, Eleanor Lord was appointed Dean of Women at
Groucher, where during the 1914-18 war she faced a troublesome
chaperonage problem. A ball was to be held for the navy, and she
was asked to supply sixty female students as partners. The war
effort demanded acceding, and so the students chose sixty of their
number. At the ball 'No name introductions were made, however,
and the dignity and poise of the college contingent, and
incidentally, the entire absence of cheek dancing so far as they were
concerned was a matter of pride and gratification' (1938: 151).

The pioneers in New Zealand and Australia were equally
vigilant. Wallis (1972: 32) in her history of the Otago Girls' High
School tells how drill classes began in 1872 in the gymnasium and
'a walled pathway was constructed so that the girls could reach it
without the contamination of contact with, or sight of, the boys'.
Similarly when male teachers were employed by the school, which
opened in 1871, the pupils' reputations were protected: 'Younger
men teachers conducting girls' classes were always chaperoned by
one of the women governesses' (1972: 25). The Presbyterian Ladies
College in Melbourne, founded in 1875, advertised for its first
principal who 'must be a married gentleman' (Fitzpatrick 1975: 38)
with the same respectability in mind.

What sense can we make of these practices in the light of
Douglas's theories? The chaperonage rules were based on privacy,
age, class, marital status and kinship. Middle- and upper-class
ladies who were unmarried were not to be seen in any public place
with any male. In private they could meet males who were married,
or relations, or chosen by their families, if a named woman was also
present. In exceptional circumstances, such as a war, these rules
could be weakened (the dance for the navy) but no social
relationship could be established (no introductions were made).
Public places, such as the street, the river, lectures, libraries, public
dance halls, and transport were so perilous that they could either not
be entered at all or only with companions approved by authority
figures. Private places, the colleges or schools themselves, had high
walls (literally or metaphorically), and any males inside them were
either kin (vouched for by the family), or teachers chaperoned by a

female staff member. The school or college thus regulated interaction with men exactly as if it were a respectable home.

The distinction between the public sphere (the outside) and the private (homes and the interior of the schools and colleges) was marked off for the pioneers by their strict rules about dress and behaviour in public places.

## Protection from the public gaze: hats and elastic

Mark Pattison, Rector of Lincoln College, advised the first principal of what is now St Anne's College 'to entreat my young women to be neat and tidy and careful in their dress and courteous in their manners' (Butler and Pritchard 1938: 24-5). All the pioneers adopted this strategy, ensuring that their young ladies dressed in the conventional ways in public, and that unconventional dress was reserved for strictly private locations. The histories and memoirs constantly refer to hats, gloves, long skirts, and decorous ways of covering up the body in ways that parallel obsessive ritual observances. If the female pupils and students wore the garments of young ladies in public, they could ward off accusations of masculinity or impropriety. Garrett Anderson decided early on in her campaign to enter medicine that ladylike behaviour and dress would advance her cause. She wrote to Emily Davies: 'I do wish, as you said, the D's dressed better....She looks awfully strong-minded in walking dress...she has short petticoats and a close round hat...it is abominable, and most damaging to the cause.' In another letter she wrote: 'I feel confident now that one is helped rather than hindered by being as much like a lady as lies in one's power' (quoted in Stephen 1927: 59).

Just as the pioneers applied the rules to their own conduct, so too they enforced them on the students and staff of the schools and colleges they founded. This led to a proliferation of rules about gloves and hats, skirt lengths and neck lines, and campaigns against jewellery and vulgarity. In the USA, the colleges were careful to enforce ladylike dress codes. Vassar started with a multiplicity of rules about dress and conduct. There was a Lady Principal to set standards and:

Everyone must change her dress for supper (if only into a clean day dress). Gloves had to be worn on formal occasions, even when reading their essays to their peers.

Miss Lyman personally inspected hemlines for platform appearances...a sagging skirt was not tolerated. (Newcomer 1959: 112)

Similarly at Barnard, when Gildersleeve (1954: 71) was Dean around 1910: 'Freda Kirchway...shocked the Barnard community greatly by actually walking across Broadway to Columbia without a hat'. Thorp tells us that at Smith, the authorities

had from the beginning tried to show a respectful courtesy to the sensibilities of a New England Community inclined to be conservative in its standards for the behaviour of young ladies...[the student] agreed to put on a hat whenever she wanted to shop on Main Street.

Abby Farwell Ferry (1931: 145) reminiscing about her time at Farmington, a famous girls' school in Connecticut, described how she had to dress to attend church in the 1870s: 'I carried the train in my left hand as I walked to church; in my other hand was my parasol, lace handkerchief, and fan: three things no lady ever went without'.

Note that initially Vassar demanded gloves inside the college for reading an essay aloud, while later the emphasis was more on ensuring that hats and gloves were worn in the town. Thus the headmistress of the Oxford Girls' High School, writing to her pupils in 1872, reported that some girls had been seen in public without gloves and: 'I have heard it objected to more than anything and it certainly gives our enemies reason to say that the High School makes girls rough and unfeminine' (GPDST 1972: 73). Similarly the girls at Cardiff High School for Girls (founded 1895) faced strict standards. Carr includes the reminiscence of one early pupil that 'gloves played a great part in our lives. We always had to carry them even on the hottest day' (Carr 1955: 165).

The early undergraduates were equally careful to keep the rules about dress. Battiscombe (1978: 82) tells how Elizabeth Wordsworth, the first principal of Lady Margaret Hall, Oxford

insisted on her students wearing gloves – 'It makes a better impression on the university'. They were also obliged to observe an already outdated convention and put on a hat whenever they went into the garden. In all circumstances, the LMH students were expected to behave like ladies.

Megson and Lindsay (1960: 44) report:

> As late as 1929 the first year students were warned by the
> mistress [of Girton] not to make themselves in any way
> conspicuous, and were told to put on their hats if they bicycled
> nearer to Cambridge than Storeys Way.

Dress became important in public, but the schools and colleges also
had to worry about what their pupils wore in private because
rumours spread. This became a particular problem when the schools
and colleges began to run activities which were novel and
potentially unladylike, such as acting in plays and pageants, and
playing sports and games. These were new activities for girls away
from the family circle, and not only were they dangerous to
ladylikeness in themselves, the clothes worn could be challenged.
The themes of publicity, ladylikeness and dress are seen as
intertwined in this extract from a Birmingham newspaper of 1876,
commenting on a cricket match held between Edgbaston Girls'
High School and another girls' school:

> We must confess to being in ignorance of the exact social
> standing of the pupils at the Edgbaston High School for Girls,
> but the name would seem to cover a good measure of gentility.
> It therefore strikes us as rather odd that the management should
> lately have allowed the school's cricket match against the first
> eleven of a kindred establishment to be reported in the sporting
> columns of the local press. The report describes the hitting as
> having been 'very spirited on both sides'. We can only hope that
> when these muscular maidens come to be married no similar
> entry will have to be made in the chronicle of their connubial
> felicity. The report does not describe, unfortunately, the costume
> of the players, but we may assume that its feminine character
> must have been greatly modified. If the exhibition was in any
> sense public, we must confess to a preference for those less
> pretentious places of education where English lasses used to be
> taught modesty, if little science. (Whitcut 1976: 43)

Here the ideas of privacy, class, costume, and ladylikeness are
inextricably linked. This is obviously why as late as 1911 in
Tunbridge Wells 'An annual gym display was started for an
audience of mothers only and fathers *who were doctors*' (GDPST
1972: 32, emphasis mine).

Shrewsbury High School for Girls opened in 1885, and began Swedish drill three years later. A demonstration was given in the music hall: 'The girls were drilled by Miss Thomas in the body of the hall and the visitors, *only ladies*, sat chiefly in the orchestra' (Bates and Wells 1962: 40, emphasis mine). Many schools remained unconvinced by the arguments put forward in favour of games and drill for girls (Atkinson 1978) – both their merits and public reaction to them. Moberly Bell (1958: 33) tells how the Church of England girls' schools in the 1880s were dubious about games because 'Our pupils were "young ladies" rather than girls, and it was expected that their legs should be decently kept from public view.'

Atkinson (1978) provides a useful commentary on the first sports day of the North London Collegiate which was organized in 1890. At that time outdoor sport for women was in most quarters an 'unheard of event', and as Scrimgeour says (1950: 65) 'An edict went forth that not even brothers were allowed on the field.' In Melbourne, too, the press were always ready to report scandalous costumes for games, and in 1904 the girls of the Presbyterian Ladies College were reported as wearing 'proper athletic costume for cricket'. The school rejected this calumny, announcing that 'our girls make no change of costume when they go from the classroom to the cricket lawn' (Fitzpatrick 1978: 121).

In these extracts the private sphere, where legs could be revealed, hats left off, and gloves were not *de rigueur*, was an all-female one. A public arena had men in it, and so activities which involved legs in knee-length skirts, or bare heads, were not suitable for such a sphere. Heads, hands, and legs were all to be covered. The gym tunic was reserved for indoors (privacy), outdoor games initially involving an ankle or floor length garment. As a pupil at St Felix School, Southwold in 1905 recalls:

> The tunic was a garment reserved for the gymnasium, and was of a decent length, covering the knee completely. Games were played in the winter in a green blouse, fitting well to the neck, and a blue serge skirt, also of a decent length. (Watson and Curtis Brown 1923: 22)

It was the boarding schools like Wycombe Abbey that adopted team games for girls most energetically, perhaps because they were set in their own grounds and so pupils could play in private. Urban schools like Edgbaston had a harder job hiding their unladylike sports clothes from the public gaze.

Gymnastic dress was not generally adopted for games played in settings more public than school playing fields in the nineteenth century and as late as 1910 a student at Dartford College caused a rumpus by wearing her college tunic when she turned out to play hockey for Kent. The rest of the players were wearing skirts less than six inches above the ground. The incident prompted the following letter in *The Hockey Field* of 7 January:

Dear Madam,
The attention of many hockey players has been drawn by their parents and guardians to the various portraits that have appeared in an illustrated paper of Kent's new outside left, who plays for the county in her college tunic. That costume is, without doubt, ideal in that it cannot hamper the movements of the wearer; *but, at the same time, does not suit itself to public grounds.* To show the adoption of this dress for public matches may prove detrimental to hockey. I quote from a letter received by a county player from her fiancé. 'Please look at page 874 of the *Sporting and Dramatic*, and see the awful apparition who plays for Kent. If there is any chance of your wearing kit like that my foot comes down bang and you have no more hockey'.
Yours obediently,
Zagazig

(quoted in May 1969)

Banner (1974) writing about America, discusses how it was only as golf and tennis became fashionable that women had really respectable games available. Certainly, American women's colleges and schools do not seem to have adopted team games, such as cricket and field hockey, with the enthusiasm of the British ones, though Thorp reports that at Smith 'The early field hockey players had conscientiously worn skirts over their bloomers when they walked up Elm Street' (1956: 249). When Phoebe Hearst, a major benefactor of women's education at Berkeley, endowed an outdoor basketball court for the women students in 1901 'a twelve foot fence *with no knotholes* to discourage observers' (Gordon 1979, emphasis mine) was erected round it. At Abbot Academy in the period 1898-9 the baseball teams actually played in bloomers, but were not allowed to be seen outside the school in them. 'The baseball nine was never allowed to play in outside games' (Lloyd 1979: 194). The school also played field hockey, in carefully chosen clothing.

Farmington, the school run by Miss Sara Porter, was exclusive and expensive, and in the spring the girls went riding. The costume Ferry had, in 1876, was very daring as it had trousers, with a skirt on top! Thus: 'The skirt came just over my stirrup as I sat in the saddle, but what really created a sensation were the trousers, the first we had seen for equestrianism' (1931: 137). This type of consideration still constrains English women's cricket in 1988 – they play in divided skirts because trousers would be unladylike. Clothing, public gaze and ladylikeness were therefore enmeshed.

In Douglas's terms the activities of academic study, and sport, were dangerous for women because they involved physical crossings of social boundaries, and once people have crossed such boundaries they become a danger to themselves and others because contamination is contagious. The insistence on dressing for dinner, on hats, gloves, and long skirts, and on shrouding PE in secrecy were strategies for warding off the contagion enforced more and more rigidly the more public the students' appearance was to be. Figure 4.1 shows the gradations.

*Figure 4.1 Precautions against 'dangerous' activities*

| Activity | Location | Potential audience | Gloves? | Hats? | Skirt length | Other features |
|----------|----------|--------------------|---------|-------|--------------|----------------|
| Church | Public | Male and female | Yes | Yes | Long | Chaperon |
| Walk | Public | Male and female | Yes | Yes | Long | Companion(s) |
| Hockey | Urban public field | Male and female | No | Yes | Long | |
| Hockey | Private school ground | Female only | No | No | Medium/ short | Bloomers possible |
| Gym/drill | Gymnasium | Female only | No | No | Knee-length | Bloomers possible |

The pupils and students of the early educational institutions not only wanted to take exercise, they also wanted to dance and act. Where a family might respectably act scenes from plays or tableaux, it was not necessarily respectable for ladies to do so outside their homes. In 1871 the Girton pioneers acted some scenes from Shakespeare in front of the staff and servants. The staff were horrified because, as Miss Gibson explained, 'Our men's clothes were a scandal and the whole performance an outrage on the proprieties which might prove fatal to the future of the college' (Quoted in Stephen 1927: 241). The acting itself was a risk; the male clothes were much worse. Throughout the first fifty years of women's academic education acting in male attire or uncovering the young ladies' legs were both scandalous.

As late as 1914 a scandal occurred in Cardiff Girls' High School when a girl acting in a Yeats play appeared on stage in bare feet (Carr 1955: 179). Similarly, the old girls of Bedford High School wanted to do scenes from the Odyssey in 1897 but 'We were hampered in the production by the decree...that no legs must be seen, nor any outline of the figure appear through transparent draperies' (Westaway 1932: 165). At St Anne's, Abbots Bromley, in the 1880s plays were done in public, with the Bishop in the audience, but 'All our plays had to be *poudre* as we were not allowed to knickerbocker; so, except when Pygmalion, I always resembled George IV in appearance' (Macpherson 1924: 45).

These conventions were relaxed in the early years of this century, as a girl who attended Oxford Girls' High School in 1900 reports: 'Dramatic performances replaced the tableaux of Miss Leahy's day and the recitations (with appropriate gestures) of Miss Soulsby's and it was no longer considered immodest for girls to take men's parts in men's dress' (Stack 1963: 59). Gradually, even bare legs became permissible. Bates and Wells (1962: 57) include a comment from an old girl who had attended Shrewsbury Girls' High School in 1914 describing the acting then, and in 1939:

A special favourite was *The Road to Bethlehem*. There were children from many lands journeying to the manger at Bethlehem. During thirty-odd years this play was repeated many times. The only difference I noticed when, some twenty-five years after appearing in it myself, I went to make up the cast for a performance, was that whereas in my day the Fiji Islander wore brown tights under her grass skirt, the present day one displayed a pair of nicely tanned bare legs.

The American literature reveals the same attitude to male dress and bare legs. Gildersleeve reports that in 1915 when she was Dean at Barnard: 'At our very beautiful annual spring festival, Greek Games, the students appeared for the first time with bare feet, that brought down upon my head reproaches from the highest authorities' (1954: 71). Bare feet caused trouble elsewhere in the same year. Plum and Dowell note: 'Vassar was criticised for allowing students in the pageant to dance in bare feet and legs' (1961: 48). Newcomer points out that Vassar women were 'at a

disadvantage in play production. In the early days women taking
men's parts had to wear skirts (1959: 121). Cole (1940: 308) reports
similar rules at Mount Holyoke where, up to 1918

> local dramatics had suffered from the administrative edict that a
> college girl should not wear the distinctive articles of male attire
> when presenting male roles – wherefore bloomers, instead of
> trousers, had lent a ludicrous touch to many a scene.

Acting, even if potentially damaging to the reputation of schools
and colleges, was at least done in private, or for an invited audience.
The advent of the bicycle, because it cried out to be used in public,
was a great problem for the educational pioneers. The cycle itself,
and the correct dress for cycling, were both much debated, as
Atkinson (1978) discusses at some length. Westaway (1932: 50-1)
tells us how in Bedford around the years 1896:

> bicycling came into fashion for women; the first High School
> girl who was seen on a bicycle was considered by some to be
> bringing great disgrace on her school and the headmistress
> received a request from a number of parents to make a rule
> forbidding such behaviour...very soon bicycling became most
> popular, but it was considered very important to have one's
> skirts of suitable length, and duly fastened down with elastic to
> keep one from showing too much of one's legs.

A similar point is made by Noake, the historian of the Alice Ottley
School in Worcester, who argues (1952: 49) that in 1895 there arose
'a nation-wide craze that affected women and girls of all ages and
classes – they took to bicycling, and it altered their whole outlook
on personal freedom. The days of chaperonage were numbered....'
Miss Ottley said her pupils could cycle 'always provided they wore
suitable skirts. This meant garments with a deep inverted pleat
behind, so that the sides of the skirt fell decently to the ankles, to
which the hem was secured by loops of elastic.'
Cycling was equally controversial in the USA (Banner 1974;
Aronson 1952; Sinclair 1965; Roberts 1977). The dangers were due
to the costume, the potential difficulty of providing chaperons, and
the fact that cycling was a public activity. The clothing rules, as
seen above, involved skirts covering the legs. Some institutions did
provide cycling chaperons. Elizabeth Wordsworth, Principal of
Lady Margaret Hall, went so far as to obtain a tricycle of her own,

and 'could be seen riding with a couple of girl cyclists alongside of her'. The activity of LMH students met with disapproval from the Vice-Chancellor, who wrote and asked Wordsworth why she had not forbidden her students to ride bicycles across the parks. She replied: 'For the same reason that Solon did not forbid parricide to the Athenians,' a suitably lofty and Delphic reply (Courtney 1934: 27)! In South Wales the headmistress of one girls' school was chaperoned on her bicycle by one of the lady governors; and at Cardiff High School the headmistress taught her head girl to ride in the playground (Glenday and Price 1974: 42). Some schools and colleges had rules that cycles were not to be ridden in public, or in certain specific places. In the 1890s students at Girton had to leave their bicycles on the outskirts of the city and walk into the town (Bradbrook 1969: 107).

Both cycling and acting were seen as potentially contaminating activities for young ladies, and so their introduction to the schools and colleges was circumscribed with multiple rules. Figure 4.2 contrasts cycling and acting with walks and gym, and figure 4.3 illustrates the way they were controlled. Figure 4.2 shows cycling, gym, acting and walking compared on two dimensions: their respectability and novelty. Walking was a traditionally respectable activity for young ladies; acting a traditional activity which was not respectable; gym and drill were novel but done in private, respectable; cycling was novel and disreputable. The pioneers reacted by framing cycling and acting very strongly, hedging them round with much stricter rules than gym and drill.

*Figure 4.2 The problem of cycling and acting*

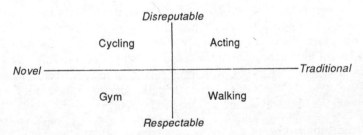

Thus far the chapter has dealt with the ways in which young ladies at schools and colleges were protected from men, and their new activities were strongly classified and framed. These precautions against damage to the social purity of the young ladies by no means exhaust the strategies of boundary maintenance in the

*Figure 4.3 Controls exercised on acting, cycling, and gym*

|  | Acting | Cycling | Gym |
|---|---|---|---|
| Classification in figure 4.2 | Trad. + disrep. | Novel + disrep. | Novel + respec. |
| Timing controlled by staff | Tight | Tight | Tight |
| Locations controlled by staff | Tight | Tight | Tight |
| Companions controlled by staff | Tight | Tight | Tight |
| Clothing | Conventional female only | Modified female | Novel, tunics and bloomers |
| Audience | By invitation, all female | Not controllable | By invitation, all female |

early schools and colleges. Even behind the high walls, in the all-female atmosphere of the schools and colleges, other potentially defiling elements were present among the women pupils and staff. Parents were fearful that the new educational institutions mixed women from different social classes and different religious denominations. There were pollution dangers inside the educational institutions too.

Young ladies who broke the strict rules of conduct in the schools and colleges were one potential source of pollution, and we have already seen that they were instantly excluded (e.g. the Vassar incident quoted on page 78 so they would not contaminate their coevals. This was one 'danger' averted, but there were more insidious ones too.

### The dangerous classes

One source of potential pollution which threatened the schoolgirl or college student was women of a lower social class. Ladies could be contaminated if they mixed promiscuously with non-ladies, and friendships across social classes were seen as undesirable. Thus the educational pioneers either excluded girls from all but a narrow class range from their schools, or kept opportunities for socializing to a minimum and discouraged friendships. The pioneers were just as confined by the rigid class conventions of their contemporaries as by their insistence on ladylike behaviour, although this is often softened and even excluded from current accounts of their activities. Their class-consciousness was not just a desire to separate 'ladies' from the working class, but comprised a subtle series of distinctions within middle and upper classes.

This point is made clearly by Curti (1959: 177) when, after describing the growth of elementary schools, the lyceum movement and the spread of seminaries in the early years of the nineteenth century in America, he summarizes the *ante-bellum* position with the education of women continued to be governed by class considerations. Curti argues that little attention was paid to educating working-class girls, and emphasizes the leisured class position of the pioneers. Emma Willard, Catharine Beecher, Mary Lyon and others 'who furnished in their seminaries' the 'proof that women were capable of pursuing the "more solid" studies' and 'did much to make the learned lady acceptable' predominantly 'belonged to the middle class...and worked for the training of girls from either the wealthy or fairly well-to-do groups'. Mary Lyon was the only one who had known poverty, and when she founded Mount Holyoke in 1837 'one of her principal purposes was to break the monopoly the upper classes had enjoyed in educating their daughters: her institution was frankly intended to make possible an education for the middle classes'. Certainly, even if there had been ample scholarships to pay for working girls to attend college, they could not have managed the entrance qualifications until late in the century. As Talbot says:

> It was not until 1852 that a public high school education of any kind was available to Boston girls, and the opening of the Girls' Latin School in 1878 gave them their first opportunity to be fitted for college. In Philadelphia no girls could be prepared for college in the public schools before 1893. (1910: 16)

Even if they had had the qualifications, it seems unlikely that many working-class girls would have been admitted to the elite women's colleges which Newcomer (1959) explicitly accuses of excluding negroes and the working class, leaving them to negro colleges and state universities. If the elite women's colleges were not for the working class, there is also some evidence that the elite groups themselves avoided them until well in to the twentieth century, and that they served the professional classes, not those with great material wealth.

Certainly, it was the emerging professional classes who sent their daughters into the new schools and colleges in Britain in far greater numbers than did the upper classes or the business world. The new institutions for women reflected the highly stratified system for men devised by Clarendon and Taunton. With the exception of Cheltenham it was the Taunton schools for girls which grew first, with the great girls' public schools, such as Roedean, Wycombe Abbey and St Leonard's, following in the last twenty-five years of the century. The development of both sections was clearly dominated by subtle class considerations which became clear for the first time in the middle of the century with the founding of Queen's College with royal patronage and upper-class support, and later Bedford College, which did not have the 'support of royalty nor of the highest social class' (Tuke 1939: 24). The founder of Bedford was forced to admit that 'perhaps half our young ladies rank as much more by good manners and ability than birth' and that there had been 'small response from the professional and other well-to-do classes' (Tuke 1939: 282).

The girls' schools for the classes covered by the Taunton Commission were revolutionary in three ways: they were day schools, they were public, and they mixed the three tiers of the middle class. The first of these public day schools were Miss Buss's two establishments which were recognized by the patronage of the Princess of Wales in 1871. Her Royal Highness expressed her desire to bring about an 'improvement in the education of girls of the poorer middle class' (Ridley 1895: 115). In the same year the organization which led to the foundation of the Girls' Public Day School Trust schools said its aim was to cater for 'the education of girls of all classes above the elementary' and the Church Schools Company, founded later that decade, said it was for 'the classes above that attending elementary schools' (Moberly Bell 1958: 3).

Felicity Hunt (1985) and Janet Howarth (1985) have begun the research task of classifying the pioneer girls' schools into a grading system parallel to, but different from, that used for boys' schools. The focus here is not the status of particular schools, but the strategies used in those revolutionary ones which mixed girls from different social strata. These new public day schools were a radical departure as Pedersen (1975) has demonstrated. The dangers that accrued from mixing the three tiers of the middle class were a matter of concern to teachers and parents. Whether or not the staff of a school were worried by mixing the girls, they had to ensure that the mingling was carefully controlled because many parents feared it. Frances Gray (n.d.) first high mistress of St Paul's School for

Girls recounts how 'I was sometimes asked by a horrid parent "Isn't the school *mixed*?" She meant by that "Won't my daughter meet girls with whom I do not wish her to go to tea?"'

The potential dangers of this social mixture were well known to Miss Buss. Elizabeth Garrett Anderson told her (in 1880) that the long morning at North London Collegiate (four hours) was too much of a strain for the girls' health. She advised a lunch break, afternoon school, and team games to lighten the load. Miss Buss was unsure about the merits of team games, but was even more worried that

> the mixture of classes which was unobjectionable as long as girls only met at lessons where talking was forbidden, or in the short intervals which were largely devoted to lunch and drill, might cause serious difficulties if the whole day were spent in school
>
> (Zimmern 1898: 152).

Miss Buss was certainly correct in her fears, because others shared them. Louisa Martindale (1951: 23), writing of her school days in the late 1880s, says:

> We were sent to school....Much to the dismay of some of our friends, mother had chosen the Brighton High School, which was under the Girls' Public Day School Trust. High schools were in those days somewhat of an innovation and catered for girls of all classes.

Miss Martindale safeguarded her daughters' gentility by employing a governess throughout their school life, who accompanied them to and from school. However, her friends' worries were not unique. Magnus (1923: 150) writing about the GPDST school at Streatham Hill founded in 1887 says:

> It took long to convince a neighbourhood of a highly old fashioned type that a *public* day school was a place in which to educate its daughters, and there was much heart-searching in such crucial matters as the social status of the girls admitted and much dread of a possible 'mixture' of social classes.

The Worcester High School for Girls, founded in 1883 with day and boarding pupils, faced the same difficulties. Noake (1952: 32) tells us:

Parents who sent their girls to school were considered rather advanced; carefully brought up children might meet others from homes of quite different kinds. And so there was a rule, formulated in consideration for sensitive parents, that pupils should not walk to and from school together without the written permission of their parents.

The girls were also forbidden to talk to boys, even their brothers, of course. The precaution of forbidding girls to mix in the streets without parental permission is reported from several of the day schools. Typically an old girl of Oxford GHS remembered:

In early days, members of the school belonged chiefly to academic families because some of the dons needed a good education for their girls, and they had helped to found the school and to people it. But by our day the field had widened and numbers had risen so that our little world of the upper third reflected faithfully the people of Oxford, apart from the very poor. I doubt if we knew what all the parents did, but among them were certainly a parson, a baker, a doctor, a printer, a dentist, a stationer, a don, an estate agent, a lawyer, a builder, and the governor of H M prison. Pocket money was trifling compared with present standards: 6d a week was usual, and we were greatly impressed when one girl told us she had a shilling. Of course the money went much further....This democratic nature of the school did not command universal approval. Some parents, especially perhaps in the academic world, would not send their daughters to such a 'mixed' school where they might pick up that hypothetical infection known as 'high school manners'. As we grew older and could reflect on these things it all seemed unfair: why should the school be blamed for bad manners when we were there for only a third of our waking hours? But no doubt it was owing to this difficulty that there was a rule against our walking home with our school fellows without the permission of our parents. Hockey was undoubtedly one of the stumbling blocks to parents – it was a rough 'unladylike' game, conducive to injury and ungainly carriage. Some parents compromised by sending their girls to the school but forbidding them to play hockey, poor things. (Stack 1963: 75)

What is clear from these accounts is both a concern about the pupils mixing, and an idea that parents were the proper people to decide who a girl's friends were to be. Time in school would be spent working; beyond the walls, parents could determine how leisure was spent, and who it was spent with. These precautions were not enough to reassure many parents. Mabell, Countess of Airlie (1956) recalled how in her youth public day schools were considered decidedly 'dangerous' socially. She was related to Lord Shaftesbury, and his progressive ideas extended to his daughters, for 'one set of cousins, Lord Shaftesbury's daughters, went to a high school' (p.22).

The Countess recalled that they 'reaped the benefits of a wonderful education' but at the cost of being socially stigmatized by their aristocratic relations. Ridler (1967: 77) quotes an old girl of Downe House whose mother 'would not send any of us four girls to the excellent education of the Oxford High because she was afraid we would "pick up accents", and it would be awkward it we became friendly with the butcher's daughters'.

Mrs Gray herself recalled (Croydon 1954: 20) how in 1872 when she and her sister began the GPDST schools 'I was asked again and again if I was mad enough to suppose that any gentleman would send his daughter to a public school.' Croydon, the third GPDST school quoted this in 1954 when it had produced 9,000 old girls, many of them daughters of gentlemen.

Among the other solutions to the mixing of the middle-class tiers was the idea of opening several schools, one for each tier of the middle class. The Truro Girls High School opened in 1880, with Amy Key as its headmistress. In 1883 she formulated a plan for another girls' school to give the 'daughters of trades-people and others, for whom the high school was not originally planned, opportunity of a similar, though perhaps simpler, curriculum at lower fees'. Clarke (1979: 44-5) reports that this plan came to nothing for a further 20 years, but the class implication of Key's plan is clear. Bedford did have more than one school, as Hunt (1985), Hutchins and Godber (1982), and Broadway and Buss (1982) have documented.

Some of the day schools tried to be more democratic (or meritocratic) than contemporary conventions. Bolton Girls' High School opened in 1879, and at an early public meeting the local committee heard a stirring speech from Professor Wilkins of Manchester University. He announced that:

He had been told of a lady in Manchester – for a lady she was in every sense of the word although engaged in the retail business

– who had been to one or another, three, or four, of the good schools, the schools in high repute, where she could get a sound education for a promising girl of hers, who had been turned back from the door of every one of them

(Brown and Poskitt 1976: 246).

Professor Wilkins believed that 'all these new public day schools ought to be absolutely free from snobbery and class distinction'. Similarly robust democratic ideas were held by David Pryde, head of the Edinburgh Ladies College, which in 1888 had 1,600 pupils from 5-20 years. The school was so successful that several of the older private schools fell into financial difficulty. Pryde reports that at a dinner party he met a teacher who was suffering from the competition. This teacher complained that the Ladies' College was too mixed, for Pryde had admitted the daughter of a cow-keeper who could be seen taking the milk round the town. Pryde's (1893: 156) response that the girl was clever and well-behaved cut little ice, for his rival retorted that he was 'doing a great injury to society by giving a high education to people of this class. Providence has placed that girl in a particular station and you are taking her out of it.'

Democratic sentiments were also expressed by one of the speakers at the opening (in 1897) of the Pontypool County School for Girls in Wales who:

hoped that no show of antagonism would be made by the better class towards those who were poorer, and if there was genius to be found among the better class of artisan he hoped that the doors of the college would be thrown open to it.

(Pontypool 1947: 15)

Such democracy, or promiscuous mixing, was exactly the reason that some parents were deeply suspicious of the new public day schools. Some day schools were exclusive, and did not try to mix social classes. Thus in Birmingham, the Edgbaston High School for Girls was originally conceived as a 'High Class Girls' School for Edgbaston' and served a social group more exclusive that the GPDST school in the same city (Whitcut 1976).

Boarding schools were more likely to aim at one class of pupil, so that in Abbots Bromley the Woodard organization actually opened two girls' boarding schools, St Mary's and St Anne's, with different fees, aimed at two segments of the Anglican middle class.

They existed side by side until 1921, sharing one chapel which they used at different times (Macpherson 1924; Rice 1947; Kirk 1937). Rice (1947: 49) explains the rationale of the sister schools. St Anne's had been founded in 1874, and St Mary's followed in 1882 because:

> Low as were the fees of St Anne's, many an application was received from parents who could not afford them, and often when the fees could be paid for one girl, they were not forthcoming for younger members of the family....Also there was the class to be considered below that for which St Anne's was intended. In those days, when England was neatly labelled into 'upper', 'middle', and 'lower middle' class, and no family was ashamed of its own label, St Anne's was meant for the 'middle class', but the 'lower middle class' knocked at the door.

So St Mary's was cheaper. The precedent among the Woodard girls' schools had already been set in Bognor Regis. The St Michael's Schools for Girls there consisted of an upper-class school for eighteen young ladies, who paid 60 guineas a year, and a larger number of middle-class girls who paid 21 guineas. The young ladies had to bring their own silver fork and spoon, and six linen napkins among their possessions (Kirk 1937). Parents were reassured that the two classes were not allowed to mingle; although they were taught the same lessons and ate together, the rest of the time they 'took their walks and amusements separately' (p.117).

The great girls' public schools had no truck with mixing social groups. In 1896 Frances Dove issued the prospectus for potential shareholders in Wycombe Abbey which made clear that 'The proposed system of education aims at doing for girls, with suitable modifications, what the existing great public schools do for boys; and it in no way interferes with the numerous high schools for girls.' In the same year prospective parents were assured that the education would be 'as complete on all its sides as that given to boys at the great public schools'. In short, Wycombe Abbey was to be a Clarendon school for girls (Bowerman 1966: 79).

The new girls' public schools such as Wycombe Abbey, founded towards the end of the nineteenth century, followed the pattern set by Cheltenham Ladies' College, opened in 1853 and dominated by Miss Beale for many years, which was careful to keep itself exclusive. Zimmern (1898: 38) tells how 'it does not receive all comers, but is distinctly intended for the "daughters of gentlemen", and references in regard to social standing are required before admission'. In her evidence to the Taunton Commission, Miss Beale concurred with the suggestion that her pupils 'come from what may be called the upper division of the middle class' with the statement that 'None are admitted but the daughters of independent gentlemen or professional men' (quoted in Kamm 1958: 82). This exclusiveness raised problems for Miss Beale when Emily Davies and her co-campaigners managed to open the Cambridge Local Examinations to girls. At that time they were 'known as the Middle-Class Examinations because they were to test standards in middle class schools' (Stephen 1927: 83). Miss Beale is often reported as refusing to enter Cheltenham girls for these examinations in the early days because of her dislike of competition and especially competition with boys. However, when discussing this issue with the Taunton Commission in 1866 she produced another drawback:

> There seems to be some difficulty in applying them to the higher middle classes. I think of our own case. The brothers of our pupils go to the universities. Now, generally speaking, those who go in for the Local Examinations occupy a much lower place in the social scale, and our pupils would not like to be classed with them, but regarded as equal in rank to those who pass at the university. These feelings are stronger in small places.
>
> (Ridley 1895: 15)

Janet Howarth (1985) has done some detailed work on the girls' schools which sent women students to Oxbridge between 1880-1914. Her conclusion about the social classes using the academic girls' schools and Oxbridge in her chosen period is that, for many women, an education was a safety-net to insure that they were not downwardly socially mobile. Many of them were the daughters of widows, or were orphans: women who needed to support themselves in jobs. Such people might well be prepared to risk a social mixture in a day school in order to get a vocational qualification. Figure 4.4 compares the public day schools' and elite boarding schools' strategies for controlling the mixture of classes. The day schools opted to ask parents to make the rules about friendships and associations outside the school, and to mix the middle- and lower-middle classes in lessons. Boarding schools, where pupils were likely to mix socially, were more likely to be

*Figure 4.4 Controlling the dangerous classes in the girls' schools*

|  | Public day schools | Boarding schools |
|---|---|---|
| Nature of intake | Mixed across upper-middle and middle classes | One stratum only |
| Pupil-pupil relations in school time | Tightly controlled – silence between lessons etc. | Relaxed control |
| Pupil-pupil relations in 'free' time | Delegated to parents | Relaxed control |
| Selection of intake | Relaxed | Strict on financial and class matters |
| Pollution dangers controlled | Inside the school by regulation | By external boundary maintenance. |

designed for one stratum only, to prevent undesirable mixtures. Class was not, however, the only problem. The other girls might be dangerous in another way too – they might be of the 'wrong' religious tendency.

## Religion: the dangerous denominations

It is hard for anyone today to appreciate how deep and bitter were the divisions between different Protestant denominations in nineteenth-century Britain. Today Muslim fundamentalists demand an education which will protect their daughters from the boys, the PE, the science and the ethos of twentieth-century Britain. In the nineteenth century, Presbyterian families did not want their daughters mixing with Anglicans or Methodists and vice versa.

In Britain, the Anglicans were active in founding schools for their daughters, with the Woodard Schools and the establishment of the Church of England's Church Schools' Company (Moberly Bell 1958). Woodard himself was not enthusiastic about girls' schools – especially the public and high schools that were opening. He wrote:

> Public schools for girls are of very doubtful merit. Religious homes, or convents are more in harmony with my ideas. The high school system and knowledge, without the grace of female gentleness and devotion, is another cloud in the gathering storm which is awaiting society.
>
> (Rice 1947: 21)

Other devout members of the Church of England disagreed, and Woodard girls' schools and the Church of England Schools' Society both grew. Within 30 years the new schooling had become not part of the storm, but for most people, a bastion against it.

Rice (1947) points out that Woodard started the Woodard boys' schools because he felt the Church of England was neglecting the middle- and lower-middle classes. His followers then applied the same logic to the girls. There was a danger that if the children of Anglicans did not go to Anglican schools they would become 'victims of political dissenters and agitators'. The Woodard girls' schools were suffused with Anglican practices, as the illustrations of processions to church and school chapel services in Macpherson (1924) and Rice (1947) show.

Moberly Bell's (1958) history of the Church Schools' Company, founded in 1883, makes a similar point. The originators of the schools were impressed by several features of the Girls' Public Day School Company, such as the academic curriculum, the public nature of the schools, and the idea of the day schools for girls, but they disliked the fact that the GPDSC schools were 'founded on undenominational lines. For those who could afford boarding schools, the Woodard Foundation provided a solution, but those who wanted Church Day Schools were in no small difficulty' (Moberly Bell 1958: 7). Both these organizations protected Anglican girls from other Protestants. All the Protestant denominations were concerned that their pupils should not be schooled with Roman Catholics, and the potential dangers of mixed denominations are revealed most clearly in the schools opened for the daughters of missionaries, soldiers and sailors.

When Walthamstow Hall was founded in 1838 to educate the daughters of missionaries, it was fairly ecumenical. It began as 'undenominational' and, while Christian, 'offered no teaching of any particular sect'. It was open to daughters of 'all evangelical missionaries' and even took Anglicans until the Church Missionary Society (CMS) opened their own school. However it did not take Catholics: mixing up Protestant denominations was daring enough (Pike, Curryer and Moore 1973: 15) There was controversy when the Royal School for Daughters of the Army was being planned. The first prospectus, for the 'Military Female School' aimed at 'Daughters of necessitous Officers of the Army', said they would be educated 'in conformity with the principles and doctrines of the Church of England' but that 'children of all Protestant denominations' would be accepted (Osborne and

Manisty 1966: 16). When the school got going in 1864 this limitation to Protestants, though recognized as probably necessary in a girls' school, cost the school money and patronage. One patron, an MP and General, withdrew his support because he thought the school should 'be open to the whole army, and separate instruction should be given to Protestants and Roman Catholics. (Osborne and Manisty 1966: 22). The Patriotic Fund refused the school a grant because they excluded Roman Catholics, and the Prince of Wales gave a relatively small donation saying he regretted that only the daughters of Protestant officers were to be included. This was apparently an issue where girls had to be more carefully protected than boys for the Royal Naval Female School was also restricted to Protestants only, but Wellington College, the army boys' school, was opened to all religions (p.23). In Australia, the same segregation took place. Melbourne, for example, saw three girls' schools, or rather ladies' schools, one each for Anglicans, Methodists, and Presbyterians. Fitzpatrick (1975: 39-40) records how the Presbyterian Ladies College (PLC), Melbourne, was intended for the daughters of parents 'who are themselves educated and in possession of means': a school for the wealthier classes. However it also had to be Presbyterian, for there were other schools which were 'luring good Presbyterian girls from the Church of their fathers'. So PLC was a large, public school – but only for Presbyterian ladies

*Figure 4.5 Controlling religious contamination in the girls' schools*

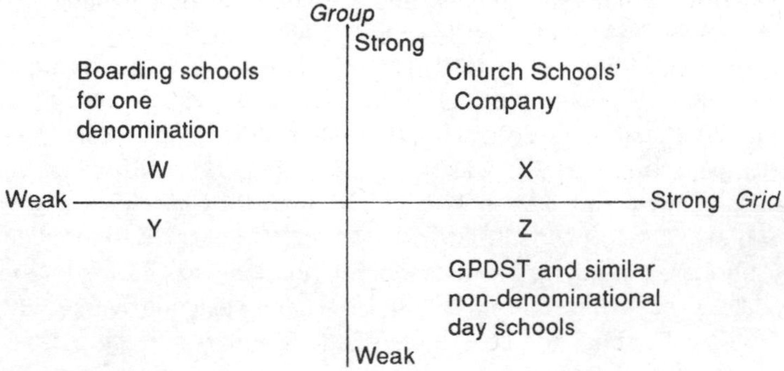

The dangers parents and teachers wished to avoid in terms of class and religion are shown in figure 4.5. Devout Roman Catholic families could send their daughters to convents (e.g. O'Leary 1936), Quakers had boarding schools such as the Mount School and

Polam Hall (Sturge and Clarke 1931; Davies 1981), and Methodists had Edgehill (Pyke 1957). As with class, boarding schools were most likely to cater for one denomination (Douglas's high group dimension) and day schools to allow a more mixed entry but hedge the pupils with rules (high grid). Figure 4.5 places the academic girls' schools, in relation to their strategies for dealing with the pupils' religions, in terms of Douglas's group and grid.

In figure 4.5 the Y quartile is empty because it was not possible to have an unregulated girls' school at that date.

## Summary and overview

This chapter has been concerned with how a group of pioneers – the heads and staff of new schools and colleges – dealt with the potential contamination of their pupils and students. Because the new educational institutions were revolutionary (large, publicly accountable, teaching games and sports, and giving girls and women a tough academic, masculine curriculum) yet dependent on parents paying fees, they were extremely careful to safeguard the gentility and ladylike femininity of their charges. The main sources of contamination were men, the public gaze, novel activities (e.g. hockey and cycling), and girls from other classes and denominations. The educational pioneers dealt with these dangers, or pollutants, by erecting strong barriers, both physical and social, around their pupils and enforcing ritual observances such as the wearing of hats and gloves, and the covering of legs. All these strategies were highly rational, part of a planned double conformity, because the freedom gained by having chaperons, hats, and rules over who could be talked to, was the freedom to learn high-status subjects. The strategy was one of double conformity: the prize was sharing cultural capital with men. The next chapter focuses upon the curriculum which was the reward for obeying the rules.

# 5

## Classics, chemistry, and cultural capital

Is the female Senior Wrangler a bright jewel rescued from the morass of down-trampled wasted capability?

(Kenealy 1899)

Latin...was sheer delight

(Park School 1930: 59)

She was clever. It had not been a lie then, that ecstasy which visited her when she read *A Midsummer Night's Dream* on top of the railway coach last summer. It had meant something. She had understood something. She was drunk with an intoxicating wine of gladness.

(Holtby 1936, *South Riding*: 128)

Lydia's ecstasy at understanding Shakespeare is, of course, the ultimate aim of education. Ideally all pupils should get pleasure from mastering bodies of knowledge and being active learners. Two issues are united in *South Riding*'s account of Lydia, for she is both a girl and from the rough working class. Access to certain types of knowledge has been severely restricted on the grounds of class and sex in the past, and the subject of this chapter is the first part of the campaign to gain access to previously forbidden knowledge. Middle- and upper-middle class women had to open the curriculum for themselves before it could be made available to working-class women such as Lydia.

This chapter examines the battles over curriculum in women's education using the ideas of Pierre Bourdieu, particularly his concept of 'cultural capital'. The importance of access to classics, to science, and to mathematics for the pioneers is examined first before Bourdieu's theoretical strength is brought into play. Cookery and needlework, and the debates over domesticity and femininity are the focus of chapter 5.

## The classics: symbolic superiority

At the beginning of the nineteenth century higher education in Britain was, as Newcomer (1959: 6) puts it 'primary professional education; and the professions, including teaching, were men's occupations'. Secondary schools were, therefore, also geared to preparation for the four professions of law, medicine, teaching and the church because they got pupils ready for college and little else. Professional education in those days bore little resemblance to that offered to law or medical students today. The curriculum was dominated by classics and mathematics and the importance of the knowledge was symbolic – a form of conspicuous consumption – rather than pragmatic. As Elliot (1972: 32) has argued:

In pre-industrial society the status professions were able to maintain a foothold among the ranks of the gentlemen by glossing over their work responsibilities and emphasising the leisured and honourable life-style which their members could adopt. Professional learning was not a specific and useful expertise so much as an acquaintance with a culture which had an accepted value in society, if no obvious vocational relevance.

Thus secondary and tertiary education were designed for an elite group of men, giving knowledge which was part of a cloistered leisured social system insulated from business, commerce, and the proletariat, and specifically intended to separate its products from the rest of society. These characteristics (cloistered, sacred, and male) were seen in their most extreme form at Oxford and Cambridge, where only members of the Anglican church could take degrees, where the college fellows were not allowed to marry, and where it was not until well into the century that law and science became full degree subjects. During the nineteenth century the celibacy rule for dons went, women students were admitted, and vocational subjects began to creep in. A similar process was taking place throughout secondary and tertiary education in Britain and the USA as mass, integrated, worldly, useful courses developed alongside the existing system. The battle for women's education, and the arguments about its content, were but a small part of the wider shifts. Classical supremacy was the symbol of the old order, and as such was challenged.

The debate between the curriculum traditionalists who defended the gentlemen's classics course, and the reformers who wanted modern languages, social sciences, English, and natural and engineering sciences, was very similar on the two sides of the Atlantic. Perhaps confusingly, the radical group in the struggle for women's education was forced to support the curriculum traditionalists in the first instance. It was only when the reformers had won their battles for the control of male education that the radical feminists could support them.

At the beginning of the nineteenth century classics dominated the colleges and hence the schools on both sides of the Atlantic. The challenge to classical supremacy began in the USA. Krug (1964) shows in some detail how in the USA throughout the period up to the 1920s the arguments about curricula were based on two points: the merits of classics and mathematics versus useful, vocational courses; and, more sinister, the demand for separate curricula for the masses, the immigrants and women. Krug says (1964: 279): 'Some of the prevailing attitude reflected the feeling that traditional subjects were unsuitable for particular groups, such as girls of any social class, or "the masses" of both sexes.' In other words, the debate was fundamentally about class and sex, as much as about classics, maths or domestic science. This was equally so in Britain where class considerations were paramount in curriculum debate. The centrality of class considerations is clear from Simon's (1974) account of the three Royal Commissions of the period between 1850-70, which examined Oxford and Cambridge; the nine great public schools (Clarendon); and the remainder of the middle- and upper-class schools (Taunton).

The evidence submitted to the Clarendon Commission shows, according to Simon, that members of the upper classes were worried that newer schools and adult education were giving the middle and lower classes knowledge which the aristocracy and gentry did not have, and that this knowledge imbalance was socially dangerous. Simon argues that these class issues were more important to many witnesses than the educational issues themselves, and quotes extensively from the evidence taken: for example, a Commission member asking a witness if he thought it a 'dangerous state of things ... that the material world should be very much better known by the middle classes of society than by the upper classes?' (p.305), and witnesses agreeing with comments implying that the imbalance 'put a certain amount of power into the hands of the middle classes which the upper classes have not' (p.306). The Commission decided that 'classics must remain the principal study of public schools' (p.307) but accepted the danger of total scientific ignorance so recommended that 'a modicum' of science be added which 'would suffice while retaining the classical "mystery" as the main mark of social superiority' (p.308). In other words, class was a crucial factor in determining who could and should receive particular kinds of knowledge.

The Taunton Commission, established in 1864 when Clarendon was published, was intended to study the education of 'those large classes of English society which are comprised between the humblest and the very highest' (p.318). They advocated a three-tier education system for boys, with separate schools for lower middle-, middle middle- and upper middle-class boys. This system of fee-paying schools was highly stratified in both form and content. There was no attempt to dethrone classics but even the potential university student was to have access to science and the other new subjects as well as the traditional curriculum. These three Royal Commissions thus left the supremacy of classics for the upper middle- and upper-class male unchallenged. Mathieson's (1975: 43) fascinating book on the history and ideology of English teaching summarizes the class basis of classical supremacy between 1850 and 1920 as follows:

> as long as English was studied only by working class children, girls, Mechanics' Institute apprentices and audiences for WEA [Workers' Educational Association] lectures, it remained a low-status subject, despised by the great public schools and universities....The curriculum controversy, arising to a considerable extent out of opposing claims made by rival social classes, took place in a climate of bitterness and suspicion....

In such a climate, it is hardly surprising that the pioneers of women's education had to plan their courses carefully and walk warily through the curriculum jungle.

One group of pioneers was careful to make its female pupils follow the same courses and take the same examinations as their brothers. If the content of those courses was bad, out-of-date and in need of reform, then they should be altered for both sexes. The other party felt that women should study different things: either because they were women, or because the male curriculum was so bad it was silly to force anyone else to study it. Elsewhere (Delamont 1978a) I called these two schools of thought the 'uncompromising' and the 'separatists', and described them as follows in the next section.

## The 'uncompromising' and the 'separatists'

The women campaigners can be divided into two groups: the uncompromising – who were determined that women should do what men did, warts and all – and the separatists – who favoured modified courses for women. The uncompromising group held that special women's courses would have no recognized standards or status, would allow employers to discriminate, and support the claim that women were mentally inferior to men. They were not necessarily supporters of the traditional curriculum, who wanted classics retained at all costs – many of them were keen for women to learn sciences, social sciences and English – but they were scared of a double jeopardy.

They realized that if girls got stuck in inferior courses, they might not only confine women's education to a cultural ghetto but also stop curriculum reform. For, as long as the new subjects were studied only by women the elite males were unlikely to consider them worth studying. The subjects would only succeed as worthwhile when elite men worked at them, and women taking them would hinder that elitist development. Some of the men pushing curriculum reform seem to have been very naive about this, for they appear to have thought that enrolling women students would help their cause. Sidgwick at Cambridge, for example, seems to have believed that women students reading English would add to the appeal of the subject for the university authorities, although the reverse was probably true – women and English were equally dubious new-fangled ideas and could have sunk together.

The separatists wanted courses for women which were particularly suited to their future as teachers, nurses and mothers. They were certainly genuine in their beliefs but played into the hands of men who did not want women to have any education at all. These men were keen to educate women in separate courses, give them separate examinations, and generally to confine them to a cultural ghetto.

These groups, the separatists and the uncompromising, existed in both Britain and the USA. The British pioneers' position is explained well by Sophie Bryant's (successor to Buss at North London Collegiate) description of Miss Buss's philosophy:

> she held that the greater liberty, as regards time of residence and studies, allowed at Newnham, was very serviceable to a large class of students....But she had, nevertheless, no doubt at all that the full university course, and the university degree as its recognition, was the end to be achieved....If the university was in need of reform, if more liberty should be allowed, as regards Greek in particular, then, it seemed to her, that question should be fought out for both sexes alike, since there was no particular reason why women specially should abstain from the classics. (quoted in Ridley 1895: 270-1)

At the school level, this meant designing a curriculum with the classics occupying a central place, and more mathematics than young ladies had ever been offered before.

In the USA there were equally uncompromising pioneers. For example, McIntosh (1974: 50) tells us 'The Bryn Mawr School in Baltimore was founded by a group of ladies....Their purpose was to provide Baltimore girls with an education equal or superior to that of their brothers.' Along similar lines were the schools called the 'curtsying sisters': Spence, Chapin, Brearley, Miss Hewitt's, Nightingale-Bamford, Sacred Heart. These schools grew up to feed the new American women's colleges. Such a school is re-created in fiction by Amanda Cross (1972: 10-11) portraying the 'Theban School' in New York, founded in 1871 by a man with no sons: 'If fate had presented him with female progeny, he would accept fate's challenge and educate them as human beings and future members of the learned professions.'

The 'Theban' is the type of school where the senior girls 'were accepted...by the college of their choice', where four years of Latin are required, and three of Greek are offered. Lloyd's (1979) history of Abbot Academy, a real school, reveals a similar pattern. As early as 1844 the girls were doing Latin and Greek (Cicero, Virgil, Xenophon and Homer), plus Euclid, German and French. The Principal and her sister/assistant who took over in 1855 had been taught Greek by their father in order to read the New Testament. These sisters, Philena and Phebe McKeen, established at Abbot on the earlier foundations a solid academic curriculum which was broader than that of the brother school (Phillips Academy) but heavily classical in nature.

St Margaret's School, in Waterbury, Connecticut, founded in 1865, was less academic than Abbot, but in the 1890s the course for those planning on college was (Ohman 1965: 37):

4 years of Latin
4 years of Maths
3 years of French or German
4 years of English Language
4 years of English Literature
1 year of Science
1 year of History

In Australia and New Zealand too, the pioneer girls' schools put classics at the heart of their curricula because it was the epitome of male, high-status, knowledge. The Melbourne Church of England Girls' School described its curriculum in 1903 as 'a sound classical, mathematical and general modern education, including regular religious instruction' (Anon 1953: 48). Similarly the Presbyterian Ladies College, founded in 1875 in Melbourne, began with a curriculum of 'Latin, mathematics, English, French, history and geography' (Fitzpatrick 1975: 60). Fitzpatrick points out that 'The only real difference' between this curriculum and that of the equivalent boys' school was 'the omission of Greek'. The founders thought Greek too extreme to open a school with, and it 'came in quietly a few years later' (1975: 61-2).

What the girls' schools began, the colleges continued. At university level Emily Davies's stand at Girton is the best known example of the uncompromising position, with her ringing pronouncements making her views clear. In Britain the uncompromising party founded Girton College, Cambridge, and Somerville College, Oxford, while the separatists founded Newnham College, Cambridge and Lady Margaret Hall, Oxford. The differences between separatists and uncompromising groups became clear when :

In 1866 Miss Davies' committee had endeavoured to persuade London University to open Matriculation to girls. This effort had led only to the offer of a Special 'women's examination', suited in the university's view to the limited capacity of females, but, of course, carrying none of the academic privileges conferred by the genuine article, and without status in the world of education.

(Brittain 1960: 35)

Emily Davies's response was unequivocal. She wrote to one of the men concerned:

> I am afraid the people who are interested in improving the education of women are a thankless crew. Instead of accepting as a great boon the admission of women to the...examinations... they have come to the conclusion that they do not consider a special examination any boon at all, and will have nothing to do with it. Please do not publish this, however, as we should not like to seem ungrateful. We are really obliged to convocation for their kind intentions in offering us a serpent when we asked for fish, tho' we cannot pretend to believe that serpents are better for us.

(Stephen 1927: 103)

The man concerned remonstrated with her, but she maintained that 'on this point I have no doubt whatever' and that 'what they call a compromise we consider a capitulation'. Emily Davies decided that she must open her own college 'which would provide for young women the same opportunities that Oxford and Cambridge offered to young men' (Brittain 1960: 35). This led to Girton College, where the students were forced to study exactly what men studied, take every possible examination (even those ignored by many male students), and complete their course inside the same time-scale as the men, even though their schooling had ill-prepared them to manage this. Her rigidity meant appallingly hard work for the students and horrified many of the onlookers, especially men working for reform. Seeley thought Cambridge was 'in a very bad state', Bryce that some of the examinations were 'really very bad and quite unworthy of a university', and Sidgwick that it was 'a pity to load a new institution...with those very vices...we deplore in an old one' (Stephen 1927: 155-6). Emily Davies was unmoved by these arguments. Until men reformed Cambridge her students would undertake the full male load, however bad it was. She was not alone in her determination. Sara Burstall, who was a student from 1878 to 1881, wrote of Girton:

> As the college made a point of keeping the regulations that the Cambridge men kept Miss Buss warmly supported it. It was one

of her principles that girls and women, if they wished to do good work, earn good pay and keep an honourable standing in the professions like men, must be allowed to take the same examinations and keep the same rules.

(Burstall 1933: 55)

C.L. Maynard, also an undergraduate in the early days, recalled: 'Three years and one term was...the time allowed to men in which to take the Tripos, and Miss Emily Davies scorned all compromises and her students must conform to the same rule' (1910: 180). As Bradbrook (1969: *x*), the mistress in the centenary year of the college, summarized it: 'Girton was founded on the clear principle of aiming at the highest education, without any modification or concessions to the inexperience of women; and for this principle large sacrifices were made.' As Kathleen Raine (1975: 11) who went up in 1926 summarized it: 'The dons of Girton believed...in the culture they had fought for women's right to share.'

While Emily Davies was establishing Girton on these principles, Anne Jemima Clough was petitioning Cambridge to set up special 'women's examinations' well suited to the capacities of women students. This petition was granted, and the students taking the special examinations were the founders of Newnham College. Holcombe explains that the separatists 'believed that the existing, severely restricted university curriculum did not represent the best possible education for either men or women, and they were interested mainly in improving the qualifications of women teachers' (1983: 47).

Oxford went through the same struggle with its two earliest women's colleges although there the issue of religion also divided the pioneers. Somerville, 'where the same refusal to compromise on intellectual aims occurred', was founded in opposition to Lady Margaret Hall which wanted 'to turn out girls so that they will be capable of making homes happy' (Brittain 1960: 36). When degrees were being considered for women after 1894 Mrs Johnson, the first principal of what became St Anne's, argued that the degree would be unfair to women because boys' schools prepared pupils in the compulsory classics much more thoroughly, and the school system wanted teachers qualified in modern languages.

At college level in the USA the American pioneers were also divided into the uncompromising, with their insistence on what Woody (1966: 1:405) calls 'slavish imitation of the curriculum of the men's institutions', and the separatists, notably Catharine

110

Beecher. Among the uncompromising was 'Z.C. Graves, the first president of Mary Sharp College, who made it clear that the only innovation at his college was providing for women the same education as men' (Newcomer 1959: 76). Other members of the uncompromising group in the USA were Mrs Lincoln Phelps, Zilpah Grant and Mary Lyon. Thompson (1947: 44) says 'These women were not content to give their students minimum essentials. They wished them to have the same curriculum of culture as that given to the boys.

In a wittier vein Cross (1965: 37) says that Carey Thomas's aim for Bryn Mawr students was to give them a training 'as rigorous and impractical as that provided at Harvard'. Smith demanded that its students had done Greek, which meant that they 'had had difficulty finding schools that could fit them for Smith's entrance requirements, which precisely paralleled those of contemporary masculine institutions' (Thorp 1956: 244). Smith started in 1875 with a compulsory Greek entrance requirement – the first women's college to do so. Thorp implies that this was hard for the first students who 'were earnest pioneers, afire with the opportunities and responsibilities that glowed before them'. Boas (1935: 249) explains this insistence on the Greek requirement in the following way.

> The reasons for requiring Greek were not hard to understand. To escape any adverse criticism, to avoid any disparagement, Smith must measure up to the New England men's colleges in every particular possible. It must be said, 'Smith is just like a man's college, *except....*' Not to know Greek was, for a man, not to be enhanced. Not to know Greek was, then, for a woman not to be college bred.

The finest example of an uncompromising pioneer was Carey Thomas. At the age of fourteen she had decided: 'My *one* aim and concentrated purpose shall be and is to show that women can learn, can reason, can compete with men in the grand fields of literature and science and conjecture...' (Finch 1947: 1). She and a friend 'felt they must try to learn Greek, since the study of Greek was regarded as harmful to girls and fitting only for boys' (1947: 20). After her first degree, graduate study and doctoral research in Europe, Thomas, involved in the establishment of Bryn Mawr, went on visits to the existing women's colleges. It is clear that she approved of the institutions which upheld male standards, writing, for

111

example, 'the secret of Wellesley's success is her inexorableness' (Finch 1947: 143). Finch includes Carey Thomas's comments on visiting Smith:

> The importance of Greek, in especial, [*sic*] President Seelye insisted upon since, regarded as a manly prerogative, its study gave a woman self-respect besides providing her with a discipline that made her, he had observed, better able to cope with the other subjects than only Latin or modern languages. (1947: 141)

In 1979 Millicent Carey McIntosh, a niece of Carey Thomas's, recalled her saying 'Don't allow those soft Baltimore mothers to weaken their daughters by insisting they drop Latin' (McIntosh 1979: *vii*). And Boas concludes that Greek was 'the framework upon which the whole framework of education was hung' (1935: 249).

In these comments from the pioneering schools and colleges we see the uncompromising group of pioneers struggling to escape what Bourdieu terms symbolic violence. In the ranking system of 1870 Latin and Greek were seen by men and women as the most important subjects. Women who wanted to be educated had, perforce, to do classics, and attempts to prevent them were a form of symbolic violence. Classical scholarship was an essential part of the *habitus* of the learned or 'status' professions, and denying classical scholarship to women was a barrier to not only jobs, but also honorific capital in the society.

At the same time as the uncompromising feminists were focusing on classics as the most important body of knowledge for women to be allowed to learn, the classical dominance of the male world was being challenged. Gradually the curricula of the men's colleges changed and then the women's institutions were freer to innovate. Once Harvard was allowing student choice, Meigs argues that Bryn Mawr was free to offer student options in which

> subjects to be specialized in by pairs, history with political science, Greek with Latin....At least half the student's work must be in required courses, and there must be offered toward the degree English, philosophy, one of the sciences, Greek, Latin and a knowledge of two modern languages. (1956: 41)

Newcomer (1959) presented a survey of the academic programmes offered by the major women's colleges in 1918; she concluded they were 'a safe imitation' of men's colleges. The convergence of courses in men's and women's colleges can also be deduced from the strong opposition expressed by the most famous believer in separate curricula – Catharine Beecher. This is well documented in Sklar (1973) and in Goodsell who quotes Beecher as follows:

> When I read the curriculum of Vassar and the other female colleges, methinks their graduates by such a course as this will be as well prepared to nurse the sick, train servants, take charge of infants, and manage all departments of the family state, as they would be to make and regulate chronometers, or build and drive steam engines. (1931: 203)

In America one can see the uncompromising view epitomized by Carey Thomas, and that of the separatist by Catharine Beecher.

The uncompromising group have been widely misunderstood although it is striking how (particularly male) commentators have reassessed this historical period since the rise of 'women's history'. For example in 1968 David Riesman, writing with Christopher Jencks, could argue that the American feminist pioneers in education were mainly opposed by other women, and that they were misguided enough to 'accept virtually all the assumptions and aspirations of their oppressors....Thus the leaders of the feminist movement were strikingly masculine in outlook and manner' (1968: 292). The colleges they opened, 'piggy-backing' on male ones, 'offered instruction almost identical to the Eastern men's colleges of the time' (1968: 302) and the feminists insisted 'on an education at least as bad as that given men' (1968: 306).

This is a damning account, which fails to represent the uncompromising position fairly. In 1976 David Riesman provided the Preface to Ann Miller's (1976) book on Bryn Mawr alumnae, and took a quite different line. Here he announces with some pride that his mother, sister and wife are Bryn Mawr alumnae and that it is the only college predominantly for women where the faculty are recruited with the expectation that they will teach both graduate and undergraduate courses. The Preface then presents the uncompromising case in its own terms concluding that 'women could no more afford spontaneity in curriculum than in contraception, for they had not yet become equal...' and that Carey Thomas needed to create 'a platform of seriousness' (1976: *xxxiv*).

In retrospect it is quite clear that the pioneers who held out for equal educational standards and curricula were correct to do so. The other course would have led to women being confined forever in an intellectual and spiritual purdah. They recognized a simple truth – that separate never means equal – which has escaped many subsequent commentators. Slavish imitation was an essential stage in the development of women's education. There were, however, two serious consequences of this victory for the uncompromising. On the one hand their success in educating bright young ladies left all other females excluded, and on the other, they failed to see that scientific knowledge was becoming an equally important area of symbolic power and cultural capital. From the vantage point of 1988 we can see that the success story of 1888 was a Pyrrhic victory.

## A Pyrrhic victory

The present state of women's education is the result of a Pyrrhic victory by the uncompromising group. Although they won access to male subjects for clever middle-class and upper-class girls, the inevitable narrowness of their social ideas prevented them from stopping separatist ideas dominating working-class education. In essence, the pattern set in the last half of the century when the uncompromising group won access to male subjects for the clever lady still stands except that scholarships mean the persistent, bright working-class girls can now follow the same path. Thus, today the bright working-class girl, and all but the stupidest women from the upper strata, do sexually integrated curricula while the majority of the working-class and the stupid girls from the middle and upper class do sexually segregated courses.

This development can only be understood in the context of the wider educational changes of the last hundred years. Arguments about women's education have been thoroughly entangled with debates about male education for at least that long, and both are permeated with class considerations. In particular, alongside the elite, cloistered, symbolic, male system of secondary and higher education, which was all that existed in the early nineteenth century, has grown up a mass, worldly, practical and sexually integrated system of secondary and higher education. The uncompromising pioneers, concerned with educating ladies, concentrated on building a parallel elite, cloistered, symbolic system and largely ignored the potential of the emergent mass system. By the time this mass system was emerging the pioneers were unable, or unwilling, to stop thinking in class terms, and so the mass system was built along sex-specific lines, with domestic subjects prominent for girls. In short, the pioneers' educational ideology was class-based, concentrated on providing ladylike education equal to men's, and was not designed to establish a sexually uniform curriculum for the working classes.

This book is only concerned with the education and professional training of elite women: clever women who are born into, or rise into, the top two classes. The consequences of the Pyrrhic victory for mass education are not, therefore addressed in this book. Scientific and technological education for elite females was a casualty of the Pyrrhic victory, and it is the focus of this chapter.

The separatists, who were not wedded to classics for women, might have been enthusiastic about science and technology but in practice tended to focus on modern languages and literature in their 'women's curricula'. The uncompromising were so determined to establish women as competent classicists that science and technology came a poor third after classics and maths. Some historians of science education have argued that science was received in a less prejudiced way in girls' schools because the classics were not so firmly ensconced there. What is undeniable is that the same split between the uncompromising and the separatists can be seen within the science curricula which were accepted for women. The uncompromising were committed to physics and chemistry (done by men) while the separatists preferred botany (a genteel topic for ladies). Layton (1984) argues that because the number of academic girls' schools grew rapidly from the 1870s onwards, and because 'nothing comparable to the dominance of classics in boys' schools constrained innovation' (1984: 34) women's educational institutions 'yielded a rich diversity of curricula'. His evidence shows that some girls' schools gave science 'an established and prominent place', some gave it only a subsidiary place in the curriculum, while many taught no science at all as late as 1918. Even in the schools which valued science there was no consensus about which branches of it should be taught. As Layton (1984: 34-5) puts it: 'The competing educational claims of nature study, botany, physiology, chemistry, physics and domestic science were familiar topics at conferences of women Science Teachers and headmistresses.' One of the problems in establishing science in girls' schools was money: laboratories were more expensive than ordinary classrooms, and classics was cheaper to teach. Parental opposition was believed to be greater, and there was a shortage of teachers. However gymnasia also cost money, and the schools managed to build these so the lack of laboratories cannot be blamed entirely on financial problems.

Jenkins (1979: chapter 5) has documented the development of science education for girls in Britain with particular emphasis on the first 50 years of this century. He emphasizes that the lack of science facilities, especially for physics and chemistry, was a serious handicap in teaching them. Quoting a survey done by the Association of Science Teachers during the 1914-18 war he points out that of twenty-eight girls' schools with between 200-300 pupils, twenty had only one laboratory, and of thirteen schools with over 300 pupils, ten had only one lab. Girls were more likely to study botany, and have a biology room, than do serious physics or chemistry. When the Thomson Committee reported in 1918 they condemned the poor quality and small quantity of physics teaching given to girls (Jenkins 1979: 178).

The histories of the girls' schools show Layton's three varieties of accommodation to science, from schools where it was always a major part of the curriculum to those where it was non-existent. In the intermediate category came Rugby Girls' High School, founded in 1919, where 'The normal curriculum was followed, Latin being introduced in the third year as an alternative to needlework. General Science was studied during the first three years, and then Botany for two years as an examination subject' (Randall 1969: 29). Richmond Lodge School, Belfast was similar, in 1912: 'The basic curriculum at that time was very much what it is today, except in being rather more limited and in placing less emphasis on the sciences. Botany and Geography alone were taught' (Robb 1969: 14). Latin was part of the compulsory, core curriculum, but Greek and German were options. The school suffered from the lack of facilities: 'When the teaching of Chemistry was introduced, about 1917, the only space available for a laboratory was the wide upstairs landing over the front hall' (Robb 1969: 14). The teacher had to cope with all the girls in the school using this landing as a thoroughfare. Richmond Lodge also faced parental opposition to science teaching: at least one family were convinced that science teaching would undermine their daughter's Christian faith. Laurel Bank School, Glasgow, founded in 1905, does not appear to have had any science teaching at all until 1930; if there was any, the school's history does not mention it (Cuthbert 1953).

116

As Layton points out, some schools did take science seriously from the outset. For example, the Park School, Glasgow, founded in 1880, had science teaching from early on: 'In 1884, upon the suggestion of Prof Young, chemistry was introduced into the curriculum, and a laboratory was fitted up – surely one of the first laboratories to be introduced into a girls' school' (Park School 1930: 11). This laboratory was upstairs in the school and 'when the enthusiastic chemists were absorbed in their investigations they were apt to leave taps running with disastrous results to the classrooms below' (1930: 42). A former pupil who left in 1904 claimed that the style of teaching was heuristic, and the science teacher 'treated us like university students' (p.62). The Newport High School for Girls founded in 1896 had problems in getting a laboratory. The official history records that, as the first headmistress put it:

> From the first we were much curtailed in our Science work by the lack of a Laboratory which fifty years ago, was not considered essential for a Girls' School. As our building was practically complete before I came to Newport I had no chance then of pleading for one. So for the first few years we had to borrow a Laboratory in the Boys' School, only available after 5 pm, a very difficult time.
>
> (Newport 1946: 13-14)

This headmistress, Mabel Annie Vivian, was a bicycling suffragist of some determination, and within five years the school had grown so much an extension was needed. It had a laboratory. An old girl, Maude Lyre (1899-1904) remembered 'the excitements of... going to our own Lab instead of the 'conducted' tour to the Boys'' (Newport 1946: 27).

In England, Redland High School in Bristol, founded in 1882, had a chemistry master from the outset, and in 1890 a Dr Cook was giving science lectures at 12/6 a lesson, 'he providing all apparatus' (Bungay 1982: 15). The early science teaching paid off for in 1900 all the City of Bristol Senior Science Scholarships went to girls from Redland High School, and two girls won science studentships to University College. In the 1920s the Higher Certificate Work was done jointly with Colston's Girls' School to produce viably-sized classes, and a pupil recalled:

> Redland had a strong science side from early days and was, I believe, one of the few girls' schools to take physics in public

examinations, at one time entering for heat, light and sound, and electricity and magnetism as two separate subjects... My group did our pure and applied mathematics at Colston's ...our physics and chemistry were done at Redland...

(Bungay 1982: 79)

At the Shrewsbury Girls' High School (1885) maths appeared on the timetable in 1886, chemistry in 1895, and physics in 1900-1 (Bates and Wells 1962). The King Edward VI High School for Girls Birmingham (1883) began to teach science in 1884 and some promising pupils went to Mason College for science. One girl was the only physiology student and 'had private lessons from one of the professors, who was always very anxious to get rid of her before his class of men arrived, and would hurry her off down the back stairs lest she should meet them' (Vardy 1928: 26). At Queen's College in Harley Street, Grylls (1948: 91) argues that science was not neglected. Chemistry was taught by a male professor and 'The freedom – and the courage – with which he allowed practical experiments to be made aroused interest in the subject.'

The familiar complaints about lack of facilities are found in Macpherson's (1924) history of St Anne's, Abbot's Bromley. In 1911 the school was inspected and the report said that 'science was still handicapped by lack of equipment and space, and also by the absence of gas, but it was becoming a more serious subject' (p.77). St James', West Malvern (Baird 1956) does not seem to have taught any science at all in that the official history does not include any account of it!

There was a continuum in the girls' schools from those like Redland which took science seriously from the early days, and those like St James' and St Anne's where it was a late addition to the curriculum and little valued. Two old girls of the Oxford Girls' High School in the 1902-32 period catch the flavour of girls' science education at the time.

My enthusiasm for Science, faintly awakened at the school I had been at for one year before coming to Oxford was stimulated and increased by Miss Macdonald. She was a delightful person, humorous and friendly. She always made us start our experiments with an open mind, instilled in us a love of discovery and eschewed any kind of text book, which certainly nurtured a true scientific spirit but made the rate of progress somewhat slow. There was an acute lack of apparatus,

118

particularly physical apparatus, and when I took my scholarship examination at Cambridge, I had never used most of the pieces of apparatus with which I was faced, though I knew their pictures and theory of their use. This shortage of apparatus cut both ways, for we became ingenious in constructing home-made things and got a great thrill when they worked, and we certainly understood the fundamental principles underlying their construction far better than many pupils of today who have only to plug in a terminal or touch a switch to get what they want.

(Marjorie Cam, in Stack 1963: 79)

This comment about nurturing a true scientific spirit leading to slow progress foreshadows the work on guided discovery science as a mock-up (Atkinson and Delamont 1976).

It seems to me that our education was very well balanced, being far more general and less specialised than was permitted in any boys' school at that date, although by the time we were ready for the University it was recognized that our attainments in classics and science were below that of boys, because in those days a classic at a public school was taught no other subject, and few science mistresses were available, nor could girls' schools afford to set up large laboratories. ...Our one teacher of natural science was Evelyn Macdonald, half Irish, full of energy and enthusiasm. She was one of the Girtonians, and therefore had the Cambridge training in three fundamental science subjects, so that O H S was more fortunate than most schools that had only one science specialist. The botany lessons were informal and seemed impromptu – we had no dull textbook to kill our interest, nor were we plagued by dictation of notes. During our progress through the Upper School we were taught the fundamental facts of elementary physics and chemistry, and my own later experience of teaching showed that the apparently informal methods were in fact the result of long practice by a teacher of genius.

On reaching Form V, I was flattered to receive an invitation to do some extra science with 'Smac' as we always called Miss Macdonald. Four close-packed years followed, full of intense interest and wide teaching, such as was then available in very few girls' schools. The one mistress had to cope with the whole of the teaching of science in the school, and manage the laboratory and keep apparatus in order with no help, giving instruction regularly in the three usual subjects, physics, chemistry and botany, and at times in geology (which with chemistry had been E M's subjects for Part II of the Tripos). Therefore, apart from extra afternoon work in the laboratory the coaching for a scholarship candidate was crammed into short periods probably filched from E M's extremely limited free time.

(Muriel Palmer, in Stack 1963: 72-3)

This enthusiasm for science is found in many other reminiscences of the 1850-1920 period, such as Kathleen Raine's (1975: 11), where she writes lyrically of her 'long enchanted hours in the little botany laboratory, learning to cut and stain specimens for the microscope'. Women who were not allowed an academic education also lament their lack of scientific experience. Mabell, Countess of Airlie (born in 1866) who was quoted in chapter 4 (p. 94) was denied an academic training and specifically regretted that: 'I had longed to study science, mathematics and other subjects barred as unfeminine' (Airlie 1956). Despite these enthusiasts, the general picture is of financial and staff shortages, few labs, and parental anxieties about physics and chemistry. Gadesden, the head of Blackheath Girls' High School, writing at the end of the nineteenth century on secondary education for girls, claimed that it was only in the previous decade that science teaching had become well established. Optimistically she went on:

Science rooms which allow of free movement, and are provided with firm benches, and gas and water supplies, are being universally fitted up....The heuristic method is adopted in most schools where a course in elementary physics and chemistry follows the nature study of the lower forms.

(Gadesden 1901: 100)

Gadesden may have been accurate in her account of science at the GPDST schools, but in the state sector things were certainly not so good, nor in many of the boarding schools, especially those with charitable purposes.

The Royal School for the Daughters of the Army at Bath only put algebra, Euclid and botany into the syllabus in the 1890s, and had no lab in the nineteenth century. In 1903 the headmistress became aware that the school needed a laboratory because 'she attended Headmistresses' Conferences from time to time and learnt what was happening elsewhere, that every year more stress was being laid on chemistry and physics' (Osborne and Manisty 1966: 83). A legacy received in 1904 was devoted to this, and the school got one lab in 1905. In the 1930s the inspectors reported that the science facilities were 'quite unworthy', and a second laboratory with prep room was needed, so in 1938 a biology lab was built.

Walthamstow Hall, the missionaries' daughters' school, was equally unscientific. Though founded in 1838 it was 1898 before a new head arranged for a visiting science teacher to come and give some lessons on Saturdays. A science room was built in 1909, and in 1928 the science teaching was reorganized to include biology. A new building was erected and this lab, 'opened in 1934, [was] said to be one of the best in Kent' (Pike, Curryer and Moore 1973: 61). The Germans bombed the laboratories in 1940, and it was 1963 before full science facilities were available, thanks to a grant from the Industrial Fund for the Advancement of Scientific Education in Schools (IFASES) (Pike *et al.* 1973: 100). In the interim, girls had walked over to Sevenoaks School to study physics and chemistry, while boys came to Walthamstow Hall for biology.

An example of the lack of facilities in local authority schools early this century is apparent from the biography of Elizabeth May Williams (*née* Larby) who suffered because her girls' school had neglected science teaching. She went from the East Ham Girls' Grammar School to Bedford College to read maths in 1911 (Howson 1982). She found that she was relatively handicapped by her 'lack of knowledge of applied mathematics' (p.177), and physics. At her school 'only heat was taught – no mechanics, electricity, sound or light' (p.177). She still managed to graduate with an upper second at the age of 19, and ended up the first married woman to be President of the Mathematics Association.

In Australia, the Melbourne Church of England Girls' Grammar School founded in 1903 began teaching science and in 1917:

> Another addition at this time was the establishment of a small laboratory ... for the teaching of physics ... and chemistry. Science classes had been held from the beginning, and as early as 1904 the Council discussed the need of a science lab, but apparently no special room was set apart until 1947.
>
> (Anon 1953: 38)

The Presbyterian Ladies College, founded in 1875, had not taught science then, because as Fitzpatrick points out 'In this omission the

Ladies' College was not really falling behind boys' public schools where it was not yet taught either' (Fitzpatrick 1975: 61-2). When a new principal was appointed in 1904 he changed this.

> Mr Bee saw at once the PLC's science teaching was hopelessly inadequate. The college had set out to give girls equal education opportunity with boys but had not kept pace with the advance of science in boys' schools and did not even attempt to teach pure science....Physics and chemistry were introduced into the curriculum and a properly equipped laboratory was built.
>
> (Fitzpatrick 1975: 120)

In the USA some of the early girls' schools had science teaching. Woods (1904) writing of the Boston Girls' High School (founded in 1852) says that in 1870 the headmaster, Mr Hunt,

> was in advance of the ordinary practice in his zeal for the thorough teaching of the sciences. Even in the dark laboratory of the Mason Street School, the teaching of text books had been supplemented by experiments performed by the teacher or by Professor Marshall of Tufts College, but in the new school the physical sciences began to be taught by specialists with well-equipped laboratories.
>
> (Woods 1904: 32)

Among the specialists was Agassiz, who taught some zoology. Emma Willard's Troy seminary (Scott 1979) had given science a place in the curriculum:

> The curriculum included mathematics, science, modern languages, Latin, history, philosophy, geography, and literature. An early enthusiast for the teaching of science, Willard had the good fortune to become a friend of Amos Eaton (a key figure in the founding of the Rensselaer Polytechnic Institute, also in Troy) who welcomed young women to his classes and helped develop a science program for the seminary.

Willard's pupils were organized to conduct experiments themselves at an early date. Lloyd's history of Abbot, in contrast, says that Philena and Phebe McKeen found, on their arrival in 1855 to run the school, that 'Science laboratory facilities were pathetic' (1979: 89). She argues that the physics and chemistry were not 'worth while' (i.e. seriously academic) until the 1880s. In general the girls' schools in the USA taught little science, and when the classical dominance of the high school curriculum was finally overthrown after the report of the National Education Association (NEA) Committee of Ten (Krug 1964), sciences were put in the college preparatory track but as electives. Relatively few girls studied college preparatory science courses in the American High Schools.

At college level, the access of women to science was rather better than at schools. Newcomer (1959) argues that when Vassar opened its science facilities they were better than in most men's colleges (e.g. Brown) at the time. Horowitz, in her study of the architecture of the women's colleges, provides useful information on their science facilities. Vassar began with an observatory and taught astronomy because it had Maria Mitchell on the faculty. The college also had a medical lecture room, and facilities for geology, minerology, and natural history (Horowitz 1984: 35). Smith built the Lilly Hall of Science in 1886, and Mount Holyoke its A. Lyman Williston Hall in 1875 for science and art. However the early enthusiasm for science was not sustained, as I show (table 5.1).

Table 5.1 Student subject choices at Vassar 1865-1957 expressed as a percentage of student body

| Subject area | 1865-9 | 1901-5 | 1927-31 | 1953-7 |
| --- | --- | --- | --- | --- |
| Sciences | 39.3 | 25.4 | 19.7 | 16.5 |
| Classics | 21.2 | 16.3 | 4.1 | 1.7 |
| Modern languages | 20.6 | 15.3 | 18.3 | 14.9 |
| Arts | 11.6 | 23.3 | 29.0 | 29.4 |
| Social sciences | 7.2 | 19.7 | 28.9 | 37.4 |

(from Newcomer 1959)

Outside the elite women's colleges female entry to the science faculties at the co-educational universities was frequently delayed long after access to arts and education had been granted. Townsend (1959) drawing on a thesis by Ragsdale (n.d.) has described women's admission to the University of Georgia. The campaign for women's admission began in 1889, and although after 1908 there were substantial numbers of women studying unofficially at Georgia, it was 1918 before they could officially be students. The Dean of Science was still opposed and announced that 'When women walk into my classroom I will walk out. I will never teach women.' However he found among his earliest mixed classes a woman from Atlanta who earned 100 per cent on a chemistry exam: the first time he had awarded that mark in 11 years teaching. Mozans (1913) claimed that when Ellen Swallow Richards was given a B.Sc degree by Massachusetts Institute of Technology (MIT) she was not only the first woman graduate of MIT but probably of any American scientific institution. In 1876, MIT officially began to admit women, first to chemistry and then to other subjects.

Overall, women keen to study science were more likely to find good courses and access to scientific knowledge in the elite women's colleges than in the co-educational universities or the specialist scientific institutions like MIT, but the women's colleges could not support good graduate schools and high-powered research teams. Women in the USA could get an undergraduate science qualification, but a Ph.D and a job were much more elusive. Rossiter (1982) has carried out a detailed historical study of women in American science, replete with examples of men in science and technology who rejected women's participation, exploited women's labour, and denied them any recognition for their work. No equivalent work has been done on science history in Britain or Australasia, but the chronology and arguments Rossiter has derived from her detailed American research are probably applicable to other countries as well.

Rossiter divides the participation of women in American science into three phases: before 1880, between 1880 and 1910, and after 1910. She points out that these three periods are different from those typically used in the history of science which relies on landmarks in discovery to divide its eras, and those used to sub-divide American political or economic history which uses wars, presidential careers, or depressions. Rossiter sees the place of women in American science developing quite rapidly before 1880, when the education of women expanded and modern science began to take its present-day structure (e.g. the American Chemical Society was founded in 1874). In this period women were able to learn science, and to practise it, in newly opening women's colleges, in observatories and in museums. Between 1880 and 1910, the sciences were trying to 'professionalize' themselves, and establish themselves in American higher education, culture and prestige. To achieve this professional status, Rossiter argues, the men scientists purified their disciplines by throwing out women already in science, and keeping in marginal and subordinate places women who qualified in their subjects.

Thus Rossiter (1982: 73) argues that while in the 1880s there were more women qualified in science than ever before, only a few were treated as professional scientists. The organizations of scientists which were being created, upgraded, made nation-wide, and claiming high status, were determined to weed out 'amateurs' and women. Because few women held high-status jobs in science they were excluded from full membership of the associations, or refused participation in their events. At the same time as the scientific associations were rebuilding themselves on exclusive, masculine lines, the growth of 'big science' created jobs for hired-hands. Women could get some employment, but only by staying in subordinate positions on other people's (i.e. males') research projects. Rossiter gives many examples of this professionalization of science, from anthropology to zoology. The pattern was for men, anxious to raise the status of their subject, to establish a learned society that demanded high standards of its members. Membership was to be dependent on having a Ph.D, a period of postgraduate work overseas, on substantial publications, or a job in a prestige college. Frequently no women could obtain these qualifications; for example German universities refused doctorates to women for many years, so any learned society which demanded a German doctorate was automatically all-male.

Engineering offers a concrete example (Rossiter 1982: 90-1). As the engineers wished to raise their status, they cut off those who were non-graduates. The engineering societies established in the 1880s had strict membership conditions which women were unable to meet because few engineering schools would admit women. Ellen Richards, who had an MIT degree, did get in to the American Institute of Mining Engineers in 1879 but her husband was a vice president at the time. No other woman was allowed into any engineering society until 1894. Nora Blatch de Forest even sued the civil engineers in 1916 for excluding her, but lost her case. It was 1927 before a woman became a full member of the American Society of Civil Engineers.

The hostility of insecure male scientists, whose subjects were not yet acceptable as occupations rather than hobbies, is recalled by writers on women students in co-educational universities after 1880. Zimmerman (1979) in a paper on the early days of Grinnel, a co-educational college in Iowa, reports that all the majors (i.e. honours degrees) were opened to women when the college abandoned compulsory classics in 1895. Women were then free to choose their major from: science, Greek, modern languages, English, Latin, history, philosophy, maths, economics, politics and education. However, between 1896 and 1914 only 6 per cent of the women students (who were between 36 per cent and 52 per cent of the total student body during that period) took science. A survey of the early women students (conducted when they were elderly) found that none recalled any hostility from men on campus except in science. One or two women who had taken some science courses recalled that 'Only in laboratories did I feel that some men felt we were an *inferior* species – a nuisance' and another suggested there was male hostility 'perhaps in physics or chemistry classes where they outnumbered the girls'.

The women scientists studied by Kundsin (1974) who were students in the 1920s and 1930s report similar hostilities and barriers from their high schools and colleges. Karle, a crystallographer, told Kundsin: 'I decided to pursue the study of chemistry in college ... my high school chemistry teacher ... tried to discourage me by saying that chemistry was not a proper field for girls' (1974: 32). Karle went to read chemistry at Michigan and 'although I graduated with highest honours, I was not encouraged in graduate studies at ... Michigan. The usual manner of supporting graduate students in chemistry ... was by awarding teaching assistantships, and none were available in the chemistry department for girls' (1974: 32).

Similarly the electrical engineer, M.S. Dresselhaus wanted to go to the Hunter College High School in New York which specializes in elite science courses. She recounts that at her ghetto school in the 1930s 'No girl from my junior high school had ever passed the entrance exam, and the teachers laughed (at me) for even thinking of applying' (1974: 39). G.T. Hunter, a black pediatrician, chose college preparatory courses at her high school and 'the courses I had elected were crossed out, and substituted with Home Economics curriculum'. Her mother complained, and the school replied: 'What is a coloured girl going to do with college?' (1974: 59). Once at Howard, a black university, Hunter found things better: 'In the Black world of Howard Medical School, I was not aware of any sexual discrimination' (1974: 59).

The meteorologist J. Simpson – the first woman to obtain a Ph.D in meteorology in the USA – found similar problems to Karle's when she wanted to do graduate work: 'As a graduate student ... my department declined to recommend me for any fellowship support whatever on grounds of sex alone' (1974: 62). R. Weiner, a chemist, was a product of the Baltimore public school where 'My high school discouraged pursuit of scientific professional careers' (1974: 73). Subsequently she became the only woman on the science staff at Temple Buell College in Denver. Such isolation is commonly reported by these eminent female scientists. M.B. Pour-El went from a women's college to do her graduate work in maths at Harvard: 'I recall very vividly my first day in class: three seats in front of me, three seats in back of me, and two seats on either side were left vacant. I was a complete pariah in that social setting' (Kundsin 1974: 36). She completed her doctorate and got a lectureship in a State University. Her new male colleagues 'were unable to interact with me mathematically because they had no social practice in doing it' (Kundsin 1974: 37).

Some universities made attempts to provide a welcoming attitude to women science students. At Berkeley, Phoebe Hearst set up a fund to hire Dr Mary Bennett Ritter, the first woman faculty member, to give lectures on hygiene to the women students and to be their medical examiner. Women students received some biological teaching from an early stage. The relative strangeness of science for women is highlighted in 1894 when women began to form subject-based clubs and societies. As well as the XYZ club for women interested in maths, there were the chemistry fiends. They pioneered 'girl-friendly laboratories' 'to make themselves feel more comfortable in the chemistry building, an all-male preserve, women practiced traditional female activities: they held evening parties there, making fudge and coffee over the bunsen burners' (Gordon 1979).

Rossiter (1982: 78 and 92-3) points out that the social side of the professionalizing learned societies was also structured to exclude women. Thus the American Chemical Society held a stag dinner in 1880 whose ' ribald' proceedings were recorded and transcribed for circulation as the *Misogynist Dinner of the American Chemical Society*. The social side of these societies was made more intimidating to women by tobacco.

> Properly bred women apparently did not smoke or enter rooms where men were smoking before the 1920s....Thus to include smoking on the programme or to allow men to smoke after dinner was, whether the men realised it or not, long an overt social message to the women not to attend.
>
> (1982: 92)

The Association of American Geographers self-consciously knew that women would not attend 'smokers'. When a group of teachers wanted to come to their annual meeting in 1915 'the men planning the meeting desired neither the 'prim schoolmarms' nor their topic, [so] they decided to hold a smoker at the appointed time and thus eliminate both vexing problems together' (1982: 93). As Rossiter points out, the women knew that they were excluded by convention: 'Thus in most instances a woman might well lose more of her reputation by going to a 'smoker' than she could possibly gain by the conversation there, however scintillating' (1982: 94).

However, as much promotion, recognition and appreciation in science depends on networks and patronage, exclusion from the social side of learned societies was an exclusion from membership of the scientific community. Hertha Ayrton was, therefore, particularly brave to attend the dinner of the British Institute of Electrical Engineers in 1900, the only woman among 359 men (Sharp 1926). As a married woman, her reputation was safer than that of a spinster. Hertha Ayrton (1854-1923) is an interesting case for historians of British science because while she won many scientific honours, and was the first woman to do so, she was also denied many others. Interestingly, when she began to win recognition and patent inventions, and these were publicized in popular newspapers and magazines, some commentators thought she proved that women were better at maths and science than at classics. *The Spectator*, in March 1899, announced that women 'have a distinct proclivity towards science and mathematics, finding them less exhausting than either history or classics ... [women] will produce a Laplace or a Lord Kelvin before they produce a Paul of Tarsus or a Shakespeare' (quoted in Sharp 1926: 137). This was not a universal view at the period, however. Carole Haslett, born in 1895, was an early woman engineer, and her biographer reports that when she was working with Mrs Pankhurst for suffrage, the latter said that engineering was not a very suitable occupation for a young girl (Messenger 1967: 26).

## Classics versus science

To summarize the argument of the chapter so far: the feminist pioneers, particularly the uncompromising group, made classics and maths their subject goal. Physics and chemistry were of less importance to them, because they were of lower status, and needed more money to teach. Access to classics and maths, and success in them, was achieved while at the same time the physical sciences were challenging the supremacy of classics and maths for men. Precisely because the sciences were engaged in attacking classical supremacy and professionalizing themselves, they were more hostile to women than classics and maths were. The physical scientists, the biological ones, and the engineers were preoccupied with building barriers between their new, paid, full-time research and the old, amateur, genteel and dilettante sciences of the first half of the century and one part of these barriers was keeping women out. The results of this were twofold. Those women who did enter science found themselves confined to teaching other women, and forming all-female professional circles; many women chose instead to study social sciences (in the USA) and English modern languages, where they could avoid barriers in science and technology. The exclusion from the informal and formal networks of science charted by Rossiter was particularly disabling for women scientists because nineteenth- and twentieth-century scientific knowledge is communicated among networks of scientists rather than through formal, published channels. (These arguments are elaborated in chapters 7 and 9.) Figure 5.1 contrasts classics and the sciences on Douglas's group and grid dimensions. While both classics and science were hard to get into (strong group) the sciences were developing a clear hierarchy and a complex set of rules to govern participants (strong grid) as well. The pollution

*Figure 5.1 Classics and sciences: pollution fears and barriers to women*

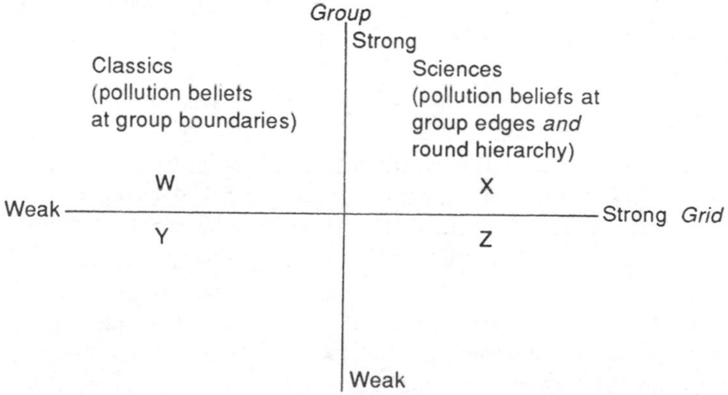

beliefs proposed by Douglas (figure 2.5), in this case enforced against women, were therefore stronger in the sciences.

Bryan Turner (1974) has argued that the disputes between science and religion in nineteenth-century Britain were not primarily about conflicting ideas at all but about opposing occupational groups: scientists and clergy. Turner suggests that once science became organized the scientists found the clergy dominated the major sources of financial support, social standing and so forth. It would not be surprising to find that the feminist pioneers, who wanted their share of the patronage, fellowships, and cognitive authority were uneasy about the organized scientists also after those things. Equally it would not be unreasonable to suggest that the scientists, engaged in a struggle for money and power with the clergy, might wish to appear conservative and pro-domesticity for women as part of their campaign.

Alternatively, classics and maths, which could be studied at home, in the family, and in private, may have been seen as more accessible for women than science which demanded long hours away from home in a laboratory among strangers of mixed sex and class. Whatever the reasons, the feminist pioneers did not give physical science the same priority as classics, and the scientists were not enthusiastic about the participation of women in their new subjects. Whatever the reasons far fewer of the pioneers' students studied sciences than classics or modern languages, and even in places like Vassar, physics and chemistry lost ground as college education spread.

Although the American women's colleges had been eager to train women scientists, by 1914 this early enthusiasm had faded. Probably because of the myriad of informal barriers and the remaining and newly erected formal ones outlined by Rossiter (1982), the initial enthusiasm for science did not persist. Instead, the students of the women's colleges and the women co-eds opted for the emergent social sciences. Newcomer (1959) provides the figures for Vassar, and they are reproduced in table 5.1. Table 5.1 shows that whereas in its earliest years arts and social sciences occupied less than one fifth of the students at Vassar, by 1957 they were the majors of two thirds. The growth of scholarship in English, history and the social sciences has absorbed the talents of women to the detriment of classics and science. The decline of classics has been general among men too, but in science the relative failure to build on the pioneers' facilities has left women far behind their 'brothers'.

The next chapter examines some of the fears men had about their scholarly domains being infested by women, and the domestic curriculum which separatists and many men thought appropriate for women.

# 6
## Domesticity or Delilahism?
## The debates over womanliness and education

Nature had no vainglorious ambitions as to a race of female wranglers or golfers; she is not concerned with Amazons.
(Kenealy 1899)

Why did the Lord create Messrs Huntley and Palmer to make cakes for us, if not to give our clever girls a chance to do something better?
(Miss Buss, quoted in Hughes 1978b: 81)

This chapter deals with two themes, cookery in the curriculum, and celibacy as a chosen lifestyle, which may seem to be unconnected. In fact, the controversial nature of women's education between 1845 and 1945 was partly due to the changing relationships between domesticity and careers, and also between marriage and celibacy, which the various protagonists were championing. Underlying the debates about the place of domestic skills and virtues in women's education, and about whether education unfitted ladies for marriage, were some deep seated fears about pollution of the sexes and their spheres. This chapter looks at the arguments over cookery and sewing for girls, over celibacy for adult women, and over fears that the practice of women entering universities and occupations was a form of Delilahism (i.e. weakening the structures to bring them down) that would result in a new race of Amazons or hermaphrodites. Kenealy wanted a domestic education for girls to protect their sexuality, domesticity and nurturance, and to safeguard the future of the race. Buss was against domestic subjects for the clever girl who could qualify as a dentist or lawyer and employ someone else to make her cakes for her. The battle lines drawn up in the second half of the nineteenth century are still affecting us today as are the deep-seated fears of Delilahism and hermaphrodites.

The vocabulary, and the symbolism it invokes, are the real focus of this chapter rather than cookery or celibacy in themselves. It is not an accident that Kenealy uses the idea of Amazons, the mythical warrior priestesses who dedicated their virginity to the goddess and fought men rather than living with them. As Vicinus (1985) has shown us, the pioneer feminists had, in their schools, colleges, orders of deaconesses, nurses' homes and settlement houses established celibate communities of Amazons in the towns and cities of Australia, America and Britain equally opposed to Victorian patriarchal domesticity as the mythical priestesses of Artemis. The image of the Amazon, and that of Delilah, more potent then when everyone would be familiar with Greek legend, the Bible story, and Milton's poem, were the twin evils held up to terrorize those who were campaigning for the education of women and especially their more faint-hearted supporters. Typical invocations of these twin images can be found in those opposed to allowing women to study at Michigan. The University of Michigan admitted its first woman student, Madelon Stockwell in 1870. There was hostility from the town, the faculty, and the other students. The local paper complained of 'Delilahism' (McGuigan 1970: 2). Three women had tried to gain admission in 1858, but the president had been opposed. He 'had set about remodelling Michigan along the lines of the German universities...' (McGuigan 1970: 18). This enterprise would, he feared, be jeopardized by admitting women, who had no place in his model university. He also feared for the women themselves who he thought would become 'defeminated', 'mongrel', 'hermaphrodite' (1970: 18). He finally gave in in 1868 largely because it was uneconomic to offer separate teaching for women. Michigan was not the first co-educational university (Oberlin 1837), and several state universities had already admitted women (Iowa, Wisconsin, Kansas, Indiana, Minnesota and Missouri). Michigan was, however, the largest university in the country and the most prestigious west of New England. The debate over women's admission to Michigan is not unusual but the vocabulary used to attack the feminists is worth examination.

The terms used were common currency in the second half of the nineteenth century, both in Britain and in the USA. Thus a British periodical, the anti-feminist *Saturday Review*, called educated women 'defeminated', 'hermaphrodite', 'mongrel', a 'species of

*Figure 6.1 The ideology of separate spheres*

| Male world | | Female world |
|---|---|---|
| Work | | Home |
| Learning | Barrier for women | Domesticity |
| Politics | | Virginity |
| Multiple sexual partners | | Fidelity |

vermin', 'one of the most intolerable monsters in creation' and a 'Plague in Egypt', among other offensive epithets. In the first part of the twentieth century, Arabella Kenealy continued the tradition of applying highly-coloured epithets to women who received an education. Kenealy argued that the girls' schools of the early twentieth century were producing girls who lost 'every womanly characteristic', who 'lapse to the biological grade, not of cultured, but of rough working men' (Kenealy 1920: p.28). These schools made girls masculine in physique so they became 'more like colts or smaller sized bullocks' (p.87) and their mental processes became mannish. Kenealy believed that 'male mental proclivities develop, obsessions to wear trousers, to smoke, to stride, to kill' (p.86).

Kenealy is an extremist, but the beliefs she held were only a more exaggerated version of what Kraditor (1968) has summarized as the doctrine of the two spheres. At its simplest, as shown in figure 6.1, this meant that men and women had separate spheres of existence, with a barrier between them only men could cross with impunity.

Men lived in both worlds, but women were confined to one. Women who crossed the barrier damaged themselves and the male sanctuaries that they polluted. The consequences for women of leaving their families and homes were twofold, as shown in figure 6.2.

The consequences for the whole society were seen as disastrous. The Amazons would not breed healthy children, and the fundamental institutions of the society were destroyed, like Samson's strength, by Delilahism. The logic of this position, such as it is, can be seen at its most coherent in the debates over cookery to which the chapter now turns.

*Figure 6.2 Consequences if women left their sphere*

| Consequences for the woman | Consequences for the male sphere |
| --- | --- |
| Lady becomes Amazon<br>Hermaphrodite<br>Monster<br>Vermin<br>Defeminated<br>Witch<br>Mongrel<br>Plague | Male sphere becomes Polluted<br>Infested<br>Weakened<br>Feminized<br>Destroyed |

## Cookery and the curriculum

There are at least four recent accounts of the debates which surrounded, and still surround, the appropriate amount of 'domestic' teaching which should be included in the curriculum of girls' schooling. Carol Dyhouse (1981) has provided the definitive research on and assessment of the debates between 1870 and 1920, and there are also discussions in Jenkins (1979), Nava (1984), and Purvis (1985). It is a debate which re-surfaces with tedious regularity and one in which many otherwise intelligent commentators frequently lose their heads. The historical arguments are not recapitulated here because of the four accessible accounts of them. Instead the analysis focuses on the symbolic issues that are raised, often unconsciously or implicitly, when the ostensible subject of debate is whether all women, working-class girls, and/or clever young ladies, should be trained in cookery, needlework, household management and childcare. Underlying debates about cookery and childcare in the curriculum are wider issues about the relationship of domestic labour to the family, and of the sexual division of labour in the society as a whole. The feminist educational campaigners were issuing a fundamental challenge to the dominant ideology of their era, so they were careful to cloak their long-term aims in a vocabulary of support for traditional domesticity. Their aims were revolutionary: the creation of a 'new' woman with a new sphere, but as a muted group the feminists cloaked their aims in the vocabulary of the traditional, dominant vision.

The developing feminist consciousness of the Victorian woman and the associated campaigns to redefine woman's sphere, gain access to education and professions, overcome ill-health, and obtain autonomy created a new woman who no longer fitted so easily into the classification system of the male-dominated society. The 'new' woman was always in danger of stepping so far outside the categories that she became an anomaly, an ambiguous abomination. The woman who deviated from the retiring domestic ideal was in constant peril: at any moment she might become one of the threatening, dangerous, unsexed, monsters incarnate, so abhorred by the conservative press. Any deviation from the male-dominated classification of behaviour could lead to labels of witchcraft, prostitution, hermaphroditism and sub-humanity, and leave the woman polluted.

The most successful feminist campaigners were those who managed to minimize hostile reactions by manipulating the classification system and not violating it. These were the pioneers who were able to reorganize the beliefs and values of the dominant male culture, who articulated their ideas in a form acceptable to that dominant male opinion, and used the dominant ideas to achieve their own ends. It is not hard to appreciate the feminist use of male-dominated ideas and understand the reasons for this as a strategy, but many commentators have misunderstood or misrepresented this aspect of feminism. William O'Neill's (1969) argument that feminism failed because it did not attack the nuclear family and embrace socialism is a clear example of a flagrant misrepresentation from an American author. In Britain one of the most polemical misunderstandings of nineteenth-century campaigns can be found in a lecture delivered by Edmund Leach (1968) which raises, and distorts, many central arguments which are discussed in this collection, especially those concerned with education. Leach made a call for women to consider an education 'consistent with domestic feminine roles' which apparently meant cookery. Leach was then a full professor of anthropology at Cambridge and is widely regarded as one of the most original thinkers in British social science. After the last war he revolutionized British anthropology single-handed by attacking the prevalent structural functionalism. Normally clear-sighted, and an opponent of functionalist theories wherever they appear, for once he managed to be both functionalist and woolly-minded. Like many other men, he could not face the educated woman with equanimity, but retreated, abandoning all his normal perspicacity.

The lecture was privately printed and is not, thank goodness, well-known. Briefly, Leach argues that higher education in Britain is designed to minimize differences between the sexes and this is bad for women, elitist, and old-fashioned. The argument can be summarized under five headings:

1. Society must have a division of labour by sex. Exceptional women may be allowed to play male roles but only in rare cases.
2. Very few people actually use what they learn, and so education cannot be justified on grounds of utility. It must be seen as having prestige value only.
3. Original feminist claims to education only made sense when women repudiated matrimony in favour of celibate careers. Nowadays, when most marry, they should reconsider the benefits of domestic training.
4. Higher education for women is 'markedly hostile to sensuality'.
5. Women who undertake higher education 'by rejecting the symbols of sex difference' are 'laying claim to a very special kind of political superiority'. That is, the notion that sex is irrelevant in education is anti-democratic and elitist.

Leach's first point is undiluted structural-functionalism which could have been written by Talcott Parsons or Radcliffe Brown, men whose theories Leach has devoted his career to demolishing! The arguments about celibacy, marriage, and sensuality are interesting, if not new (indeed, of the five points only the last is in any sense novel for all the others can be found throughout the history of campaigns for and against women's education). If an education which minimizes sexual differences is elitist now, this represents a marked change from the nineteenth century, when it was working-class education that was relatively undifferentiated by sex, and middle higher-class and upper-class education that was sharply divided, as I have discussed in my paper 'The domestic ideology and women's education' (1978b).

Leach appears to be adopting the functional argument that the family needs a strict division of labour by sex, with the man playing instrumental roles and the woman expressive/emotional ones. If social stability depends on women restricting themselves to the home, educating them in anything but domestic skills is uneconomic or positively harmful. Higher education is a particularly expensive and highly dangerous form of education because it is most likely to make women unwilling to stay in the domestic sphere. Leach argues that in stratified, literate societies such as Mandarin China and the capitalist West 'higher education is a device for excluding the unworthy from the privileges of a governing elite'. In other words higher education is as much a form of conspicuous consumption as a useful qualification for work – it has high prestige, but is often of little use. In general only those with money and leisure can enter higher education, and their doing so is evidence of their fitness to become members of the elite strata in society. Indeed, Leach argues that society would be a happier place if everyone were taught cooking instead of just stupid women. In practice 'male education is not much use to the men'. (Leach is conveniently ignoring here higher education in law, medicine, engineering and so on, and referring to pure mathematics, classics, and so forth which is a misrepresentation of higher education.) Leach admits: 'I suppose...that it is quite understandable that the later [feminists]... should have considered it a measure of female emancipation that women should establish the right to jump through the same educational hoops as upper-middle-class men.'

However he regards it as odd that anyone in 1968 should still have the same ambitions, although he admits that 'the rules are still rigged' to stop women entering certain professional schools and occupations! Thus he seems to want the women to abandon their struggle before they have actually won it, but offers no reason except the uselessness of male education.

The whole lecture is very odd. Leach argues that domestic skills are low in prestige, and useless subjects are highly valued, but then wonders why women still want the high prestige courses! He ignores the fact that not all male-dominated subjects are useless and calls on women to see men's education as a sham and opt for something more sensible. This clarion call to women's good sense ignores the harsh facts of hierarchy and power in society. The people at the bottom of the heap cannot redefine the goals of the society; the losing side cannot change the rules of the game. If men like Leach really believe that cookery would be better for men's souls than anthropology, they must start teaching men to cook. Women are powerless to alter the male prestige hierarchy in education, except via a female revolution which falls outside Leach's vision.

Leach argues that it is only in the most socially-privileged group – those who are receiving a university education – that the sexual division of labour can be relaxed. The rest of society still adheres to separate sex roles and so the lack of sex divisions in higher education is elitist. Leach does not consider whether the strong sexual divisions in the less-privileged strata are good or bad, although the tone of the paper suggests that he regards them as functional and useful for society. In fact the reverse is the case. British education for the majority of pupils has accentuated gender divisions to hide class distinction. Wolpe (1974) has shown in an analysis of official thinking on the education of teenagers in Britain since the Second World War that:

> Girls were seen to comprise a homogeneous group on the basis of their gender...although pupils in general were considered in a hierarchical structure in regard to their future positions in stratification terms, female pupils were not even considered as people who have a position in any hierarchy except on the basis of what they might attain through their husbands.

Thus the stress on domestic skills for all women but a few exceptionally able ones not only limits the horizons of the pupils and hides their class position from them, it also produces a pool of unskilled labour whose talents are untapped. If this did actually serve to mitigate against racial, religious, regional, and class conflict it might be considered essential, if tragic. As it is, domestic education for women is a denial of their human rights – part and parcel of the injustice the Grimké sisters set out to fight in the 1830s.

Leach completely fails to understand the complex problem which faced the nineteenth-century feminists in redefining women's sphere and the reason why they adopted the male-prestige system in education. However, the underlying ideas about social stability, domestic roles, and feminism are worth a more detailed examination. The idea that a rigid separation of sex roles was essential for social life, democracy, and economic welfare was widespread in the nineteenth century and formed one of the chief barriers to the feminist campaign. One of its chief proponents was Catharine Beecher, whose statement of the 'separate sex roles' theory is particularly suited to an analysis following Mary Douglas.

Opinion is divided about Catharine Beecher's credentials as a feminist. She campaigned for women to become teachers when public opinion thought teaching a man's job, and founded several good schools, However, she was opposed to suffrage and preached subordination to men. A recent intellectual portrait by Sklar highlights the many contradictions that make it hard to decide on her inclusion or exclusion from the gallery of 'founding mothers' of feminism. Sklar's (1973: xiii) judgement is that feminism was 'mixed with anti-feminism in her lifework' and that she 'accumulated a tremendous amount of animus against male cultural dominance' although this animus was usually expressed indirectly. Beecher's version of feminism became apparent when 'In the 1830s, the core of the feminist dilemma took shape – whether to assert female influence as a function of their difference from men, or on the basis of their human equality' (Sklar 1973: 137). Sklar shows how the Grimké sisters opted for the second path while Beecher chose the first, but argues that both courses must be seen as feminist. Beecher's views were more popular in the short run, although the Grimké views triumphed in the end.

Beecher was the most articulate of all female separatists and her ideas foreshadowed American functionalist theories of the family. In 1841 she published her *Treatise on Domestic Economy* which was a best seller for decades and gave her financial independence. Among the hints on cooking, laundry, and home nursing lie Beecher's central tenets: her theory of women's role. The ideas came from de Tocqueville's *Democracy in America* but Beecher added flourishes of her own. In essence Beecher argued that women must be restricted to the domestic sphere as 'a political expedient necessary to the maintenance of democracy in America' (1841: 156). She saw American society as being full of tension – religious, regional, racial and economic – and was sure that society would explode if no safety valve were found. She reasoned that 'by removing half of the population from the arena of competition and making it subservient to the other half, the amount of antagonism the society had to bear would be reduced to a tolerable limit' (1841: 156).

In other words, Beecher argued that gender distinctions should be emphasized to such an extent that class, race, religion and region became relatively unimportant. The rapid social change America was experiencing was so disruptive that some stable force must be found to counter-balance it, and for Beecher this stable force was a fixed division of labour by sex. Thus Beecher argued that women must be subordinate to men in society but she also maintained that, in return, they must have complete hegemony in their homes. Their public subordination and private supremacy were essential not because women were inferior to men but because they would safeguard American democracy.

Beecher argued that the home was experienced by all members

of American society, irrespective of class, religion, race or region and that this universal experience could be a focus for a new national identity. All women were fundamentally similar across America and by creating identical homes, uniformity of culture would percolate America, healing dangerous fissiparous tendencies. The culture of the universal home was to be Beecher's middle-class, Puritan morality, of course, and this was to be spread as a set of unifying, democratic values throughout the USA.

Domesticity of women and for women could create a stabilizing force in society in two main ways: women would set a good example of voluntary submission to authority which could be copied by men in the wider society; and the values of the home would compensate for the commercial and acquisitive values prevalent in the wider society. Thus the home would form, as Sklar (1973: 61) puts it, 'an oasis of noncommercial values in an otherwise acquisitive society'. Women would be making great sacrifices by confining themselves to domesticity, but these would be willingly undertaken to safeguard democracy, lessen class-conflict, and produce racial harmony. To become saints, martyrs, and guardians of the national culture all women had to do was 'reject aggression and embrace deference as a style of social interaction' (Beecher 1841: 163). There were small shifts in the details of Beecher's ideas later in her career, but as Sklar says, Beecher always 'made an effort to retain the old ideological goal of domesticity by continuing the belief that society's fundamental social divisions were the "natural" ones of sex, rather than the pernicious ones of class' (Sklar 1973: 211).

These ideas about women survived for at least a hundred years after Beecher first declaimed them, and turn up, surprisingly unmodified, in the structural-functional sociology of the 1950s. In many ways the male-dominated belief-system or model held by the middle classes in Britain and America supported the ideas of Catharine Beecher. Not everyone would accept the visionary ideal of the martyr, but the subordination, domesticity, and submission of the woman, kept severely away from commerce, politics and controversy, was an appealing picture. Yet this very rigid division of the sexes led directly to many of the problems associated with relations between them and to the complex systems of theories about health, illness, and sex which are discussed by Duffin (1978a, 1978b) and Atkinson (1978, 1985a).

At the end of the nineteenth century, and between the wars, the same ideas were rehearsed to argue against women's emancipation

*Figure 6.3 Traditional and feminist views of woman's place*

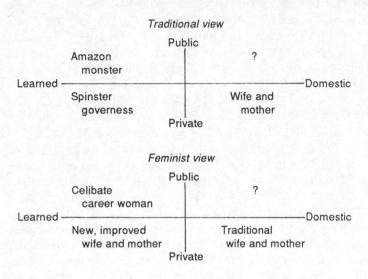

with the stress not so much on democracy as on the survival of the Anglo-Saxon race by eugenicists such as Kenealy (1920), and Meyrick Booth (1932). The beliefs about the purity of women and the dangers threatening it outside the home on the hockey field, in the laboratory, or on the Stock Exchange were essentially similar. The problem for the feminists of the 1920s was, however, that the strategy which had worked for their predecessors in the 1850-1900 period was no defence against the eugenicists and Freudians who attacked careers for ladies after the First World War. The chapter explains the successful strategy of the 1850-1900 period, and then examines why it, in turn, was then challenged.

## Successful challenge to the 'spheres' ideology

The successful pioneers of feminism in the mid-nineteenth century made public statements that they supported domesticity for young ladies while quietly establishing two new lifestyles for educated ladies: the celibate career woman and the learned wife. Figure 6.3 shows the only role for ladies in the traditional, dominant world view, and the alternatives developed by the pioneers. Until the rise of the eugenicists and the Freudians, this alternative world view, in which some women were freed to adopt the new roles of learned

*Figure 6.4 Old and new girls' schools compared*

|  | Old, private schools | New, public schools |
|---|---|---|
| Numbers of pupils | Small | Large |
| Numbers of staff | Small | Large |
| Modelled on: | Domestic, family life | Boys' school |
| Academic work | Different from boys' (accomplishments) | Similar to boys' (academic) |
| Audience for achievement | Private, domestic | Public – examiners speech days prizes |
| Main aim | A 'style' of accomplishment | Vocational exams competitive |
| Mode of control | Personal/familial | Impersonal, bureaucratic |
| Welfare of pupils | Personal supervision | Impersonal – PE medical inspection uniform measurements |
| Ownership | Private | Public – trustees, companies |
| Visibility and accountability | Low | High – inspection governors speech day uniform |
| Teachers' qualifications | Personal | Bureaucratic / publicly vetted |

wife or celibate career woman, achieved support from a segment of the middle class who paid fees to send their daughters to the new schools. Howarth (1985) has shown that the daughters of widows and orphans were particularly likely to study for degrees before the 1914 war because they knew that a vocational qualification was a safety-net. That is, a good schooling and a degree would enable a lady to earn her own living in a new, but respectable, role. This novel role, as schoolmistress, headmistress, or don was different from that of governess because it was public: the governess and the old-style headmistress had been working in private (Pedersen 1975; Peterson 1972), in homes, or schools run like homes. The new celibate role was played out in a public arena: the large 'girls' school. Figure 6.4 shows the differences between the small schools of the old order and the new, public girls' schools.

The pioneers' main aim had been to demonstrate that while education did not make the majority of its graduates unfit for marriage, and therefore that many men quite liked having wives who had read a little Caesar and heard of Euclid, it also provided a vocational qualification for those who did not marry. The feminists had to alter the equation of women's sphere and domesticity yet most of them never challenged the domestic ideology itself; they merely tried to establish an alternative: the girls' schools and colleges where women remained womanly but had previously undreamed of freedoms to be active, learned, and healthy. Vicinus (1985) offers an intriguing account of the educational communities, and those set up for nursing, for social work, and for religious observance.

The pioneers, then, established both a new life style for a celibate lady in a female community where moral standards were impeccable, and a new kind of wife: beautiful and learned. Indeed, from the earliest days of college education men had snatched the graduates away into marriage. Thus one of the first women to attend Girton, Miss Cook, married C.P. Scott of the *Manchester Guardian*; and Mary Paley, a pioneer of Newnham, married Marshall, the great economist. Admittedly Marshall first saw her in a domestic milieu; as she recalled, 'my first recollections of Mr Sidgwick and Mr Marshall...were the evenings when we sat around and sewed the household linen' (Paley Marshall 1947: 11). Later she forced him onto the dance floor, got a second in moral sciences (which included economics at that period), taught other students for a year, and then he married her, although it meant resigning his fellowship and moving to the new university at Bristol. Newnham was run by separatists and perhaps Mary Paley's second class degree was not intimidating.

Agnata Frances Ramsey was a different matter. Leaving St Leonard's for Girton she took the only first-class degree in classics in 1887. *Punch* took this seriously enough to give a whole page to an illustration showing a gowned lady being ushered into a first-class railway compartment labelled 'Ladies Only' with the caption 'Honour to Agnata Frances Ramsay'. The Master of Trinity, Henry Montague Butler, 'had been much interested by this lady's success, as was to be expected from one who cared much both for the classics and for the education of women' (Butler 1925: 29). Butler took forty-two seats for a performance of *Oedipus Rex* and made up a party including the Mistress of Girton and Agnata. In July 1888 they became engaged. He was a widower with grown children, but still a distinguished 'catch'. Butler wrote to a friend that it was Agnata's 'goodness...not her Greek and Latin, which have stolen my heart', but on the honeymoon they 'read a great deal of Greek together' (Butler 1925: 30-2). In 1890 Agnata had the first of her three sons and established a new style of married life. *Punch* carried another cartoon in which a young mother identified as a Girtonian tells her friend she is ordering a crib for Herodotus. The friend asks 'Is that what you are going to call the dear little baby?' The reader is obviously meant to see the mother (Agnata) who had published a book on Herodotus as wise and the friend a fool.

If this was proof that the Cambridge bluestocking could be marriageable, Oxford was not far behind. In 1888 Barbara Bradby achieved Lady Margaret Hall's first double first and caused a young man to lament:

> I go every day to my crammer,
> And he marks all my verses with 'gamma';
> While that girl over there
> With the flaming red hair,
> Gets 'alpha plus' easily, — her,

Barbara Bradby went on to marry J.L. Hammond and a famous academic partnership was born. In the 1890s Frances Crawley emulated Agnata by marrying the Warden of Wadham. Thus, although the Oxbridge women's colleges sent forth a stream of professional, careerist, celibate graduates, there was also a series of beautiful and brilliant graduates who made excellent marriages. Indeed Leavis goes so far as to suggest that 'women's colleges...had an equally important function in providing distinguished academics with suitable wives' (1968). Her evidence for this claim is an anecdote of Mrs Fawcett's. The wife of a distinguished Cambridge man had expressed thankfulness that Newnham had not existed in her husband's youth 'because if it had been I am sure he would have married one of them instead of me'.

Thus the educational pioneers created two new female roles, the celibate career woman and the wife who was an intellectual partner to her husband, an articulate companion who could swap Greek epigrams or scientific formulae. This was, of course, an elitist solution to feminist dilemmas. Neither pattern was of any immediate use to working-class women; rather both new types of educated women needed a houseful of servants to live out their new life styles. Nor had these two new styles for adult women challenged in any fundamental way the Victorian domestic ideal. Many commentators have argued that the feminist campaign failed ultimately because it did not challenge the nuclear family. Such criticisms show a lack of understanding of the ideological climate.

It was only by continuing to glorify the Victorian domestic ideal, as the educational pioneers all did, that any educational progress could be made and the two new variations of the pattern created. Women's education could only progress if the family was not threatened.

Of course many people were unconvinced by the pioneers. They did not want their daughters educated, and the image of the careerist celibate was more powerful than the Agnata Butler/Barbara Hammond one. The verse quoted by Thomas Woody (1929) still had many believers:

> One did commend to me a wife both fair and young.
> That had French, Spanish and Italian tongue.
> I thanked him kindly and told him I loved none such,
> For I thought one tongue for a wife too much,
> 'What love ye not the scholar?'
> Yes, as my life,
> A learned scholar, but not a learned wife.
>
> (Vol.1, 195-6)

By the 1880s and 1890s enough parents had lost their earlier fears about schools, so that on meeting Dorothea Beale in 1884 Janet Courtney could write that by then she 'had fought her fight for girls' education some twenty years earlier and won through. The days when parents threatened to remove their daughter if set to study such "masculine" subjects as mathematics were in the distant past' (1934: 13). Yet fears about ruined marriage prospects had not been stilled in 1912 when a government inspector reported that not all the pupils at Roedean were working as hard as they might be; as Zouche comments (1955: 137): 'One must remember that a number of parents still held the view that a daughter's excessive education, particularly a university education, would lessen her opportunities for matrimony.' In other words, school was no longer fatal, but university studies probably would be. Vera Brittain, who attended St Monica's in Surrey before the First World War, says that most of her peers were only preparing to 'come out' and marry, and Naomi Mitchison, although growing up in a scholarly family in Oxford, had no secondary schooling but shared an incompetent governess with four other girls. She writes:

> All were definitely young ladies whose brothers or male cousins went to reputable and expensive public schools, where various kinds of learning were shovelled into them...but whose own

education was mainly in the hands of a governess with no particular qualifications

(1975: 13).

This was in Oxford, where one of the best GPDST schools, with an Archbishop's sister as its first headmistress, had flourished for thirty years with many dons' daughters among its pupils!

Certainly the generation of women who went up to university in the years before the First World War was still suffering from the prejudice that they were strange creatures who would never marry. Hamilton, at Newnham in this period, wrote: 'Before the war, when I was at college, people used to say to me "You are at college?" and stare, as though they quite expected to see horns and a tail peeping out from under my skirt' (1944: 24). When Vera Brittain was working for Oxford entrance in 1913 her mother's friends exclaimed: 'How can you send your daughter to college, Mrs Brittain! ...Don't you want her ever to get *married?*' (1933: 73). These public fears were reflected in an expectation of celibacy in the student body itself. According to Dalglish who was at St Hilda's during the war:

> The fact that we had been chosen for a university career meant, according to the world-outlook of the authorities who had chosen us, that it was probable that a high proportion of us would not marry. We could not all expect to become headmistresses, nobly planned, but to be such was the ideal. In Oxford we were, more obviously than we had been at school, part of a movement still not far removed from pioneer stages.
>
> (1938: 93)

The same problems had dogged the American pioneers. In 1889, when the first 36 students started at Bryn Mawr, Meigs says that going to college 'meant turning a deaf ear to the innumerable warnings that four years spent in institutional life would be a death blow to matrimonial prospects'. In America, too, prospective college women had to face a barrage of 'experts' who told them that their health would never stand the strain of study, education would ruin their reproductive systems, and race suicide would ensue. The turn of the century saw a series of hysterical authors bewailing the low marriage and birth rates of college women which was thought to herald the downfall of the white middle classes (see Dyhouse 1981; Burstyn 1980; Atkinson 1978, 1987; Duffin 1978b).

Three currents of opinion came into fashion at the turn of the century, and flourished in its first three decades, that damaged the success of the pioneers. First were the Social Darwinistic ideas of race suicide and eugenics; second the rise of Freudianism with its emphasis on repression; and thirdly the post-war hedonism that led to a revolt against Victorian convention. These combined to form a climate in which the two new roles which had been so daring only thirty years earlier, seemed old-fashioned and even perverted. The highly educated wife was under attack for having few children too late in life, and not reproducing her class, race and intelligence fast enough or prolifically enough. However she was relatively safe from the Freudians and the hedonists. The celibate woman was vulnerable to all three types of attack. The hedonists saw her as imprisoned in Victorian conventions that had no meaning in the 1920s – students in the 1920s wanted to smoke, drink, ride unchaperoned in cars, pet, and discuss sex with men (Fass 1977), and could no longer see any reason for the confining regulations of the schools and colleges. Fass has excellent material on this period in student life, and it is a great pity no equivalent research has been done on Britain or Australasia in this era.

The Freudians, and the sexologists who became fashionable, were deeply suspicious of the spinster. If she was heterosexual, then she was repressing her sexuality by remaining unmarried or virginal and this was bound to make her neurotic and hence unfit to live. If she was homosexual, then she was an invert and such a dangerous creature that no other female should be allowed near her. Jeffereys (1985) in an overstated and badly researched, though interesting, book provides some fascinating material on such writers as Havelock Ellis, Ernest Carpenter and Iwan Bloch. Jeffereys claims, quite wrongly, that no previous writer has understood or explained the celibacy of the Victorian feminists; and she fails to mention Joe and Olive Banks (1964), Constance Rover (1970), Delamont (1978a), Sigsworth and Wyke (1972), or Haller and Haller (1974). However she does present accounts of the purity crusaders of the late nineteenth century and their complex ideas on women's sexuality and its place in social harmony. Jeffereys's main complaint against the pioneers of sexual liberation (Haverlock Ellis and Ernest Carpenter) is that they regarded both celibacy and lesbianism as perversions and held out heterosexual intercourse as essential for women's mental and physical health. As a lesbian she finds this position both personally offensive and academically unsound, pointing out in passing that for a man like Carpenter, who was erotically aroused by women urinating, to set standards of normality for women was presumptive to say the least. The reasons for the pioneers' celibacy, and the way it lost favour in the first thirty years of the twentieth century, are now discussed, followed by the moral panic which arose over lesbianism at the same time.

## Celibate women

Grant Allen (1889), author of *The Woman who Did* and opponent of Victorian marriage, was convinced that the feminists were all arguing from 'the point of view of the self-supporting spinster [who is] an abnormity [*sic*], not the woman of the future'.

He was a campaigner for 'free love' and wanted all women to be sexually active and to be mothers while rejecting the traditional patriarchal marriages of their parents' generation. His solution to the oppression of the Victorian marriage – free love – was more outrageous than the feminists' answer: they had upheld the ideal of marriage while themselves choosing celibacy, and the all-female communities (Vicinus 1985).

Certainly the educational pioneers concentrated on creating an alternative role, that of the public, professional, celibate woman but they did not challenge the domestic dream. In short, celibacy, actual or potential, was the price paid for entry to the male fields of secondary and higher education. Celibacy was a common form of revolt against the traditional female sphere; as the Hallers argued, the Victorian lady 'sought to achieve a sort of sexual freedom by denying her sexuality, by resorting to marital continence or abstinence in an effort to keep from being considered or treated as a sex object'. Celibacy was, therefore, a form of liberation: 'the woman today flaunts her sexuality to achieve the same end that many Victorian women could only achieve by denying theirs' (Haller and Haller 1974: xii). Celibacy was a way of subverting conventional marriage, but only if the woman lived a pure life. The pioneers' own lives were, as we have seen conducted along lines of the strictest decorum. In addition, many of them were celibate, either from choice or necessity. Some saw the educational campaign as a higher calling, while others were hostile to sexuality even in marriage. Thus, for example, 'M. Carey Thomas assumed a conflict between womanliness and intellect' and thought that 'sexual instincts, marriage, and children...interfered with woman's higher achievements' (Cross 1965: 32-3). Indeed Finch (1947: 57) says that she took to calling herself Carey Thomas rather than using her first name because 'the added dignity and especially the sexlessness of the name were symbolical'. In Britain, Frances Buss, Dorothea Beale, Emily Davies, C.L. Maynard, Louisa Lumsden, and the Lawrence and MacMillan sisters all stayed single, and they and hundreds like them were taunted in the well-known rhyme:

> Miss Buss and Miss Beale
> Cupid's darts do not feel.
> They are not like us
> Miss Beale and Miss Buss.

In fact it is clear from their biographies that both Dorothea Beale and Frances Buss received proposals but chose to stay single and work. Rhoda Nunn, in Gissing's *Odd Women* is a fictional example of such a woman turning down an eligible husband to work for women's liberation.

Roberta Frankfort (1977) draws an interesting distinction between celibacy and domesticity as ideologies among collegiate women in the USA at the turn of the century. She contrasts the lives and beliefs of Alice Freeman Palmer and Martha Carey Thomas, the former epitomizing the 'new' career where the educated woman married an intellectual and shared his interests; the latter embodying the celibate who spent her life in a female community. Frankfort (1977: 33) summarizes Carey Thomas's position as follows: 'She was an isolationist with respect to men, living most of her adult life with close women friends surrounded by a college filled with women students.' Marion Talbot was a similar career celibate, and when she left Boston (her home) in 1892 to go to Chicago to the brash new University of Chicago to be Dean of Women she saw this as a quasi-marriage: 'There were clothes to be bought, suitable for many kinds of occasions, and enough to last several months, and even seasons, for there would be no time or strength for shopping or dressmakers' (1936: 56). Those clothes were 'almost like a modest trousseau'. She summarized her feelings: 'the impression I was about to change my state...from spinsterhood to matrimony'.

Popular manuals on health and sex publicized the idea that women who wished to use their brains should be celibate. Macdonald who has compiled a selection from the books of the 1880s includes the following:

Q  Should the Girl who wishes to fulfil her Maternal Duties avoid the influence of Education? And should the Educated Woman remain Celibate?

A  On the whole, the answer is yes, to both questions. Girls who are natural and would like to be well married, would do well to avoid education, remembering that the personal advantage to the highly educated woman impairs her usefulness as a mother. Those who overtax their vital energies by an intellectual strain, likely to produce ill effects on their offspring, ought to accept a voluntary celibacy. They are self-made invalids and must accept the penalties of the position.

(Macdonald 1981: 16)

Vicinus (1985) in her sensitive discussion of the use of celibacy and all-women communities in the nineteenth century feminist campaigns has pointed out that by 1920 celibacy had become distinctly unfashionable. The ideals and practices of the generations of women who had chosen celibacy and all-female communities were challenged by imperialism, eugenics, the depression, and the Freudian revolution. Vicinus (1985: 289) states that

American historians have noted how singularly ill prepared Jane Addams and her generation were for the Freudian revolution; they simply could not understand, nor were they sympathetic to, the psychological interpretation of social behaviour. A similar level of misunderstanding seems to have characterized women leaders in England.

Vicinus argues that not only did the celibate women find themselves ill-prepared for the Freudian onslaught; they had no defence against it. She goes on: 'Single women had no weapons with which to fight the labeling of their friendships as deviant because they had understood sexual activity as heterosexual' (p.291). The growing acceptance of Freudian ideas raised another 'danger' lurking in schools and colleges to imperil girls – the lesbian – discussed later in the chapter.

The 'new' psychological theories were used by Meyrick Booth in the 1920s and 1930s to criticize the education of girls which he saw as out of date. He characterized the ideology of the girls' schools as 'the sterile rational doctrinairism of the J.S. Mill – Olive

Schreiner – Buss and Beale school' (Booth 1932: 143). This sterile doctrine was pernicious, as Booth saw it, because it was not informed by psychology.

> The great boys' schools, despite their defects, embody a long tradition, an immense experience of boyish ways and needs. The girls' school of today on the other hand, is a new-fangled creation evolved for the most part under the unpsychological ideals of pre-war days. (p.162)

Booth accused the women running schools of being ignorant of psychology, especially of the work of Havelock Ellis and G. Stanley Hall. Their ignorance, he claimed, meant that:

> all over the country countless thousands of young girls are being forced through examinations and encouraged in the playing of all sorts of strenuous games and sports at an age when in the opinion of competent medical men *and psychologists*, it is essential that they should refrain from all severe mental and physical strain. (Booth 1932: 169) (emphasis mine)

Among the 'authorities' he cites is Kenealy (1920) who wrote on similar lines. Booth did not include among the psychologists Helen Bradford Thompson Woolley or Leta Stetter Hollingworth. The former had carried out research which found no consistent sex differences in mental abilities or performance, and Hollingworth showed that menstruation had no effect on women's performance at mental and motor tasks (Rosenberg 1982). Indeed Booth quite failed to take account of any psychology which differed from G. Stanley Hall's. Booth repeats himself a good deal, claiming that the big girls' schools were 'dominated by an absolute doctrinairism alien to reality' (p.177). He claimed that the head of at least one women's teacher training college did not believe in fundamental sex differences, and that such women had grown up with 'a large area of [her] innermost personality violently repressed' (p.177). He feared that the girls' schools were not designed to produce wives and mothers and 'it is by preparing girls for celibacy that we make them celibate' (p.179).

There were then two aspects of Booth's critique: he claimed that the new science of psychology showed the nineteenth-century pioneers to have been wrong, and that spinsters were suppressing, or repressing, their true nature. This latter point was particularly harmful to the cause of women's equality because it is impossible to refute.

Ronald Walters has analysed the sexual advice offered to 'Victorian' America. He shows that it was predicated on the idea that 'young women...had to beware of the man of loose morals whose greatest delight was in dragging innocent females to his own level of sensuality' (Walters 1974: 50). One doctor in 1880 even argued that tight corsets restricted the blood flow and thus limited sexual desire while heavy knots of hair pressing on the brain increased it. Walters summarizes the image of the lady offered by these manuals as follows: 'The Victorian lady, icily aloof from all dangerous impulses, loomed like a white-clad mountain amid the world's moral debris' (1974: 65).

The change in attitude between the Buss/Beale/Davies/Thomas/Talbot generation with what Booth called their 'sterile rational doctrinairism' and their immediate successors was not just a shift over celibacy. The generation of Sayers/Mitchison/Holtby/Brittain wanted something different. They saw, with a shocking clarity, the problem at the heart of the previous generation's views. Naomi Mitchison (1975: 86) puts her finger on the logical flaw:

> My mother told me that if anyone proposed marriage...I must ask whether he had ever had anything to do with another woman and if he had I must refuse him. This was straight feminism of the period, an attack on the double standard for men and women....It was asking for trouble, especially on the assumption that the man was normally at least five years older than the girl he married. If he was still a virgin nearer thirty than twenty, then there was likely to be something wrong.

## The feminist challenge to the double standard

Mitchison's mother held a logical position, which was opposed to the Victorian double standard. The generation of Sayers/Brittain/Dora Russell/and Naomi Mitchison, if they rejected their mothers' and teachers' views, had either to revert to the Victorian double standard, opt for celibacy, or embrace a new morality in which women, too, were free to be sexually experienced. Figure 6.5 plots the contrasting views on male and female purity before marriage.

*Figure 6.5 Contrasting views on male and female purity*

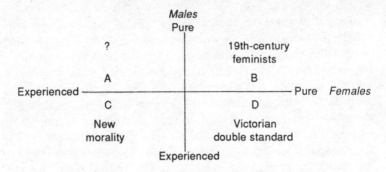

The women who benefited from the pioneers such as Dora Russell and Naomi Mitchison rejecting the position 'B', opted instead for a different challenge to the double standard – position 'C'. This was espoused in their own lives, and in their fiction. Dorothy Sayers had a baby outside marriage and in her fictional *alter ego*, Harriet Vane, she created a woman who publicly lived with a man outside marriage and eventually married a man who, sexually experienced himself, did not expect or want her to be a virgin (*Strong Poison, Have his Carcase, Gaudy Night,* and *Busman's Honeymoon*). Similarly Winifred Holtby's heroine in *South Riding* is sexually experienced outside marriage. Neither woman is portrayed in a way that suggests they are wrong, or that they have suffered by rejecting traditional virginity. Holtby (1934: 127) made this position clear when she challenged the Freudian, anti-feminist idea that spinsterhood was wrong.

> Now the identification of this frustration with virginity (for it is commonly though erroneously presumed that all spinsters are virgins) is a comparatively modern notion....The woman's movement ...has improved the social and economic status of the spinster, and, in some still limited circles, removed her moral obligation of virginity.

The existence of such radical views among intellectual women would have been a threat to the educational institutions as bad as the new fear of lesbianism if the exponents of it had not been kept far from the schools and colleges by the headmistresses and Deans of Women. Paula Fass (1977) has shown how firmly the educational authorities in the American colleges kept to the old double standard, or to the old feminist position, and their British and Australian equivalents almost certainly fought the same battles on the same issues: curfews, bans on driving, and most fiercely, prohibitions on smoking. Paula Fass argues that the double standard was only slightly weakened on the American college campuses in the 1920s, for very few students rejected the ideal of female purity entirely. She claims that although petting became more common, the majority of girls remained virgins, and believed that college girls should remain so. Fass then goes on to show how another battle on the campuses of the 1920s – over smoking – was related to the sexual double standard. Most colleges forbade women students to smoke on or near the campus. Bryn Mawr was an exception when Marian Park, in 1925, opened smoking rooms on the campus. Her gesture 'provoked consternation among Deans of Women throughout the country' (Fass 1977: 295).

Fass explains this revulsion among the Deans of Women in the following way:

> The right to smoke was denied to women as part of the double standard of morality. The implicit fear was that smoking would have an immoral effect on women because it removed one further barrier from the traditional differentiation of the roles and behaviour of the sexes. Smoking implied a promiscuous equality between men and women and was an indication that women could enjoy the same vulgar habits and ultimately also the same vices as men. (p.294)

The woman who smoked was crossing the line from the feminine to the 'hermaphrodite', a concern expressed by Kenealy (1920). Smoking became in the 1920s and 1930s, on the American campuses, a new-fangled and contaminating idea, much as suffrage and other revolutionary feminist ideas had been a generation earlier. Chapter 3 discussed how, and why, the educational pioneers handled the innovations of hockey, bicycling, and the gym tunic so carefully, with real and symbolic precautions against them contaminating pupils. These symbolic protections seem to have worked in that parents went on paying the fees to keep the girls at school.

There was, however, a more dangerous sort of pollution: feminism. If bicycles, acting, and cricket were potentially damaging for a lady's reputation, far worse were associations with other feminist campaigns.

## The dangerous women

The educational pioneers were not all feminists, but those who had such interests suppressed them. There were genuine fears that the educational cause would be damaged by association with suffrage movements, and so Emily Davies gave up her suffrage work in case it affected the founding of Girton. Emily Davies was certainly wise. Annie Rogers (1938: 107) tells how in Oxford:

> Nearly all the educational women were moderate but convinced suffragists, but so strong was the fanaticism of certain anti-suffragists that the holding of a meeting...at Somerville led to the resignation of the Secretary of the Council of the college, the loss of her husband's subscription, and the withdrawal of a scholarship given by an Oxford resident.

Miss Dobell, the first headmistress of the County School for Girls, Pontypool which opened in 1897, was a suffragist (and an opponent of the Boer War) and 'took part in a Woman Suffrage procession a few hours after seeing a Harley Street Specialist, from whom she heard what her fate was to be' (Pontypool 1947: 30).

The next headmistress, Miss Jones, who had attended Aberystwyth in its earliest days, was also 'an ardent suffragist' (Pontypool 1947: 32). These women were able to show their sympathies in 1910-14 where their predecessors of the 1870s had not been able to. Miss Dobell had retired by the time of the march so could no longer be a real danger to the girls' school. Similarly once Dorinda Neligan, the head of Croydon GPDST School from 1874 to 1901, had retired, she was free to take 'part in the battles for women's suffrage' (Croydon 1954: 23). Mabel Annie Vivian, the first head of the girls' high school in Newport (who cycled) was also a suffragist. An early member of the staff recalled in the school's jubilee book how 'Miss Vivian...stimulated the interest I already possessed in the Women's Movement and I left Newport to work for the enfranchisement of women' (Irene Ashton Jones, teacher, 1909-13, in Newport 1946: 34).

Similarly, in the USA, Gildersleeve tells how, when first Dean at Barnard,

> the mother of one of our leading seniors came to see me and implored me to prevent our students from marching in the suffrage parade. She said that to march in a parade would be a

shocking and shameful thing for them to do and would injure the college greatly.

(1954: 71)

Thorp (1956: 242) in her biography of Neilson of Smith, describing the college in the period 1910-17, says 'the only embarrassing request President Burton's students made of him was permission to found a suffrage discussion club – and that he denied'. And, from the same period, Newcomer (1959: 76) recounts:

> When I, as a brash young instructor, chaperoned some Vassar students to a suffrage rally...in 1917, I was reproved by the head of my hall, herself a classmate of Harriot Stanton Blatch....Women's education was still on trial and must not be confused with other doubtful causes.

The contrast here, between being chaperoned and being a suffragist, is particularly telling to contemporary readers – taken for granted by Newcomer in 1917.

Not *all* suffragists were beyond the pale for all educationalists for Thorp's biography of Neilson (president of Smith) describes a 'modern woman' he knew at Harvard who 'was...a suffragist; she even rode a bicycle, but Cambridge approved of her. They never applied to her that opprobrious epithet "strong-minded" ' (Thorp 1956: 76).

In general, however, the risks were too great. Campaigns to do with sexual matters were even more dangerous to the educational cause than suffrage, and riddled with even more contradictions. Josephine Butler's campaigns about veneral disease and prostitution had to be jettisoned from the educational battle. George Eliot, whose ambivalent relationship with feminist thought and campaigns is discussed elsewhere (McGuinn 1978), also presented problems for the educational pioneers because of her irregular liaison with Lewes. Emily Davies, the founder of Girton, decided 'it is justifiable to go and see Mrs Lewes herself, but not to meet people at her house' (Stephen 1927: 171). Sara Burstall reports how, though she was a benefactor of Girton, George Eliot could not visit the college openly. Instead 'it was said that she visited the place, but incognito' so as not to prejudice the educational experiment, 'which shows how extraordinary prudent everyone concerned with Girton had to be then' (1933: 77-8).

157

In the USA, too, the wise educational pioneer was circumspect about airing other radical views. Thus M.C. McIntosh, a niece of Carey Thomas's, attended the Bryn Mawr School in Baltimore, and the Bryn Mawr itself. She tells how Carey Thomas:

> introduced us to many areas of her own concern: women's suffrage, the infant trade-union movement, progressive education. As her niece, I shared her more private views which she was wise enough not to expound in chapel – on birth control.
>
> (Kundsin 1974: 50)

The strategies that had served the girls' schools well in the pre-Freudian era – insisting on privacy and avoiding men, eschewing feminist causes, fallen women, and upholding celibacy from heterosexual contacts for both sexes outside marriage – all failed when the moral panic over lesbianism in the girls' schools and colleges began.

## The lesbian

Vicinus (1985) argues that once Freudian ideas became known among the intelligentsia, the celibate woman was automatically suspected of lesbianism in a manner quite inconceivable in Victorian times. Thus novels such as Clemence Dane's (1917) *Regiment of Women* were seen as indictments of girls' schools and colleges where innocent girls might be corrupted. However unlike the earlier dangers to pupils, which were genuinely feared by parents and staff alike (e.g. mixing with males without chaperons or dressing immodestly), the newly discovered – or newly mentionable – danger of the school as a den of lesbians does not seem to have deterred parents from paying the fees, or encouraged schools to set up elaborate precautions. The writers of the 1920s and 1930s start to mention the supposed danger of lesbianism but do so to dismiss it. Thus Theodora Benson (1934: 38) describing Cheltenham in the early twentieth century says that 'we were almost incredibly innocent' about heterosexual and homosexual practices, and that the crushes girls had on one another were a teenage phase 'of no significance in the post-college life of the girls'. She reassures her audience that everyone she subsequently met had 'turned out as normal as can be'. Elizabeth Bowen, at

Downe House during the 1914-18 war, emphasizes that she and all her friends 'intended to marry early' (Bowen 1934: 52). E. Arnot Robertson who loathed Sherborne also stresses the girls' total innocence of masturbation, lesbianism or heterosexuality (1934: 180). Antonia White claims that although at the Sacred Heart they all prayed for their purity 'we were all a little hazy as to what purity really meant' (1934: 237). These four novelists, chosen by Graham Greene to contribute to what he envisaged as an obituary for the English public school, all stressed that there were no lesbians lurking behind the ivy-clad walls.

Winifred Holtby (1934: 123) claimed that none of her school contemporaries 'knew the precise nature of lesbianism', and that when she taught she only came across one case 'where a student was suspected of lesbian practices, but nothing was proved, and the bulk of the students appeared quite ignorant of the supposed nature of her peculiarity'. This superstitious dread that girls' schools were miniature Lesboses, heaving with seductions and betrayals, seems to have worried two old girls of Downe House particularly. In her foreword to Ann Ridler's book about the school, Elizabeth Bowen (1967: 2) stresses that there were 'few or no cases of *schwärmerei*' there. Ridler herself (1967: 10) is not only contemptuous of the nineteenth-century headmistresses but seems obsessed with convincing her readers that 'the respect which Miss Willis inspired in her pupils had nothing in it of morbid fear or of a homosexual excitement'.

Such denials have not stopped various hysterical men seeing lesbians under the beds in girls' schools throughout the last fifty years, most noticeably Gathorne-Hardy (1977: 258) who announces that 'teaching at girls' schools attracted a considerable, but quite incalculable, number of lesbians'. Gathorne-Hardy then ridicules those schools which set up rules and procedures designed to prevent lesbian liaisons in schools, claiming that 'on the whole the ravening couples the patrolling schoolmistresses expected to stop in the corridors existed in their imaginations; if they were not indeed themselves the only candidates' (1977: 263).

In an analysis such as this a girls' school cannot win, because if it ignores the possibility of lesbianism it is naive, if it sets up precautions, its teachers have morbid imaginations. Such double binds are the most pernicious effect of Freudianism: if you admit to something you are sick, if you do not, you are repressing it.

## Overview and conclusions

It may seem a long distance from cookery to lesbians, or from needlework to the sexual double standard. In fact what was happening in the debate over whether or not middle-class girls should be trained in cookery, needlework, and childcare was actually the rise of the 'new' middle class (Bernstein 1973a) with its novel pattern of family life and child rearing centred on the transmission of symbolic property. The old middle class, where a woman had to bring material goods and then run a household, did not need a committed believer to function. The new middle class, where the mother became a crucial source of the symbolic and cultural capital and the main vehicle for its transmission, was dependent on the wife/mother being committed to the role. For these families, a woman who was unwilling to become fully absorbed in the role was better occupied in another role – as paid worker supporting herself. It was, therefore the old middle class who seized on 'eugenic' arguments and called for middle-class girls to be trained as wives, while the new middle class initially embraced the alternative female roles of either marriage to an intellectual equal, or the celibate households and community in the 1850-1900 period. They then produced the 'bohemian'/'progressive' vanguard who began the campaign against the sexual double standard. The old middle class had a vested interest in believing the arguments of Catharine Beecher and Meyrick Booth, because the stability it promised would benefit them. The new middle class, without property and capital, had an equally strong interest in cultural interruption, and creating novel roles for women. When Kenealy (1899) argued that Amazons were unnatural, this would be a mark in their favour for the new middle class not, as Kenealy intended, a damaging condemnation.

# Part III
Exploring structuralist sociology
of education:
A critique of sociological accounts
for the period 1945-88

How much of the nature of science is bound up with the idea of masculinity, and what would it mean for science if it were otherwise?

(Evelyn Fox Keller 1985: 3)

Placing women's experience at the centre of inquiry challenges basic theoretical frameworks in most academic disciplines.

(Abel and Abel 1983: 2)

## Introduction

The period straight after the Second World War seemed to be one of triumph for women. Eighty years after Girton opened, Cambridge finally gave in and during 1947-8 the first women became full graduates. The College's song book includes a 'Triumphal ode' for 21 October 1948:

Hail, long expected Day!
When, each a true M.A.
(No longer 'tit')
Girtonians sit
In senator's array!

(Girton College Song Book: 11)

This was the victory for which the feminist pioneers had been working for a century in the face of scepticism and even hostility. A song from the North London Collegiate (Scrimgeour 1950: 125) expressed this vision:

'Put not your trust in Girton's pleas;
These girls will never get degrees.'
So spake irate MAs in scorn;
The answer came on east winds born,
'We work in hope.'

At the same period the 1944 Education Act opened up the possibility of academic secondary education for clever working-class girls, and several of the London hospitals were forced into taking women students or losing their financial support from the University Grants Committee (UGC). In this period, too, the

163

sociology of education began to grow and develop in Britain as Halsey (1982) and Banks (1982) have shown, and in the USA (Hurn 1978) and Australasia (Connell *et al.* 1982). This section contains four chapters which apply the structuralist theories both to the events of the last 40 years and to the sociology which developed to analyse them. Chapter 7 deals with schools and focuses upon both pupils and teachers in them since 1945. Chapter 8 concerns itself with the role women have played in high-status occupations since 1945, and the way in which sociologists have addressed it. Throughout these two chapters the theoretical perspective of the structuralists is applied both to the data on women and to the sociology that developed around those data. Chapter 9 deals with debates about social mobility. Chapter 10 examines the sociological work on 'the professionals' and highlights a paradox which lies unexamined at the heart of the literature. Both focus on the notion of 'cultural capital' and women's role in its reproduction to illuminate aspects of the sociological literature on social stratification and 'the professions', which have in common a concentration of attention on men and a history of being researched by separate 'schools' of scholars who ignore each other's work. In both areas of literature the neglect of women is not just a scandal in itself, it is also a serious handicap to progress of the research area because women are actually an integral part of the area and neglecting them has limited the explanatory power of the whole field. Incorporating women, via the structuralist ideas of Douglas, Bourdieu, and Bernstein, provides new angles on the topics of stratification and 'professions'. Bourdieu (1986: 133-4) pointed out that:

> The very rapid growth in girls' and women's education has been a significant factor in the devaluing of academic qualifications ...women now bring academic qualifications onto the labour market which previously were partly held in reserve (and were 'invested' only in the marriage market).

That growth is the focus of this section, together with social science's failure to analyse it. Chapters 7 and 8 are relatively under theorized, 9 and 10 more heavily structuralist.

# 7

## A country fit for heroines?
## Schooling and teaching 1945–88

Truth-loving Persians do not dwell upon
The trivial skirmish fought near Marathon

(Graves 1966: 147)

This chapter deals with six themes in the education of clever women, and their subsequent careers, in the period since 1945. What the chapter chronicles is as uncomfortable for a feminist as the story of Marathon for a Persian. The themes are the loss of feminist faith in the elite girls' schools, the unintended consequences of co-education for girls and teachers, and the failure of science educators, novelists, and social scientists to pay attention to the fact that the feminist education campaign had lost momentum.

## Schooling loses its way?

In 1977 Gathorne-Hardy's populist book on British public schools announced that by the 1950s 'The girls' schools still tended to think that merely by existing at all they were doing something revolutionary' (Gathorne-Hardy 1977: 355). Gathorne-Hardy is convinced that by 1945 the girls' schools were anachronistic, resting on their laurels. He is in fact totally wrong. As most of the great girls' schools were less than 75 years old, and many less than 50, they were actually still revolutionary just because they did exist. As one old girl of Croydon GPDST wrote in the volume commemorating 50 years of her school, reflecting on her life as a headmistress in the north of England: 'the fallacy dies hard, in Yorkshire, that money spent on educating a girl who may marry is

165

likely to be wasted' (Croydon 1954: 104). That fallacy had been alive and well in Yorkshire immediately before the war, as Holtby had displayed in *South Riding*. Her child-heroine, Lydia, dreams of an academic education denied her by poverty and her gender:

> She wanted to pass examinations; she wanted to take her matric. History, chemistry, algebra, maths and Latin....She could do all these things and essays too. English was easy. She wanted problems, formulae, long tables and categories to master.
>
> (Holtby 1936, *South Riding*: 389)

Here Lydia, the daughter of the unskilled labourer, dreams of the curriculum at the girls' high school. She is portrayed as a person who deserves an academic education, deserves it all the more because her father is feckless, her mother burdened with multiple pregnancies, and she lives in a slum. Winifred Holtby's generation had a determination to open up academic learning to bright, motivated, working-class girls.

It was dreams such as Lydia's that lay behind the 1944 Education Act. While it is currently fashionable for feminist commentators (e.g. Wolpe 1974; Deem 1978) to attack the official reports of the 1920s and 1930s (Hadow and Norwood) for their sexism, and to see that sexism carried on into the reports of the post-war period (Newsom, Crowther and Robbins), this chapter takes a rather different view, that the official perspective leading up to the 1944 Act, and the reports between 1945 and circular 10/67, both benefited and betrayed the cause of women's equality.

The perspective of this chapter is similar to that adopted by Elizabeth Wilson (1980) in her history of British women from 1945-68. Wilson is extremely skilful at showing how there were genuine differences of opinion about the merits of every aspect of law and policy relating to gender between women who can all be seen as feminists – but of different types. Wilson does not spend much time on education but points out that John Newsom's infamous statement about domesticity for the majority of girls was only an elaborated version of 'what feminists such as Eva Hubback were saying after the war' (p.33). The material in the chapter on the girls' public and direct-grant schools, on co-education, and on the loss of a career path for women in teaching all has to be understood in this way. What was hailed as liberating by one group of women has to be seen as destructive of female opportunities by today's feminists. The sociological research on education almost all comes in this period (for the discipline scarcely existed before 1945) and the fifth theme of this chapter is the invisibility of gender in the sociology of education (Acker 1981; Banks 1982). There is also a brief excursion into the 'realistic' or 'naturalistic' fiction of the period – a double abberation in a structuralist book, but one that is necessary to make a point about the absence/invisibility of women from educational debate in the period. These five issues, together with the material on the lack of scientific education for women (and the failure of *anyone* to be concerned about that lack) make a somewhat bleak picture.

## Losing their way, or losing their friends?

Vicinus (1985: 210) has argued that in their first 50 years the boarding schools for girls 'were probably the most successful of all women's total communities'. However she then turns on them saying they were not sufficiently 'flexible': 'Frozen in time, girls' schools became subject to satire and amusement – and worst of all – irrelevance.' She noticed that 'What had been liberating for one generation', such as the gym slip and lacrosse, 'became stultifying for the next'. Her only source for this condemnation is Judith Okely's (1978) much cited paper on her life as a pupil at a girls' boarding school in the 1950s. Vicinus summarizes Okely as follows: 'girls' boarding schools were so narrow and out of date as to destroy all that had once been intellectually exciting and socially freeing'.

There are several points one can make about Vicinus's loss of insight, but perhaps most odd is her failure to use Wober's (1971) data on girls' boarding schools. His sexist condemnation of them for concentrating on classics rather than cookery, and science rather than sewing would probably have sensitized her to the continuing importance of such schools. They, and only they, kept up the supply of science and maths students during the long period from 1950-80 when co-educational state schools were failing to enthuse girls about science or teach it to them effectively (or both). Vicinus also neglects other published work on the elite girls' schools but the omission of Wober is the most striking.

The popularity of Okely's paper, which has been reprinted several times is odd, particularly when few commentators have noticed that her school (if she represents it correctly) was rather bad. The way in which many women have sided with Wober to attack the only feminist sector of the whole education system of the UK is startling. It is true, as I have argued elsewhere (1978a, 1980a), that some of the girls' boarding schools had allowed the double conformity trap to enslave them rather than using it as a self-conscious strategy for the advancement of women, but they still taught difficult, academic subjects to high standards. Hours on a cold hockey pitch are still a small price to pay for proper maths teaching. Okely's paper is interesting for its total disregard of the fact that the single-sex girls' school with academic standards actually carried the feminist torch onwards between 1945 and 1980 – perhaps against the will of many pupils, and perhaps unconsciously – while it was extinguished everywhere else.

The achievements of the feminist educational pioneers in establishing the right of young ladies to study nearly every conceivable subject and play a range of sports plus the organization of a secure and respected career structure for women teachers in the academic girls' schools were both allowed to run down in a few short years. The cause of the equality of women in education lost out to a 'reform' which was never thoroughly debated: co-education. This chapter examines the negative impact of co-education on schools and teaching careers, and then addresses the ways in which the achievements of the feminists were betrayed in the surviving schools themselves and by three sets of scholars: novelists, scientists and the supposedly iconoclastic sociologists.

## Co-education

Not only did women turn on the elite girls' (boarding) schools and berate them for faults. There was a widespread revulsion against single-sex education. Sutherland (1985a) has pointed out that although co-education has been 'one of the major changes since the 1944 Act in England' it came about without serious discussion at either Local Education Authority (LEA) or national level as an 'absent minded' 'side effect' of comprehensive schooling. Scotland, Wales and Northern Ireland differ from England here, because the former two have traditionally had mixed schools in the maintained sector, while Northern Ireland has kept single-sex schools to the present.

In England the 1944 Act produced new 'secondary modern' schools, which were often single-sex. In 1947 there were 1312 mixed secondary moderns and 1707 single-sex ones. Gradually this pattern changed so that by 1960 most secondary moderns were mixed, and this pattern was followed as comprehensive schools grew. In 1982 there were 2885 mixed comprehensives and 473 single-sex ones. Single-sex schooling in the maintained sector has been common only in ILEA and in those LEAs which have kept grammar schools. Roman Catholics have been most likely to retain single-sex schooling in denominational schools because there have been encyclicals (1929 and 1957) condemning co-education.

Sutherland's (1985a) paper then goes on to discuss the side effects of this shift towards co-education, and produces a list similar to those of other commentators although failing to cite Shaw (1976, 1980), Delamont (1980a), Walford (1983) or Deem (1984). In fact the contemporary criticisms of the effects of co-education were foreseen by Alice Zimmern nearly a century ago. Back in 1898 Alice Zimmern viewed the advocates of mixed schools with suspicion. She wrote that the education of girls had become established 'as a right' but 'in some cases, happily rare', this led to 'a subordination of the girls' interests', 'under the pretence of equality' (Zimmern 1898: 243). Co-education, or the running of two separate schools under one structure, was the awful spectre at which Zimmern was hinting. She went on to elaborate her fears:

> The attempts recently made...to economise by teaching boys and girls together, abolishing the headmistress and putting a headmaster over boys and girls alike...letting the girls do the best they can with it, is only a revival, under a new guise, of the old idea, that girls are not entitled to the same consideration as boys.
>
> (Zimmern 1898: 244)

This concern was taken up by Clarke in 1937 who said that although 'in theory' co-education was an ideal system in practice it was not. She wrote:

> In Scotland co-education is the rule and single-sex schools the exception, women as independent human beings are at a disadvantage, socially and economically, in adult life....Moreover...so-called 'co-education' is as a rule education for boys of which girls are permitted – or forced – to partake.

Over 30 years, then, women concerned about the education of girls thought that co-education was likely to mean second-best for girls, and for woman teachers. Much later the research by Dale (1969) found that it was women teachers worried about their promotion prospects – or lack of them – in mixed schools who were the most hostile to co-education. Dale's research is our main source of evidence on all aspects of co-education, and what we can say about the issue has to be based on his work. Dale concluded that mixed grammar schools were superior to single-sex ones on social and academic grounds. Yet as Jenny Shaw (1976) has pointed out: 'although Dale...has dedicated his professional career to championing the cause of co-education and especially to showing that mixed schools are superior to single sex ones on social grounds, the evidence is far from consistent'.

Indeed, as Eggleston (1974) pointed out, while the evidence that boys do better in mixed schools is 'overwhelming' it is 'less convincing' for girls. Indeed it seems possible to argue that boys benefit socially and academically from going to co-educational schools but girls are better off in single-sex ones.

Walford's (1983) data reveal that the senior staff of those boys' public schools which had admitted girls to the sixth form have been motivated not by a desire to improve girls' chances at 'A' level and university entrance – which given the better science facilities (and classics teaching) available there would be plausible – but by a desire to counter falling rolls in a manner least disruptive to the school.

When we examine the impact of co-education in schools and colleges on the careers of teachers, it is clear that the fears expressed by Dale's (1969) women respondents were far from groundless. The teachers surveyed about co-education by Dale included women teachers opposed to co-education because of poorer career opportunities for women. Dale says: 'No men made comments in this section. Typical of the first objection is: One aspect of co-education that seems to me unfair is that in such a school there is less prospect of promotion for women teachers' (1969: 48). Dale says later in the book that

> an important section of women teachers in girls' schools oppose co-education for reasons which are not educational...but are concerned with careers and promotion, some women feeling strongly that there would be little hope of women gaining headships if...schools became co-educational. (p.228)

He proposed that there should be a senior mistress post with deputy head status because 'Opinion in the country is not ready for more than the exceptionally good headmistress to be placed permanently in charge of a mixed grammar school, nor do there appear to be many women who would desire it' (pp.228-9).

No evidence whatever was offered for either statement, but 20 years later the fears of those women have been confirmed. Women entering school teaching, and teacher-training institutions had, in 1945, possibilities of two types of top job. They could aspire to become a headmistress, or the principal of a women's training college. Both were well-paid occupations with considerable social cachet, and led to other work – the magistrate's bench, committees, local councils, and so forth. Even if one did not reach the top of these parallel trees, one could become a head of department in either a school or college. Admittedly, in 1945 there was no equal pay for women teachers, but there was a career structure. By 1985 equal pay had become legal in theory – although rarely achieved in practice – and the career structure had gone with the coming of co-education.

In 1937 Muriel Davies who was then headmistress of Streatham Secondary School for Girls wrote that 'to be responsible for a big school is one of the most absorbing and interesting things a woman can do'. Fifty years later it appears that only a minority of women agree with Muriel Davies, for men out-number women as heads of secondary schools by 3:1. Yet school teaching is still widely seen as a 'good job for a woman', and women outnumber men in the classrooms of schools in Great Britain.

Sutherland (1985a) has pointed out that co-education was adopted as an undiscussed adjunct to going comprehensive. No sustained public debate took place at national or local level about the consequences of co-education for the careers of women in teaching. Yet what women teachers gained with the award of equal pay they lost with the coming of co-education because no provisions were made to safeguard their career ladder in the co-educational school. It is easy to forget that teachers only got equal pay in 1961, and that in Scotland, and in England and Wales, there existed men's unions opposed to equal pay up until the Sex Discrimination Act made single-sex unions illegal. The struggle for equal pay, described by Partington (1976) was long and bitter, and it should not surprise us if entrenched positions adopted during that struggle have not disappeared.

The principle of equal pay in teaching was established in 1955, with a settlement then planned to phase it in over 6 years. The National Association of Schoolmasters (NAS) campaigned to have the decision reversed, while the National Union of Women Teachers (NUWT) campaigned to have equal pay adopted at once. During this period an NAS man wrote in the *Times Educational Supplement* (12.4.57) that women only came into teaching 'to get a husband to get them out of it. The women's staff room has become a waiting room for the bridal chamber and an ante-room for the maternity home!' The NAS line was that men had dependants to support, and they gradually swung their efforts towards a campaign for a dependants' allowance after 1961. Terry Casey, who later became the NAS general secretary, called for an extra £200 per year for men in 1958. The NUWT disbanded in 1961 and gave its remaining funds to New Hall, a new women's college in Cambridge. Partington argues that the award of equal pay and the failure of the campaign for a dependants' allowance were due to the shortage of teachers, and the high birth rate, in the post-war years, especially the shortage of women teachers. Certainly those who had claimed that giving women teachers equal pay would discourage men from entering the occupation were proved wrong. The number of men becoming teachers, and their proportional share of teaching jobs both grew between 1955 and 1972, the period when equal pay was newsworthy enough to create interest.

The battle for equal pay was long – it began with a resolution put to the NUT conference of 1904 – and extremely bitter, as Partington's history shows. However it would be hard to argue that the sexual inequalities in pay and promotion which are found in school teaching and in teacher-training institutions today are a legacy from that struggle. Rather the rapid spread of co-education has, as Zimmern (1898) and Clarke (1937) feared, closed the main career and promotion path for the woman teacher – in the girls' school – without providing equality in the co-educational one.

Thirty years after the principle of equal pay was gained, women teachers are clustered in the lowest-paid sectors of teaching, and within each sector, in the lower-paid parts of it. Thus if we examine the Department of Education and Science (DES) Education Statistics for 1983, and take women secondary teachers in England and Wales, we find women bunched on the lowest scales (table 7.1).

The HMI (1979) survey found that 20 per cent of senior teachers were women, 22 per cent of those on scale 4, and 58 per cent on scale 1. It looks as if the sex balance is roughly equal among scale 2 teachers, and men become the majority in each promoted grade above scale 2. The NUT/EOC survey (1980) revealed a similar point when they compared the percentage of all male and female

*Table 7.1 Percentage of posts held by male and female teachers, January 1983*

| Type of post | Male | Female |
|---|---|---|
| Head | 84 | 16 |
| Deputy head | 63 | 37 |
| Senior teacher | 81 | 19 |
| Scale 4 | 78 | 22 |
| Scale 3 | 63 | 37 |
| Scale 2 | 50 | 50 |
| Scale 1 | 37 | 63 |
| No: | 132,308 | 110,308 |

teachers who had reached promoted posts. Data gathered by Wells (1985) and Davidson (1985) show similar patterns inside two English LEAs.

The percentage of women who have been promoted to senior positions, especially headships, within any one LEA is an important factor in the promotion prospects of other women candidates for headships in the LEA. The research project by Morgan, Hall and Mackay (1983) found that there was a vicious circle which could prevent women becoming heads in LEAs which had few women headteachers already. The authors report that, in England and Wales, in the early 1980s 'the selection of headteachers is carried out in an arbitrary and amateur way'. (Morgan *et al.* 1983: 145). A substantial part of the selection involves committee members matching candidates against stereotypes of heads they have encountered. 'Many more models of men headteachers are available to selectors, as a basis for stereotypes' (p.77). In the three LEAs where there were already a larger proportion of women heads than the national average 'officers also reported a more favourable attitude to women candidates' (p.73). If there are women around to provide the selectors with models, or stereotypes, of women heads, more possible styles are available for future candidates to be matched against.

The research team had detailed data on thirty-six headships being awarded between 1980-3, and their data on women candidates are shown in table 7.2. Women actually got appointed in exactly the proportions in which they applied. There is, therefore, some grounds for accepting the complaints of some LEA officials and researchers that not enough women apply. Morgan *et al.*

173

*Table 7.2 The fate of applicants for 36 headships*

|                        | No. of applicants | No. of interviewees | No. of appointments |
|------------------------|-------------------|---------------------|---------------------|
| Total no. of candidates | 2,753             | 96                  | 36                  |
| Percentage of women    | 11%               | 12%                 | 11%                 |

(1983: 67) conclude that the LEA officials went through three phases when considering women candidates for headships:

1. at the first stage of sifting the applications they welcomed any from women;
2. at the stage of getting ready to interview they expected women to be of a higher quality than men to make the same shortlist;
3. at the final stages they anticipated hostility from the lay people among the selectors to appointing women to mixed or boys' schools.

The data Morgan *et al.* (1983) present support these conclusions and they call for more systematic, and job-related, selection procedures not only to make the appointment of heads more equitable and efficient but also to allow women a fairer chance.

The career structure of the girls' grammar and direct grant schools has largely gone, and the suggested safeguards of the senior-mistress post at deputy-head level are a poor substitute. The career in the women's teacher-training college has also been changed out of all recognition by the coming of co-education, and then the closure and merger of colleges. Sheila Fletcher (1984) has chronicled the changes in the Bedford women's PE training college from a cloistered total institution (see Walker 1983) of the type described in *Miss Pym Disposes* (Tey 1947) to a mixed, multi-site institute of higher education. Apart from this one account, we are short of information about these college principals and their careers. Howson (1982) has written a biography of Elizabeth Williams who was principal of Whitelands and Homerton, but we have little information about Williams' coevals and their successors. A whole career avenue for women has been swept away without any public debate, and without any rescue archaeology on the lives of women who chose that career.

Browne (1979) has written a history of the Association of Teachers in Colleges and Departments of Education (ATCDE) from 1943 until it was absorbed into the National Association of Teachers in Further and Higher Education (NATFHE), and as the ATCDE was formed by amalgamating the Training College Association (founded 1891) and the Council of Principals (1913), her book includes data on women college principals this century. Women were in a majority in the Council of Principals, and between the wars there was an abortive move by a few men to form a separate association to escape a perceived female dominance (Browne 1979: 9). In the period 1918-39, lecturing in a college of education, though a respectable occupation for women, was not a highly-paid one for the salaries were the same as those for teaching in elementary school (p.26). Even the principals did not receive generous salaries, because until 1965 there was no agreed national-salary scale for them. As Browne comments wrily: 'before that the salaries were based on gentlemen's agreements in each college. As the majority of the gentlemen on the principals' side were ladies, they did not do very well' (1979: 134). So it would be wrong to claim that lecturing in a teachers' training college, or being principal of one, was a well-paid occupation but it was a career, and gave women autonomy. In 1957 there were 108 two-year teacher training colleges, nineteen for men, fifteen mixed, and seventy-four for women only. As many of these had women principals these were a source of status for women.

Historically, the experience of women staff in co-educational colleges was not particularly happy. When Winifred Mercier served under a male principal at the mixed college in Leeds she found her position intolerable. She and nine women staff resigned because of the principal's – James Graham – public criticism of and lack of respect for his female staff and their work with the female students. The commotion lasted from 1916-18, and although the inquiry vindicated the women this would have given other females little confidence in mixed colleges. However after 1944 the criticisms of single-sex colleges grew in strength, so that gradually they became seen as anachronisms. In 1969 one retiring principal of a women's college told Browne that her generation were 'the last of the lay abbesses' (Browne 1979: 134). They were, and a whole career path went with them.

From the end of the emergency training scheme until the mid-1970s, women outnumbered men in teacher-training colleges (by 7,500 to 1,900 in 1976). After 1974 there was a dramatic change in higher education provision, which affected women particularly. The government decided that teachers should no longer be trained in specialist colleges, isolated from other students, and that a falling birthrate meant that there was a slackening demand for primary teachers immediately, and for secondary ones later. This meant that women's higher-education opportunities were curtailed, and a career path for college lecturers almost vanished. The *Times Higher Education Supplement* (*THES*) (19.8.77) commented:

> The drastic reduction in places at the colleges of education which have traditionally provided education as well as training for both young and mature women is a setback to the slow progress which women have been making in the world of higher education....Three times more women than men entered teacher education last year, more than half of them with one A level. Many must now turn elsewhere for higher education.

The *THES* went on to argue that alternative arenas for women's higher education should be found, a call also made by Turner (1974) and Scribbins (1977), but nothing was done, and no public campaign resulted.

Thus in 30 years two career paths for women were lost, and nothing was done to replace them with alternatives in the new co-educational schools and multi-course tertiary colleges. Similar analyses can be made for nursing, librarianship, and social work where reorganization and bureaucratization have led to senior posts increasingly being held by men. As Heath (1981) pointed out: 'school-teaching, nursing and social work...the helping professions provide a definite channel of upward mobility for career-orientated women' (p.120). If senior posts in these occupations are becoming monopolized by males, then women will be trapped in the lower-paid grades of these occupations with little chance of promotion. The sociology of education and professional socialization has not yet begun to focus on the consequences of this for these occupations, for social mobility, and for women's lives and careers.

Carol Dyhouse (1985) has shown that while a few nineteenth-century feminists favoured co-education others were anxious about its deleterious results for girls and women. The fears of that group have been amply justified. However, the surviving girls' schools in the period since 1945 have also betrayed the campaigning zeal of their foremothers, not least by allowing double conformity to become an end in itself, rather than a strategy.

## Double conformity revisited

By the 1960s many girls' schools had become trapped by 'double conformity'. Whereas it had been a conscious strategy adopted by the pioneers as a means to an end, it had become in some girls' schools an end in itself. Dale's three-volume attack on single-sex schools (1969, 1971, 1974) captured this complaint from the alumnae of the girls' grammar schools. They reported to Dale (1969: 168-74) that their schools had enforced large numbers of 'petty' rules about dress, deportment and conduct.

> This even went so far as having a fine to pay if we appeared without lace-up shoes, fawn socks, white gloves, no hat.

> Absolutely ridiculous. If nails were long they had to be cut. No carrying satchells on shoulder. Same hair style all term etc.

> Too much attention was paid to trivial matters of uniform, e.g. black lace-up shoes, girls wearing ankle socks till they were 18.

> If one didn't wear a hat out of school whilst in uniform, one had to wear it all day in school for all activities for one month.

Dale showed no understanding of the reasons why girls in secondary schools are obliged to wear school uniforms, and the insistence on gloves, hats and leg coverings. Yet, this care for the public appearance of female pupils can be easily understood as part of a continuing concern that girls should be 'respectably' dressed, which can be traced back to the period of founding schools and colleges for women in the nineteenth century.

While it demands an exercise of imagination to see that:

1. the tunic of thick serge...without pleats...'three inches above the knee when kneeling'
2. thick brown stockings
3. two pairs of knickers – white 'linings' and thick navy blue baggy knickers complete with pocket
4. lace-up shoes, striped shirts, blazers, ties and tie-pins

described by Okely (1978) with loathing were once liberating, it is essential that this be grasped. Ties, panamas, and such garments were an important part of the feminist campaigns for education. The educational pioneers did not have any kind of uniform for school, although they tried to discourage unhealthy garments, especially the corset. Standardized clothes came in first for games. The early PE clothes were carefully constructed to be decent and were not to be seen in public. Gradually, the newer clothing styles began to be adopted for school work, and as Atkinson (1978) points out 'the young ladies had escaped the confines of stays and skirts, only to encounter the institutional control manifested in the...uniform'. That there is a continuity from the time when the new clothes were a proud symbol to their restricting and annoying existence today, can be seen in the histories of many girls' schools. Carr's (1955) account of the City of Cardiff High School for Girls from 1895-1955 will serve as an example. In 1900 there was no school uniform except for gym for which ankle length skirts of navy serge and black stockings were worn. Uniform began to appear around 1907, with special uniforms for prefects and sub-prefects (Carr 1955: 82). Carr traces the growth of uniform, and the attention to appearance down to 1955, commenting about 'fashion distorts uniform as the moon distorts the sea' (1955: 165). The degree of control over pupils' self-presentation in 1955 is then summarized as follows:

> the charging staff's battle-cry, as they wage war on safety pins, bangles, and rings...over-elaborate hair, and hair unkempt, high heels, down-at-heels, and the thousand divagations (*sic*) from the golden mean that are frowned on much more severely in school*girls* than are the corresponding lapses in school*boys*. The battle cry is always on. (p.160)

It is the legacy from those far gone days of 1870-1914 which kept the school girls of the 1950s grammar schools complaining to Dale about gloves and hats. The schools still believed that ladies wore hats and gloves, and therefore that grammar-school girls should too. The dying throes of these ideas about clothing concern trousers for women in schools. The reluctance of many schools to allow either teachers or pupils to wear trousers is a legacy from the period when trousers were immoral. Amelia Bloomer's abortive attempt to introduce trousers for ladies in the nineteenth century and the cocktail pyjamas of the 1920s and 1930s worn by 'fast' women must be colouring those heads who still ban trousers. *Spare Rib 89* devoted an article to the issue, and Wolcott (1973: 25) quotes a typical headmaster's view. Three girls had come to school wearing 'neatly pressed pedal pushers' and the head tells them not to do so again unless there is a 'lesson in tumbling' or a trip, because 'I want you to dress like ladies'. This legacy also affects teachers, for King (1978: 72) records how in two of the infant schools he studied

> the headmistresses constrained how the teachers dressed. At Burnley Road the principle was suitable dress for school; this excluded trousers. The headmistress of the Langley school also banned trousers. This was the cause of some ill-feeling among the teachers, who complained to me that they often had to 'get down with the children' and so had blackened knees and ruined tights. Trousers, they thought, would be more practical and dignified garments. One day I was surprised to see most of them wearing trousers. They had made another appeal and to their evident delight the ban had been lifted.

These teachers were luckier than those at Guy Mannering (9-13) Middle School, studied during the ORACLE project in the late 1970s (Delamont and Galton 1986). One of the research team recorded the following staffroom conversation about the head, Miss Tyree's, ban on female staff wearing trousers:

> There was also a discussion about whether the women teachers could wear trousers. Apparently Miss Tyree won't have the staff wear them and when she was asked by the deputy before she said 'No' and then 'Are they all transvestites?'

> 'Anyway' says one young male teacher, 'she would soon let you wear trousers if she knew the boys stand at the bottom of the stairs looking up your dresses'. 'I bet they keep a book on the colour of our knickers' says the deputy.

Guy Mannering had been a girls' secondary-modern school until shortly before the research, and was still under the same head. Dale's sample were equally vociferous about the vestiges of the chaperonage rules which were still being enforced in the girls' grammar schools of the 1960s.

> You weren't allowed to talk to boys, you mustn't work in Woolworths. (Dale 1969: 174)

> Silly rules such as not talking to boys at the school gate. (p.172)

> Not supposed to wait for boys at neighbouring school to walk home etc. (p.173)

Too strict over petty things like being outdoors at lunchtime, not going down to the school wood in winter, not talking to gardeners. (p.172)

It was a bit fussy over little details such as we were not to eat ice cream while in school uniform. (p.176)

The headmistress disliked girls talking to boys. We had to wait behind after school until we would just be able to catch the bus in order to prevent us from talking to the boys in the bus station. (p.173)

Couldn't look out of the windows that looked out onto the male section of school. (p.174)

These rules looked ridiculous to girls at school in the 1960s, but both the insistence on ladylike behaviour (e.g. not eating in the street) and the strict segregation from males are conventions which can be traced directly from the nineteenth century. The early schools had to show they were educating ladies, and that their moral standards were high, as we have seen earlier in the book. The headmistress keeping girls away from the bus station quoted above is a direct descendent of the first headmistress of the Bedford Girls' High School quoted earlier, who started her school at a different time to avoid boys (Westaway 1932: 23).

What Dale found, and signally failed to understand, was the last throes of the nineteenth-century pioneers' care for ladylike standards. The impact of double conformity in girls' schools in the 1950s and 1960s was influenced by the academic aims of the school and the staff's perceptions of the class background of the intake, so that it bore down most strongly in the grammar schools. In elite, expensive schools the pressures to be ladylike would be less because the pupils were already ladies, in secondary moderns the academic pressures were lessened. Thus we can separate four types of schooling for girls as in figure 7.1. This figure has certain similarities with the model proposed by King (1971) in his important statement about sexual inequalities in educational achievement.

Figure 7.1 shows how the staff of the girls' grammar schools saw themselves with the most demanding task: turning working–class girls into ladies who could fit into the superior occupations their academic success would lead them to.

A colleague at Cardiff recalls how when a teenager at grammar

*Figure 7.1 Class background of pupils*

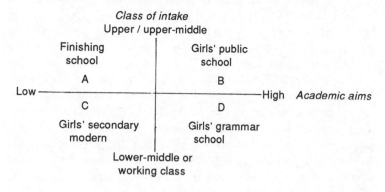

school she was seen by a teacher in school uniform but hatless, eating a bun, seated on the crossbar of a boy's bike as he carried her along the road. At the time she did not realize why the headmistress considered this behaviour so appalling. Readers of this book can both identify with a teenage life style which enjoys eating in the street, meeting boys and going hatless, and see why to a professional woman of the early 1960s, the school was shamed by such behaviour.

The attacks on girls' boarding schools, on single-sex schooling, and the total failure to understand the double conformity system as a legacy of nineteenth-century battles were three hostile arguments ranged against women's real emancipatory needs. Even more damaging to women's education and careers, however, was the way in which three segments of the intelligentsia in Britain ignored the subject in their writing.

## Three betrayals or *la trahison des trois clercs*

The schooling of clever girls received a boost from the 1944 Act, which by removing fees at least allowed many girls access to the academic subjects that fees had priced out of their mothers' reach. However, the high hopes of the Brittain/Holtby generation were betrayed. Not only did many commentators, including many women, turn on the girls' schools as old-fashioned, and the policy makers introduce co-education without safeguarding the academic needs of girls and the careers of female teachers, and the previously liberating use of double conformity as a strategy become a moribund end in itself, there were three additional betrayals. The new disciplines of the social sciences in educational research ignored women's schooling; so too did both the two groups of intelligent people highlighted by C.P. Snow (1959): the literary and the scientific intelligentsia. That is, both the novelists and the scientists of the 1950s and 1960s left women invisible – or saw them in a one-dimensional way as lovers, wives and mothers – not as learning, working, thinking people. The first of these three groups to be considered is the novelists. As Bourdieu has pointed out, novelists lack actual power in society but they have symbolic capital: they can make topics part of the discourse of national debate. In the period from 1850-1945 men and women novelists had seen the education and careers of women as a topic worth writing about. After 1945, they no longer did.

## The vanished heroines?

The education of women vanished from the fictional agenda in the post-1944 period. Novels and plays which treated education, social mobility and careers were male-centred (androcentric). There are problems in 'reading-off' from the fiction of the 1944-84 era to the events of contemporary life, as Elizabeth Wilson (1980: 148-9) has pointed out:

> In singling out a few novels and a few authors I have run the risk of considerable distortion. In any case, it might not be relevant to relate the novels too closely to the period in which they were written...these novels seem to relate to other social and cultural trends. I have also run the risk of using them as documentary evidence of the state of feelings....Although most remained within the realist tradition of the psychological, confessional, sometimes openly autobiographical novel, this approach does raise problems. I can only say that I am aware of them.

It is arguable, however one feels about the relations between novels and their social context, that if writers fail to address a topic at all, then that subject fails to become part of the national agenda. Thus the predominance of fictional heroes who are shown in educational institutions achieving social mobility, and living as scientists, and the total absence of heroines in such situations, can be used as evidence that the education of women was not a matter of concern among the educated middle classes in post-war Britain.

When post-war novels featured men succeeding in education, and achieving entry to high-status jobs because of that success, they were following in a tradition which already existed. Thus both Hardy's *Jude the Obscure* and Lawrence's *Sons and Lovers* were centrally concerned with men, social class, education and social mobility. These perennial themes were picked up by novelists after 1945, most noticeably by C.P. Snow in his decameron *Strangers and Brothers*, by William Cooper in *Diary of a New Man*, by J.I.M. Stewart in his *Staircase in Surrey* sequence, by Kingsley Amis in *Lucky Jim*, Malcolm Bradbury in *Eating People is Wrong*, *Stepping Westward*, *The History Man*, and *Rates of Exchange*, by David Lodge in *Changing Places* and *Small World*, and by Howard Jacobson in *Coming from Behind*. In all these novels, many of them widely read, male characters are shown using educational success to rise in the world: the boy from the working-class home who masters science, or medieval history, or epic-verse forms, and enters elite institutions such as the civil service, Oxbridge colleges, and higher-education lectureships. The British elite is portrayed as relatively open to the talented male outsider as long as he is prepared to conform to its arcane values.

The plays of the post-war period have also included variations on this theme, as in *Look Back in Anger* (where the anti-hero is a graduate from a redbrick university) and *Butley* with its chaotic English lecturer at London University. All these fictional forms make the educational achievements of males part of the public consciousness, an issue that deserves serious thought. Jimmy Porter in *Look Back in Anger* has echoes of the young men uneasy with their social mobility discussed by Earl Hopper (1981). Whereas in C.P. Snow social mobility is seen as a benefit to the society and the individuals; in Osborne and Amis both benefits are queried; in both the topics of male academic success and social mobility are placed on the intellectual agenda. There is even a sub-species of novel dealing with the trials of boys from poor homes sent, because of academic ability, on scholarships to elite public schools. David Benedictus's *Fourth of June* deals with the miseries of being a misfit at Eton, because of one's poverty, class or race, and is a typical example of this genre.

These fictional works are all by men, and centred on heroes. There are no equivalent books with heroines using their brains to achieve scholarships, Oxbridge fellowships, peerages or professorships. Not only is there a total lack of plays and novels by men with heroines gaining social mobility through physics or

Icelandic epics or medieval French, there is also a complete absence of such heroines in the fiction written by women. The male writers not only ignored the educational achievement and mobility of women in their fiction, but also created, in their occasional educated women, a gallery of grotesques.

The absence of fictional heroines who achieve social mobility, or even interesting jobs, because of their educational success, is a striking feature of British post-war novels. There were such women in the fiction of the pre-1939 era, and the wider issues of female education were central concerns in the nineteenth-century novel. George Eliot had the education of women at the centre of her canvas in *Middlemarch* and *The Mill on the Floss*, the Brontë sisters used educational issues in *Jane Eyre* and *Villette*, and the topic was also important for many lesser women writers. Winifred Holtby's *South Riding* was the last great novel in which the educational or career ambitions of women were seriously addressed. Lydia is the only working-class girl who is shown climbing out of a slum into a satisfying career by ambition, brains, and the support of a sponsoring teacher. No female writer since the 1944 Education Act has written about her successors and fictional women scientists, doctors, and engineers are conspicuously absent from post-war novels.

There are a few novels in which the schooling and higher education of women forms a backcloth to action which is not achievement-oriented. Thus *The Prime of Miss Jean Brodie* takes place in one of the elite Edinburgh girls' schools in the 1930s, Ruth Adam's heroine in *I'm not Complaining* is an elementary school teacher, and the protagonists in both A.S. Byatt's and Margaret Drabble's novels are frequently Oxbridge graduates. However in none of these does the educational success or the careers of the women take the centre of the stage; that position is occupied by the women's sexual and marital fortunes, or their roles as mothers. Thus in *The Millstone* the heroine is supposed to be doing a Ph.D (in an arts subject) but the pregnancy occupies the reader's attention, there is no evocation of the actual struggles necessary to complete a high degree, or consideration of the heroine's vocational future. Similarly in *Jerusalem the Golden* Clara, although bright enough to escape a grim unintellectual home and reach university, is shown mesmerized by an intellectual family and quite without ambition or career plans for herself. A.S. Byatt's clever sisters in *The Virgin in the Garden* are also shown dissipating their intellectual gifts in either marriage and pregnancy, or an unrequited passion.

The heroines of most of the female novelists of the post-war period were obsessed with marriage, sexuality, and motherhood to the neglect of any educational achievement, social mobility or career. There is no post-war equivalent of Rhoda Nunn, choosing celibacy and a political, philanthropic or feminist career rather than love, marriage, and domesticity. Indeed the only heroines who are shown to be concerned with issues beyond the personal are those of Doris Lessing, where the female characters do become engaged with ideas, both political and intellectual. The career woman, the dual-career family, and the heroine who cares about her work, vanished from serious fiction for thirty years, except in Lessing, and only survived in the detective story. Thus the only heroines in fiction whose own jobs actually mattered were Sayer's Harriet Vane, Marsh's Agatha Troy, Allingham's Amanda Fitton, and Jessica Mann's Thea Wade. These women all marry, each has at least one child yet continue their careers as detective novelist, painter, aircraft engineer and archaeology professor respectively. Amanda Fitton is the only woman engineer in fiction, and the only woman whose career is seen as important enough for her husband to refuse a job overseas because it would interrupt her work. No such heroine, occupation or husband appears in any serious British post-war fiction. There is not room in this volume to examine equivalent fiction in Australasia and the USA but the same general picture seems to hold. Amanda Cross's detective heroine, a full professor at Columbia, is a more positive role model for American women than any character in a serious novel. American men had *The Graduate* and *Goodbye Columbus*, their sisters had nothing.

For thirty years the education and careers of women, especially in science and engineering, vanished from the consciousness of the opinion-forming classes, ceasing to be an issue worth addressing. The education, social mobility, and careers of men never left the popular consciousness in the same way.

The absence of women's education and careers from the consciousness of the literary intelligentsia might not have had any consequences if it had not been matched by an equal lack of concern about women's role from the scientific elite.

## A sad reflection?

When Elizabeth Williams became Principal of Whitelands College in 1951 she discovered that 'physical science and mathematics were not properly recognised and had no proper accommodation'. This was, Williams felt, 'a sad reflection on what can be done by highly intelligent women in discouraging girls from taking up maths or physics' (Howson 1982: 192). The next chapter examines the role of women in science while here the material on science in girls' schools is presented.

The scientific education of girls was largely ignored after 1945 until the late 1970s, although science and technology was an important issue on the educational agenda as far as boys were concerned. The scientific and technological training of boys was seen as a matter of general, public, national concern – that of girls was relegated to a topic only of interest to a few teachers in girls' schools. The national debates about science and technology in education have been the subject of several books, such as McCullock, Jenkins, and Layton (1985), Layton (1984), Waring (1979) and Jenkins (1979). These have been used extensively in what follows.

Two main themes can be seen in the debates over science and technology in schools in post-war Britain: one centred on the shortage of scientists and the scientific ignorance of many school leavers; the second on the balance between 'pure' and 'applied' science in the curriculum. Neither debate was seriously concerned with the possibility that schoolgirls could ease the manpower shortage in science, needed to be scientifically knowledgeable, or should be given a technological education. Few bothered to argue that science or technology were *unsuitable* for schoolgirls but fewer still argued that the nation's problems would be eased by improving science and technology in girls' schools.

McCullock, Jenkins, and Layton (1985) deal with both debates in their book on science and technology education in secondary schools in England and Wales since 1945. They point out that ever since the Second World War a series of august bodies and distinguished individuals have made public calls for more attention to be paid to science education in the UK, and argued that the nation's future is imperilled by the low status of engineering and the shortage of scientifically qualified manpower. Their analysis reveals both the complexities of the issues and the invisibility of girls in the debates.

McCullock *et al*. (1985: 23) point out that the most influential organization of school science teachers was heavily biased against applied science in schools, because they were still struggling to establish science – as opposed to classics – in the boys' schools. The authors say: 'In the immediate post-war years, the Science Masters' Association [SMA] was the effective guardian of pure, academically-oriented school science education in England and Wales.' The SMA was based in boys' grammar and direct-grant public schools, and had always (i.e. since 1901 when the Association of Public School Science Masters began) emphasized that science was a fit subject for gentlemen, and had been hostile to its mechanics-institute/technological applications. These men campaigned for science on the grounds that it 'was liberal in approach, cultural in scope, and rigorous in its intellectual and academic demands' (p. 31).

Through the period from 1945-75 the male science teachers and the various public committees and pressure groups were much more concerned with establishing science in boys' schools and discussing boys' curricula. Thus when several large industrial companies set up the Industrial Fund for the Advancement of Scientific Education in Schools (IFASES or the Fund) one of the leading lights saw its purpose as increasing 'the flow of able *boys* into science and technology' (McCullock *et al*. 1985: 32 – emphasis mine). The fund channelled £3.25 million into laboratories and equipment for independent schools between 1955-63 (and did actually include girls' schools as well).

When the SMA and the AWST (Association of Women Science Teachers) set up panels to re-design the school science syllabuses in 1958 Boulind of the SMA while announcing of their target pupil that 'he (or she) is the sixth-form student' (McCullock *et al*. 1985: 82) went on to state that 'he' will occupy responsible positions and become 'men of affairs' – the girl is never mentioned again. Similarly the Rector of Imperial College, Linshead, in 1962, spoke about his concern for 'the clever boys, the university material' (p.85). In 1964 the *Times Educational Supplement (TES)* was concerned that the new-style, Nuffield syllabuses might damage recruitment to engineering because 'the better the Nuffield course is made in pure science alone, the more firmly it will direct *boys* away from engineering' (p.109). The man who chaired the FBI education committee from 1953-5 complained publicly that 'grammar school education tended to turn a *boy's* mind from the concrete to the abstract' (p. 118 – emphasis mine) and that there was an urgent need to 'convince the *schoolboy* and *his* parents' (p.119 – emphasis mine) of the desirability of a career in engineering. In 1963 one of the professors of engineering at Sheffield was arguing that the 'sixth form *boy* is impressed by the prestige of The Royal Society' and so there was a need for a Royal Society of Applied Science for improving the prestige of engineering 'in the eyes of school *boys*' (p.121 – emphasis mine). Boulind admitted later that the SMA 'gave no particular thought to the special needs of sixth formers in girls' schools' (p.192) and Page that, when doing a survey for the Institute of Mechanical Engineers, he did not visit any girls' schools because there was 'no time'. The only exception to this male world view in which the nation's manpower needs can only be met by clever boys was K.H. Platt, speaking for the I.Mech.E. in 1965 when he wanted a future in which 'every little boy and girl would not grow up' (p.125) ignorant of engineering. Platt is, of course, married to a woman engineer.

McCullock *et al.* (1985: 192) say that the needs of girls were 'overshadowed by what were seen as more urgent national issues'. The authors, however, compounded this perspective and conducted their research on the period entirely from a male angle in that they only examined the private papers of men, only interviewed men, and only corresponded with men – so that the historical reconstruction leaves out women science teachers, the women practising engineering and science at the period, and women industrialists.

The invisibility of women in debates about science has even led Gathorne-Hardy (1977) to state that the IFASES excluded girls' schools. In fact the Fund gave financial aid to eighty-two girls' schools, including Walthamstow Hall whose laboratories had been bombed in the war (Pike, Curryer and Moore, 1973). Both McCormick (1986) and Layton (1986) have argued that girls' schools benefited less than boys' ones due to the terms and aims of the IFASES. McCormick says that girls' schools did not receive help on the same scale as the boys' because 'there was 'Matthew effect' (to him who hath shall be given). They wanted to put money where it was likely to have some immediate effect – small 6th forms were thought uneconomical.' Layton points out that

the specific aim of the Fund being to increase the numbers of chemists, physicists, mathematicians and geologists (oil money!) other departments of science such as biology were

Table 7.3 Schools funded by the IFASES in England and Wales,
1955-62

|  | Equipment grants only | Building and equipment grants |
|---|---|---|
| Boys' schools | 42 | 164 |
| Girls' schools | 53 | 14 |
| Co-ed. schools | 10 | 2 |
| Totals | 105 | 180 = 285 |

excluded except insofar as they were part of general science
teaching up to Ordinary Level. The Fund's Apparatus Brochure,
with suggested apparatus for science teaching, lists items for
physics, chemistry and geology only.

The Final Report of the Fund (1963) lists the contributing firms,
and the terms of the Fund, together with the details of the
disbursement of the money. They began by considering 'those
schools with 250 or more boys (or girls) over the age of 13, and with
ten per cent or more of their number in the science and mathematics
divisions of the sixth forms' (p.5). Later these conditions were
relaxed so that eventually they were able to give funds to 'almost
every school which gave promise of expansion on the science side
of the sixth form' (p.5). The Fund were concerned that

although the output of scientists was increasing, an insufficient
proportion of them were embarking on careers in
engineering....That the pure sciences should be so much more
attractive to boys leaving schools gives us some concern. (p.6)

Summing up their effect on schools, the Report says that 'every boy
from the time of entry up to the Ordinary Level of the General
Certificate studies a science subject' (p.7). No effects on girls'
schools are mentioned. The Report lists all the schools which had
received building and equipment grants – and the eighty-two girls'
schools are listed in Appendix 3. The breakdown of grants between
boys', girls' and mixed schools is shown in table 7.3.

This table (taken from page 19 of the Final Report) shows that
very few girls' schools got new buildings from the fund, most of the
eighty-two receiving only equipment grants. Late in its life the fund

installed engine test beds in seven schools to encourage boys towards applied science – these were all boys' schools in England. The Fund was disappointed with the fourteen girls' schools which had received building grants because their science sixths had not increased in size taking the schools together. The trustees announced that:

> In girls' schools interest in science clearly depends on factors other than the material ones of space and equipment. Staffing is one problem but generally it is to be feared that, except for the medical profession and its ancillary services, girls do not envisage careers for themselves in science. (p.22)

The trustees felt that headmistresses did not expect girls to go on to be scientists. They noted, though, that those girls who did do science in the sixth were 'highly successful....As a group they secure a higher percentage of passes in all science subjects than any other group with which this report is concerned' (p.22). The success rate in 'A' level biology was 95 per cent. Girls' schools also differed from boys' in the relative passes in the different sciences. In boys' schools, as the successes in physics and chemistry rose, biology declined: in girls' schools 'increasing success in the physical sciences is not accompanied by a decline in biology – quite the reverse. Doubtless improved standards in the basic physical sciences have reacted favourably on the work in biology' (p.30).

While the Fund was unhappy about the small impact of their building grants on the fourteen girls' private schools they had aided, they found that the position was much worse in the maintained sector. The percentage of girls doing advanced work in maths and science in grammar schools and grammar streams was smaller (4.1 per cent) than in the elite schools they had helped (10 per cent). No proposals were made by the committee to encourage girls into science or technology, despite the high standard obtained by those who did study science at 'A' level.

The lack of any planning or proposals from the science teachers, or the trustees of the Fund, was paralleled by a lack of positive leadership from government reports. As I have argued elsewhere both the Hadow (1926) and Norwood (1943) reports had been largely indifferent to women studying sciences – their attitudes was *laissez-faire*: if a bright girl wished to study sciences that was permissible, but no enthusiasm was evinced (Delamont 1980a).

It would be anachronistic to criticize Hadow, or Norwood, for failing to propose a radical change in direction in the education of women when the idea of secondary education for the workers in previously 'elite' subjects was revolutionary. However, the leaders of women's education could, and should, have seen that a positive leadership was necessary and campaigned against a view of education for girls planned on an uneasy compromise between society's 'needs' and 'individual interests' in favour of more interventionist strategy. They should have appreciated that the Hadow proposals would lead to separate and unequal curricula for men and women in which girls did humanities and languages, and domestic science which led to poorly-paid jobs, while boys did science and technology which led to better-paid work.The leaders of female education should have seen the economic implications of Hadow and Norwood and it is legitimate to highlight the failure of the leaders of women's education to take a feminist line in science and mathematics for women, and to point to the consequences of that failure subsequently. The few women who did manage to enter science and engineering between Hadow and the present have been seen as oddities, and faced hurdles which a sustained campaign might have alleviated.

The lack of positive leadership from the Hadow (1926) and Norwood (1943) reports to pull, push, cajole, bully or direct girls into maths and science has had long-standing consequences which are with us all today. Byrne (1975) studied resource allocation between 1945-65 and the achievement of boys and girls related to that allocation. She found that both better resources, and resources of different kinds, were automatically considered to be necessary for male pupils rather than females, for urban rather than rural, for the able rather than the stupid, and the older rather than the younger. Byrne concluded that the less-able girl in a rural school had a triple chance of deprivation and this was reflected in the poor employment she entered. Byrne then looked at resource allocation in terms of material facilities (buildings, specialist rooms, etc.), finance and staffing. She found that of 133 schools in her sample (88 mixed, 20 boys' and 25 girls') all the girls' schools were short of science laboratories. Over half the mixed schools (which were all secondary moderns) had a shortage of laboratories and all but four 'solved' the problem by teaching the girls biology in classrooms while the boys did physics and chemistry in the proper laboratories. Fogelman's (1976: 43) survey of 12,676 sixteen-year olds carried out in 1974 asked their headteachers whether their schools were lacking in, or had inadequate, facilities. Only a third of the heads said their schools were adequately provided with all the facilities, and only 23 per cent said their schools were adequately provided with laboratories. Fogelman's data did not show who suffered from the lack of laboratory facilities, but it will not have been able boys.

The IFASES clearly did not expect girls to be interested in engineering and so did not provide any facilities in technology in girls' schools. Whereas science and maths had been available to a clever and committed girl from the nineteenth century, if she were lucky in her schooling, and to all bright girls after 1944, the chances of her learning 'male' craft subjects were slim. The teaching of domestic science, needlework, woodwork, technical drawing, and metalwork was until very recently the most sex-segregated area of the curriculum.

From 1944 until the passing of the Sex Discrimination Act the 'failure' of science and technology to attract girls in numbers commensurate with their potential was not a matter for public concern. The invisibility of gender in discussion of science education is particularly interesting when examining the research on the 'Nuffield-style' changes in the science syllabuses for the most able planned and implemented from the late 1950s onwards. From the historical work of Waring (1979) and the empirical investigations of Nuffield science in practice (e.g. Eggleston, Galton, and Jones 1976), we can find a further area where the issue of gender divisions was invisible until very recently yet was actually rather important (Galton 1981). The issue of girls and Nuffield science is complex, and discussed elsewhere (Delamont 1986) using the theoretical ideas on indeterminacy and technicality (Jamous and Peloille 1970) and of the new history and sociology of science (Collins 1985) introduced in chapter 8. The neglect of women by the literary intelligentsia and the scientific decision makers was paralleled by an equal purblindness from a newly-emerging third intellectual group: the social scientists.

## The social scientists

Appendix 1 contains details of the way in which the sociology of education failed to address sex equality issues or indeed women's education between 1944 and about 1974. The sociologists of education were not alone in this: similar blind spots can be found in all branches of social science. This was very different from the nineteenth century when social science had been a forum for women's emancipation to be discussed and acted out. As the social science intelligentsia rose in size and influence to rival the literary and scientific ones, it failed to conduct research on, or debate, women's role in society. Elizabeth Wilson (1980) has outlined the impact of Freudian psychology and Parsonian sociology but the work still has to be done for economics, anthropology, political science, and so on. In each discipline the contemporary role and status of women were left unchallenged and unexamined. Women vanished from the discourse.

Basil Bernstein was one exception whose theories left women with a place in the discourse and provided a framework for re-examining their role. Mary Douglas (1975: 174) has suggested that Basil Bernstein is not a conventional sociologist, but rather he is 'Neither fish, flesh nor fowl'. She goes on:

> Some tribes reject and fear anomalous beasts, some revere them. In sociology Professor Bernstein is to some a fearsome scaly monster, cutting across all the tidy categories. The light he sheds on thoughts we would prefer to keep veiled is often cruel. No wonder he holds an anomalous place in his profession.

Bernstein's analytic power – which appeals so highly to Douglas – comes from looking at any social process in four stages. Bernstein always concentrates first on the control system, then the boundaries it sets up, then the ideological justifications which come to surround those boundaries, and finally the power which underlies the whole system/process. If we think about the growth of co-education, the changes in science education, and the concerns of the post-war novelists, using Bernstein's approach alongside the ideas of the Ardeners, sense can be made of the changes chronicled in the chapter.

In Bernsteinian terms, boundaries were being changed for males, and male benefit, with particular emphasis on boundaries of class and wealth. The coming of co-education was a consequence of going comprehensive (mixing children of different classes, wealth, and ability ranges); the abolition of the single-sex teacher-training college was a consequence of an expansion of tertiary education and a mixing of student categories in it; the novelists were addressing the issue of educating working-class men. Bernstein repeatedly said that women's lives were changing and being changed by these shifts in boundaries but women were a very muted group in the period and no one else noticed. The shifting of boundaries between the classes damaged women's educational and career chances as an unintended consequence, and those boundaries that should have been broken down (double conformity and lack of maths and science) were not challenged because they only constrained a muted group. Also, the implications of the changes were indeed veiled: it is with hindsight that we can see – thanks to Bernstein – how the feminist hope was betrayed. Mary Douglas likened Bernstein to an anomalous beast. She was thinking more of his status within sociology than his radical ideas about the role of working mothers as cultural interrupters. It is, however, in the ideas of Bernstein about the experiences of working-class women taking paid employment in bureaucracies and bringing the language of bureaucracy back to their childrearing that we find the earliest questioning of the otherwise taken for granted theories of women's role in industrial societies.

# 8

## Excluded from the elite?
## Women and top jobs 1945-85

A womanly occupation means, practically, an occupation that a
man disdains.

(Gissing *The Odd Women*, p.135)

There are a few professions, the stage, journalism, the law, and
certain branches of medicine where men and women receive
equal pay for equal work, though in all but the first,
opportunities are by no means equal.

(Holtby 1934: 86)

Chapter 7 discussed how two career paths (towards being
headmistresses and principals of teacher-training colleges)
vanished in the period after 1945. Similar analyses could be done
for nursing, social work, and librarianship. These were occupations
opened up, or created, by the nineteenth-century feminists to
provide respectable jobs for ladies in which they could support
themselves with dignity. The exceptionally talented or ambitious
woman could rise to a public position of power in these jobs as
headmistress, college principal, matron, and so on. Even for those
who stayed in the lower grades, as Heath (1981) points out, these
occupations were the main avenue of social mobility for the single
woman. The loss of these sex-segregated careers in separate,
female institutions/spheres, would not have mattered if other
occupations and professions had become more open to women at
the same time. If the potential matron had been able to become a
hospital consultant and the potential headmistress a solicitor, then
justice would have been done. Instead, there has been a 40-year
period in which the original career paths vanished, and new ones
did not open. This chapter focuses upon elite occupations which

remained relatively closed to women between 1945 and 1975, and are only beginning to become more open to them in the last decade. Four occupations are selected for particular attention: teaching in universities; research, especially in science; medicine, and law. University teaching, research activity in general, and scientific research in particular, are rare topics in the sociology of education. However the study of how careers are built on the making of new knowledge is, or rather should be, an important issue in the sociology of education. Medicine and law do not usually feature in sociology of education books yet these are the very occupations that the most successful school boys aim for. An analysis of the recruitment patterns of these four occupations is as valid a part of the sociology of education as YTS (Youth Training Scheme) or CPVE (Certificate of Pre-Vocational Education).

The chapter, and its material on women in four occupations, is somewhat undertheorized. An understanding of the basic facts about gender divisions in these occupations is necessary to follow the more theoretically complex analyses in chapters 9 and 10. The sociological data on social mobility and recruitment to these top jobs are analysed in chapter 9, and the sociological theory on 'the professions' in chapter 10, so that this chapter focuses upon some of the basic facts about the sexual divisions in those occupations and the place of women in them. The analysis begins with material on women in university teaching, then moves on to science and technology as careers, following on from the data on schooling in the previous chapter, and then looks at medicine and law. Bourdieu (1986: 108) points out that:

> an increase in the proportion of women indicates the whole trend of an occupation, in particular the absolute or relative devaluation which may result from changes in the nature and organization of the work itself...or from changes in relative position in social space....

Two theoretical issues underly the discussion of the four occupations therefore: how the cultural capital and symbolic power of those jobs is changed by shifting gender divisions, and how far women in them (a minority in all four) form a muted group whose perspective has been neglected by scholars focusing on the profession. Readers should bear both in mind during what follows:

## University teaching and research

There are relatively few data available on those whose careers take place in universities, polytechnics and colleges in either Britain or the USA. To discuss the *habitus* of the occupation certain data are necessary and they are not readily available. The most recently published data on women's position in the USA are from Bogart, Wells, and Spencer (1985) who looked at both two-year colleges and institutions offering the BA degree and beyond. Women are a more substantial proportion of the lecturing force (36 per cent) in the two-year college than in the higher-status institutions (19 per cent). In the degree-granting colleges women staff are clustered in the lower-status, non-tenured jobs, so women are 45 per cent of the instructors, 43 per cent of the assistant professors, 17 per cent of the associate professors, and 6 per cent of the full professors. In the UK the equivalent figures for 1973 and 1983 are shown in table 8.1.

*Table 8.1 Percentage of female staff in universities*

|                  | 1973 | 1983 |
|------------------|------|------|
| Professors       | 1.7  | 2.4  |
| Senior lecturers | 6.6  | 6.8  |
| Lecturers        | 10.6 | 16.8 |
| Total            | 10.6 | 14.9 |

There are several studies of women teaching in higher education, although none is very recent. Before examining the evidence on women who teach in higher education it is worth examining the nature of the job – because it is possible that men and women perform the role differently and/or occupy different roles in the same occupation. There are three aspects of the job – teaching, administration, and research – but each of these has several facets. Teaching, for example, can include a wide range of activities from seeing a single, frightened first year who cannot write an essay, or supervising a Ph.D project, to lecturing 300 students in a vast hall. Administration can cover being a dean, representing a faculty of 300 staff and 3,000 students on senate, or dealing with the pastoral care of a new student who does not know how to deal with the mice in his bedsitter. Research can mean running a research project with a multi-million pound budget employing twenty people, or spending 20 years all alone in the archives of an Austrian family and ultimately writing a book only 200 people will read in the next 20 years. The world of the full professor in science who attracts big

197

grants and is on many committees is quite different from that of the new lecturer in art history who will never hold research funds or lecture to more than forty people.

The occupation of university teacher is then a deeply-segmented one (Bucher and Strauss 1961) and the evidence we have is that men and women occupy rather different segments of it and experience it in different ways. In both the USA and the UK women in universities are found to be doing more teaching, especially at the lowest levels (that is, introductory and service courses rather than Ph.D work), more pastoral care, less administration and committee work, and less research and publication. This last area is the one where the differences between males and females in university work are most significant because the size and prestige of research grants and the list of publications are the two most visible, and easily measured, criteria for judging job performance. Teaching and administration are invisible, and despite lip service being paid to their importance, promotion and recognition are actually based on publications and research to a great extent because they can be quantified, compared, and assessed most easily.

The first and most significant feature of research and publication is that large numbers of people in the occupation do little of either. Although it is widely believed that in higher education one must 'publish or perish', in fact substantial numbers of men and women publish very little and do not perish. Cole and Cole (1973: 92-3) use a fourfold typology of publication patterns where they look at high and low quantities of publications and high and low quality. (Their criterion for 'quality' is based on citations: if a paper is cited a great deal it is classified as of high quality. This is a controversial criterion, but for the purposes of my argument here, I am not going to dwell on that!) Using their two dimensions they can classify four types of author as shown in Figure 8.1.

In quartile A is the perfectionist, who publishes a small amount of highly-cited work, in B, the 'star', who publishes a great deal which is significant to colleagues. In D is the mass producer who produces a lot of publications which are largely ignored by other writers. Finally in the 'C' quartile is the 'silent' scholar, who publishes very little and what appears is not cited. In the sciences, Nobel prizewinners (Zuckerman 1977) are nearly always 'prolifics', who publish far more than their peers and are cited more frequently long before they become Nobelists. Most people teaching in higher education are silent: men as well as women. For

*Figure 8.1 Four types of scholarly author*

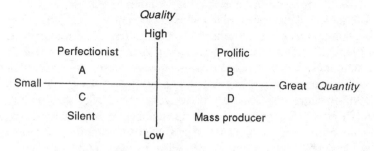

example Cole and Cole looked at the published output of 499 matched men and women in chemistry, biology, and psychology who had gained Ph.Ds in 1957-8 up to 1970. They found that the average lifetime output of this group was nine papers over the twelve years and that the typical male's papers were cited eleven times a year while the typical woman's were cited four times. The men in this sample were more productive than the women, whether married or single. The relative lack of publications and citations of work which characterizes most workers in higher education is thrown into relief by a comparison with Nobel Laureates. Zuckerman found (1977: 145) that they published an average of thirteen papers while still in their twenties, and their work is cited forty times more frequently than the average scientist who is ever cited. Gaston (1978a: 18) found that the variation in the number of publications among the scientists he studied in Britain and the USA was from zero to over 100 (and one man had published 768 papers).

There is then a wide range of productivity between scholars in higher education and many publish very little. Against this there is consistent evidence that women publish less than matched samples of men in the same disciplines, that what women publish is cited less, and that in at least one discipline women's publication patterns are different in an important respect. A typical finding here is that of Reskin (1978) who compared 450 men and women with Ph.Ds in chemistry sampled in 1965 and 1970. She divided these chemists into the categories shown in figure 8.1 and found that she had to divide her categories in different places for men and women. The figures for the prolific scientists reveal the pattern of sex differences. Prolific men had published an average of twenty-four in 10 years and been cited 116 times. Prolific women had published fifteen papers and been cited seventy-one times.

Statistics such as these turn up in many of the studies of scholarly productivity done by the Columbia School (see Gaston 1978b) on American women in science and social science. In Britain we lack recent data, but the research of Williams *et al.* (1974: 399) found that women published less than men in all disciplines, but that married women were more productive than single ones. In the two years before the research was done (i.e. 1967-9) more than half the single women had published nothing while only one quarter of the married had been silent. Similarly one in six of the married women had produced six or more publications while only one in twelve of the single ones were that productive.

The American studies have found women carrying bigger teaching loads than their male colleagues, and especially less-prestigious ones. In the USA women are more likely to be teaching introductory and service courses while men supervise Ph.D students. The Williams, Blackstone, and Metcalf (1974) research found that in the UK women did not carry bigger loads than men but did do the less prestigious work. In Britain, therefore it would not be possible to 'explain' lower publication rates by heavier teaching loads. There is, however, a feature of publication in the social sciences which could tie in with fewer Ph.D students and lower publication rates, and that is co-authorship. It appears from American sociology, and from the whole non-science area in Australia and the UK, that men are much more likely to publish jointly than women are. University teachers may publish collaboratively with graduate students so if women have fewer higher-degree students they have fewer potential collaborators.

The finding that men are more likely to publish jointly than women has been reported spasmodically in the literature but not been the subject of a systematic research project. Chubin (1974) looked at a sample of men and women with Ph.Ds in sociology from American universities. She found that there were many silent women, and that the vast majority of those who were ever going to publish had done so for the first time within 5 years of their doctorate. Among those who had published she found that women were much less likely to be co-authors than men; that is women were more likely to have only publications of which they were the sole author. When women did co-author, they were rarely listed first and women's publications were cited less than men's. Mackie (1977) examined the articles published in fourteen sociology journals in 1967 and in 1973 and found that: 'In 1967 and in 1973, women sociologists were more likely than men to publish alone'

Table 8.2 Single and joint-authored articles by men and women in 1967 and 1973

|  | 1967 | | 1973 | |
|---|---|---|---|---|
| Men | N | % | N | % |
| Total | 695 | 100 | 724 | 100 |
| Single | 332 | 47.8 | 286 | 39.5 |
| Joint | 363 | 52.2 | 438 | 60.5 |
| Women |  |  |  |  |
| Total | 90 | 100 | 153 | 100 |
| Single | 51 | 56.7 | 73 | 47.7 |
| Joint | 39 | 43.3 | 80 | 52.3 |

(p.286). In the period he studied, the proportion of articles that was jointly authored was rising steadily. The actual figures Mackie discovered are shown in table 8.2. In C.P. Snow's (1934) novel about crystallography, *The Search*, two successful scientists are described advising an unsuccessful one how to build his career so that he will become eligible for promotion. The failure is told that he must 'Publish a great deal, some in collaboration, some by yourself. If it's all by yourself, the jealous men will say you're impossible to work with; and if it's all in collaboration, they'll say you're no good on your own' (p.324).

It may be that women academics are falling into the trap of seeming to be 'impossible to work with' by going it alone on too high a proportion of their publications. The data from University College, Cardiff, reveal that the women in arts, education, and social science are more likely to publish alone than jointly when compared with their male colleagues.

Cole and Zuckerman (1984) have reviewed over fifty studies of publication differences between males and females and reported their own latest findings. They have found that in more recent generations of scientists, women's productivity has risen and the proportion of women among 'prolific' scientists has risen from 8 per cent to 26 per cent. They did not find that women in science were less likely to publish collaboratively.

The research on publication and collaboration is therefore unclear. Women academics may publish less and in a different pattern from men but this is far from clearly established. There is some evidence that men placed a higher value on publication than women but that too is inconclusive.

What is lacking from the literature (Halsey and Trow 1971; Williams *et al.* 1974; Blackstone and Fulton 1975; Acker 1980; EOC 1982; Burrage 1983; Acker and Piper 1984; and Sutherland 1985b) is any sense of what being a member of the occupation feels like to its women members. There is no research which deals with women in academic life, controlled by subject specialism, which approaches the empathy of Epstein (1983) on lawyers or Lorber (1984) on doctors. This lack is particularly acute because, as chapter 10 argues, it is the indeterminate aspects of occupational performance in elite jobs which prove elusive to women. There is a need for a study of how women conceptualize the indeterminate aspects of the task of lecturing in higher education, and whether, like law and medicine, there are parts of the occupational identity and performance which are obscured from unsuccessful male, and all female, members of the profession.

The issues which have prevented women from occupying half the posts at all levels in university teaching are particularly acute in science. Hilary Burrage (1983) had done one of the few British studies of women university science teachers, and that is based on 164 usable replies to a questionnaire sent out in 1971. Her demographic data showed that the typical woman scientist in a university came from a middle-class home and girls' school, had a Ph.D, was married, and was only a lecturer. It is a serious indictment of the sociology of science that there are not more recent, more detailed, more qualitative, and more sociologically informed research studies of women in science. As the next section shows, women in science are so unimportant that they have been left invisible.

## Women and science – pure and applied

In 1959 C.P. Snow delivered his famous lecture on *The Two Cultures and the Scientific Revolution*. His argument was that a dangerous gulf had opened up in most capitalist countries between the literary intelligentsia, who were not only ignorant of science and technology but despised them, and the scientific and technological intelligentsia, who were ignorant of all the arts except music. Other issues were raised in the lecture as well, such as the rich-world/poor-world divide, nuclear war, and the English distaste for applied rather than pure science. However his claim that in literary circles scientific ignorance was normal and even encouraged became widely quoted. Between 1964 and 1968 there were eighty-eight English language articles about his thesis (Snow 1971: 81)

Snow's evocation of his two elites, divided into uncomprehending camps by their training, is vivid. They are 'comparable in intelligence, identical in race, not grossly different in social origin, earning about the same incomes' (1971: 14). Yet they are quite unable to communicate. Re-reading the essay in the light of contemporary fears about third-world poverty, cruise missiles, star, wars, and the government's desire to change the balance of university places towards science, many of its concerns are strikingly contemporary.

This is not the place to discuss whether Snow was an accurate social commentator on his times, far less on the literary merit of his novels. Yet one aspect of both his commentaries and his fiction deserves attention: the total invisibility of women in science and technology. Throughout the original 'two cultures' lecture, and two subsequent pieces on its reception written in 1963 and 1970, the scientific worlds evoked are entirely male. Not one woman scientist is mentioned. The 1959 piece contains a long list of famous names in science and literature in which only one woman – Jane Austen – is mentioned. Particularly striking is the omission of George Eliot and Mrs Gaskell whose novels *Middlemarch* and *Wives and Daughters* captured the nineteenth-century beginnings of the very scientific culture Snow so admired. Women are mentioned three times, once concerning Russia, praised for educating its 'men and women' in science and technology on a national basis (p.35). There is also one footnote, which follows the comment on the USSR and reads:

A third of Russian graduate engineers are women. It is one of our major follies that, whatever we say, we don't in reality really regard women as suitable for scientific careers. We thus neatly divide our pool of potential talent by two. (p.45)

Ignoring the scientific potential of women may have been a major folly but was not discussed in the body of the essay. Nor did Snow return to it in his 1963 piece where he defends his argument against criticism or his 1970 one where he finally attacked Leavis and the authors of the Black Papers.

Snow's novels are the same. He dealt with science, in the sense of everyday life in the laboratory and career-building in *The Search*

(1934) and the *The Affair* (1960). *The New Men*, dealing with the race to build the bomb is rather different, and is not discussed here although there is the same absence of women. *The Search* is an insider's view, in that the narrator is himself a crystallographer, and is interesting for its portrayal of laboratory life in the 1930s. Women are completely absent from that life. None of the scientists is a woman: the women are scientists' wives and mistresses. The possibility of a woman being a scientist is only raised twice in the whole book. At one point a man who has a reputation for flirting is being groomed to become a professor at Leeds. His friends require him to promise not to make passes at women. He agrees 'not a scientist's wife. Not one. Not even a woman scientist' (p.325). As this character is an unethical scientist, who falsifies experimental results, the feeling that he might seduce women scientists is presumably all part of his defective character.

The scientific world described in Snow's novel is, then entirely male – even though the actual scientists working on crystallography in the 1930s included several women. The hero is portrayed facing a choice between science (an all-male world) and people (life with his wife) in a simplistic way. The omission of women from the London and Cambridge laboratories of the 1930s is particularly odd when one of the central characters in *The Search* – Constantine – is modelled on J.D.Bernal, according to Philip Snow (1982). Bernal was notoriously pro-women in his laboratories:

> he held to the rather old-fashioned communist notions about the equality of male and female workers, and was well-known for his willingness to accept women students, to encourage them, to promote their careers, to find opportunities for them
>
> (Sayre 1975: 174)

No hint of this comes through in *The Search*.

Snow returned to non-military science for *The Affair*, set in the 1950s. This book is a reworking of the Dreyfus Affair, with communist beliefs replacing Jewishness, and scientific fraud instead of espionage. Everyday laboratory life is only mentioned in passing, and the scientific action has taken place in 'a Scottish university' before the story begins. The Dreyfus figure, Howard, is accused of fraud but claims that his deceased supervisor, Palairet, actually carried out the falsification of results. Among the parallels to the Howard/Palairet fraud drawn by the characters in Snow's fiction is the work of Barkla, a physics professor at Edinburgh from

1924-44. Barkla believed he had discovered a 'J-phenomenon' and fourteen research students successfully got Ph.Ds for work on this, non-existent, phenomenon (Wynne 1979). Snow may well have had the Barkla department in mind but if so he did not represent it faithfully, for Barkla had women students, and no scientific women appear in *The Affair*. Despite the footnote to the 'Two Cultures' lecture, this omission probably reflects Snow's views of women – common in scientists of his age – captured when his niece was born in the immediate post-war period. He wrote to his brother: 'one advantage of a girl is that you don't have to bother about her education' (Snow 1982: 93).

Snow was by no means alone in his perception of science and engineering as essentially male fields where manpower needs could only be met by men. The material on schooling set out in chapter 7 shows that most of his contemporaries shared that world view. The public debate around the Swann and Dainton Reports was equally purblind. In the late 1960s the British government became frightened about the rapid growth of arts and social science in the universities and the much slower growth of science and technology. There was a widespread belief that too many 16- and 17-year olds were specializing in arts and social sciences and were going on to study those subjects at university. Conversely, too few sixth-formers were taking Advanced Level exams in science and too few were studying science and technology at university level. A shortfall of graduates in science and technology was expected to cause problems in industry and lower the standard of science teaching in schools, thus producing few science specialists at school and so perpetuating the shortfall.

Two official government inquiries investigated this 'swing from science'. Both produced gloomy prognostications spiced with desperate remedies (Dainton 1968; Swann 1968). Both reports drew on statistics compiled by Celia Phillips and later published as a book (Phillips 1969), so outsiders can study both their conclusions and their source. Doing so reveals serious flaws in the two reports. McPherson (1969) in a telling article called 'Swing from science or retreat from reason' pointed out three major mistakes. Both reports led to calls that the narrow, specialized English curriculum for 16-18 year olds be replaced by the wider, more generalized Scottish one. McPherson showed that this call was based on total ignorance of the Scottish system and its results in practice. McPherson then pointed out that far more potential scientists and engineers were 'lost' through selection at 11 and 12, early leaving, lack of grants for sixth-form studies, and other barriers to clever working-class pupils than were lured into non-science courses in sixth forms. Third, he showed that both committees ignored one of Phillip's main findings, a finding which would have solved the 'scientific manpower crisis'. Phillips had shown that the universities were failing to tap one source of science students: women. Only half the qualified girl school-leavers actually reached degree courses as opposed to 70 per cent of qualified boys. Yet girls who specialize in science were likely to have received worse teaching in worse laboratories and less encouragement from school, home, and society. As Phillips said, 'they may well have a higher capacity for a university science course than boys' (p.119).

In short, there was a large pool of potential science students who never entered university, not because they did not try but because universities did not take them. McPherson went on to point out that women science graduates were much more likely to enter teaching than men, so the pool of students was likely to become a pool of teachers. The vicious circle of no students – no teachers – no students could be broken. Yet neither Swann nor Dainton urged universities to recruit these girls or encourage others to join them as science specialists. Swann recommended paying science teachers more than their colleagues (just the thing to produce harmony in the nation's classrooms and staffrooms), the resurrection of the retired (whose science had been learnt before the atom was split), and the transfer of burnt-out cases from industrial and university research (at protected salaries, of course). This is a typical example of educational debate. Women are invisible. If the answer staring you in the face is women there is no solution to the problem. Better an elderly man who has failed to become a senior lecturer in a university than a young girl graduate with up to date scientific knowledge and a commitment to the subject fired by struggling to study it.

In retrospect, it is clear that in so far as there was a shortage of scientists and engineers in 1968, a serious campaign on the lines of Girls Into Science and Technology (GIST) (Whyte 1985) and Women Into Science and Engineering (WISE) would have been more useful than any of the 'solutions' proposed by Swann and Dainton.

Since the era of Swann and Dainton the invisibility of women in science has been unchallenged by sociologists. The sociologists of science who have claimed to treat science in ways which challenge its popular and Popperian image have actually failed in three respects to do so. The New History and Sociology of Science (NHSS) group has developed a body of research and theory which has left three noticeable gaps:

1. A failure to address the concerns, both methodologically and theoretically, raised by the sociology of the 'learned professions' which are relevant to the sociology of science.
2. A total lack of attention to the learning of science and to the sociology of learning environments in science.
3. A complete omission of research on gender in science in all its manifestations.

Sociologists of science, whatever their methods and theoretical persuasion, have neglected to compare the work of scientists and their occupational identity with those of other occupations, even those demanding similar standards of training, such as law and medicine. This is true of the Mertonian scholars from the Columbia tradition, the ethnographers of laboratory life, and the ethnomethodologists. Although the Columbia school of the sociology of science grew out of work on the learned professions, contemporary work in this tradition pays little attention to research on other occupations. For example the Gaston collection (1978a) which includes papers by most of the sociologists of science from the Columbia school contains no comparisons of science and law or medicine, let alone any discussion of less exalted occupations. The researchers who focus upon everyday life in laboratories have not made principled comparisons with the working lives of other occupational groups. For example the two chapters in the Knorr-Cetina and Mulkay collection (1983) which are about everyday life in scientific settings contain no references at all to ethnographic research on other workplaces or social settings. Research in courts, wards, and clinics is not utilized to illuminate laboratory life, still less are comparisons made with factories, dance halls, massage parlours or building sites.

The exception who proves this rule is Susan L. Star, who does ground her work in the Chicago School work on other occupations (see Star 1985, 1986). Those sociologists of knowledge in science have failed to incorporate work on professional knowledge from outside science, or that on knowledge from other settings. Similarly, the two chapters in Knorr-Cetina and Mulkay (1983) which focus on knowledge contain only one reference to an anthropological study and one to medical sociology. There is no discussion of knowledge in other occupational cultures, no references to studies of them, and no hint that they might be relevant to the NHSS programme (Oldroyd 1986 is an honourable exception). These failures to compare and contrast scientists with other workers makes the sociology of science vulnerable to precisely the same criticisms that have been justifiably levelled against the sociologists of the professions. As Everett Hughes, Julius Roth, and others (Freidson 1986; Hughes 1971; Roth 1974) have pointed out the sociologist who fails to make principled comparisons across a wide range of occupations falls into the trap of giving 'the professions' exactly that exalted, separate, privileged, 'sacred' status which the sociologist should be subjecting to critical scrutiny. That is, the sociologist must not treat 'professions' as a type of occupation *sui generis*, but examine claims to professionalism in a sociological manner. If sociologists of science fail to compare and contrast science and scientists with other bodies of knowledge and members of other occupational groups they are implicitly treating 'science' and 'scientists' as a unique phenomenon. Such a treatment accords science and scientists the very exalted and privileged status which the whole sociological specialism was designed to make problematic. The sociology of science is losing out by its failure to assimilate the findings of research on lawyers, doctors and other groups of similar class origin, education, income, and lifestyle.

Equally serious is the absence of research on learning environments in science and on socialization into science. There are no sociologists of science from any of the contemporary schools studying school laboratories, undergraduate laboratories, the training of science teachers, and little work on graduate students. Sociology of science is not informing the separate disciplines of 'science education', or school ethnographies, and these specialties are not being used by the sociologists of science. Here there is a striking contrast with the sociology of occupations which has always included research on socialization into the culture alongside studies of qualified practitioners. (See Atkinson 1983 for examples.) Many aspects of any occupational culture are most visible in studies of neophytes, and here the sociology of science is missing out.

The lack of research on learning environments and socialization by sociologists of science is odd, given the emphasis in the sociology of science on the production and reproduction of knowledge. As everyday, routine 'science' goes on in educational setting (schools, Further Education colleges, polytechnics and universities) it is in such settings that the reproduction, evaluation, and legitimation of much of the knowledge, methods, beliefs, and attitudes takes place. As Addelson (1983) puts it: 'Most of us are introduced to scientific knowledge by our schoolteachers, in classrooms and laboratories, using textbooks and lab manuals as guides.' There is a need for sociologists of science to examine normal science and paradigms inscribed in curricula, and the ways in which scientists' tacit knowledge is reproduced through 'craft' apprenticeship.

At first sight the lack of attention to gender divisions in science by most of the sociologists of science may seem to have little in common with the two previous gaps identified. Once this third omission has been described, however, the ways in which it relates to the neglect of comparisons with other occupations and of socialization will become clear.

There are six major issues related to gender divisions in science which are all missing from NHSS scholarship. The absence of gender as a topic in the sociology of science has prevented it being riven with disputes, which may be a bonus. Other empirical areas of sociology are suffused with controversies about gender while sociology of science appears calm. Yet there are six issues which deserve attention from sociologists of science, as follow:

1. Why are there so few women working in the sociology of science; such a small proportion of publications in the field by women; so few women on the editorial boards of the journals?
2. Why has the study of women scientists been left entirely to the Columbia School, whose work is widely regarded as inadequate on other issues?
3. Why does the field neglect/ignore the serious scholarship by women on women and science that does appear? For example Margaret Rossiter's (1982) and Evelyn Fox Keller's (1985) publications have been ignored by mainstream NHSS.
4. Although the majority of 'names' in science are male, there are many women around them who are totally neglected by NHSS. No studies exist of laboratory technicians, secretaries, wives, and daughters. Yet the two former groups of workers may be crucial for the production of scientific knowledge; the latter are sociologically interesting.

209

5. There has been no discussion in the NHSS literature of campaigns to recruit and retain more women in science and engineering such as GIST, GATE, WISE and so on. Other areas of science policy have been carefully scrutinized, but not those relating to women.

6. A substantial feminist literature has grown up attacking science as 'masculinist', and inherently hostile to women. While much of this can easily be dismissed as unscholarly there are issues embedded in it which deserve serious scrutiny.

Each of these points can be discussed at length, but the main issue here is that the NHSS scholars have, by their neglect of gender divisions and women in science, missed two important sources of insight into science.

First, focusing on gender divisions is a very powerful strategy for making the familiar strange (Delamont 1981). Precisely because gender divisions are regularly taken-for-granted, making them problematic is a useful way of highlighting previously unconsidered features of an institution, occupation or body of knowledge. Margaret Rossiter's historical research on the learned societies in American science and Evelyn Fox Keller's on genetics both exemplify this phenomenon. Scientific work and knowledge are frequently assumed by practitioners to be male domains, and for sociologists to treat this as a problematic assumption can be illuminating.

The second reason for examining gender divisions in scientific work and knowledge is closely connected to the reasons advanced above for remedying the other two *lacunae*. Much of the work women do in science is mundane and routine (as technicians, secretaries, students, and schoolteachers). Focusing on such ordinary activity would help to redress the balance of the sociology of science. Currently its emphasis is on studying the novel, the elite, and the frontiers of discovery and controversy. Researchers from all schools show a bias towards exciting, high-status men working in elite centres of 'big science' excellence. Most science is not of this kind, and by focusing on elite sites the sociologists are in danger of accepting scientists' own relative evaluations of the Noble prizewinner compared to the undergraduate when the whole rationale of the sociology of science is to challenge scientists' taken-for-granted assumptions. Given the six serious questions about gender divisions and the sociology of science, it appears that the NHSS has been less affected by the rise of 'feminist' sociology than any other empirical area of sociology.

An outsider who wanted to use the perspective of the NHSS to re-invigorate the sociology of education is left at a loss. When searching the literature on science for material relevant to a study of women's roles in the cultural reproduction of elites, only material on experienced male scientists appears – nothing on socialization into science or on women's roles in science that was sociologically reliable. For example the work of Jonathan Cole (1979) claims that science is universalistic and if a woman publishes as much as a man, and what she publishes is as good (in his terms, gets cited as often) she will receive nearly equal honours, recognition, and esteem. All the non-sociological, feminist writing on science denies that women are treated equally even when they do work of equal quality. The published studies from other sociological perspectives have not addressed sexual inequalities in science. The research on women in law and medicine could be used if it could be assumed that the practice of science was similar to the practice of law and medicine, but those principled comparisons have not been made. One could turn to the sociological research on the schooling of scientists and their socialization into roles to compare material on the schooling and occupational learning of women in other areas, but that too is missing.

In short, the tasks chosen by the researchers of the NHSS are a very limited sub-set of all the interesting problems in the scientific and sociological worlds. There are three major topics for sociological research which would be interesting in their own right, make useful links to other areas of sociological research, and, most importantly, serve to make some currently taken-for-granted features of science problematic. Research on the life of the scientist as a 'professional', on the school and college experiences whereby scientists are socialized into the lifestyle, and on the gender divisions in the field would highlight aspects of science which are currently invisible.

The occupations of university lecturer and scientist are similar in at least one important respect to those of lawyer and doctor. All four jobs demand a long training (6 years after school at least) and have power that comes from knowledge rather than material wealth. As women's career opportunities have declined in the 'semi-professions', where caring and dealing with people are believed to be the skills most needed, the ambitious women have turned to these elite occupations where knowledge is power.

There are three lessons here for the sociology of education. First there is a need to ensure that the occupational destinies of clever school leavers are included in the boundaries of the subject; second that attention is paid to the indeterminate features of occupations and the *habitus* of each; and third that research is needed on how recruits to elite occupations who do master the indeterminate features succeed in piercing Saturn's Rings and reaching the core of the profession. A sociological study of education which encompassed these three tasks would make substantial progress: examination of law and medicine makes this clear.

## Law and medicine

The legal profession was closed to women in Britain until 1919 and the passing of the Sex Disqualification (Removal) Act. Compared to medicine, where there are many histories of women's role, and many biographies and autobiographies, there are very few published materials on the early women lawyers. Elizabeth Garrett Anderson is much more famous than any pioneer woman solicitor or barrister. Until 1980 the number of women training for legal careers was very small, and the percentage of lawyers who were female was under 3 per cent. Since the rise of feminist sociology there has been a small amount of research conducted. Cynthia Epstein (1983) in the USA and Spencer and Podmore (1987) in the UK are among those who have provided data on women lawyers. In both countries the number, and the percentage, of women among law students and practising lawyers has grown remarkably since

Table 8.3 Women in the legal profession in the USA, 1940-80

| Year | No. | Percentage of total occupation |
|------|------|-------------------------------|
| 1940 | 4,447 | 2.4 |
| 1950 | 6,348 | 3.5 |
| 1960 | 7,543 | 3.3 |
| 1970 | 13,000 | 4.7 |
| 1976 | 38,000 | 9.2 |
| 1980 | 62,000 | 12.0 |

Table 8.4 Women lawyers in the UK, 1955-85

|         | Solicitors | | Barristers | |
| --- | --- | --- | --- | --- |
|         | No. | % | No. | % |
| 1955-7  | 337   | 1.9  | 64  | 3.2  |
| 1967-8  | 619   | 2.7  | 138 | 5.8  |
| 1973-4  | 1,299 | 4.5  | 252 | 7.4  |
| 1979-80 | 3,700 | 9.8  | 447 | 9.7  |
| 1983-4  | 5,497 | 12.3 | 641 | 12.3 |
| 1984-5  | 6,262 | 13.5 | 696 | 13.0 |

1940. Table 8.3 shows the rising number of women in the legal profession since 1940 in the USA, and table 8.4 figures for the UK since 1955.

Epstein reports that about one-third of women lawyers in the USA stayed single, and the figures in Britain are similar. Law, too, shows a pattern of specialization, in that women lawyers tend to specialize in certain areas (such as divorce) rather than others (such as taxation). In the USA many women have made careers in public agencies rather than private practice or in capitalist corporations. In Britain the division between solicitors (writers to the signet) and barristers (advocates), restricts the possibility of women becoming judges (only open to barristers) compared to the USA. As late as 1976 the majority of chambers had never had a female as a pupil barrister. The figures for women in the legal profession in the UK in table 8.4 show a rapid rise in the female percentage, and should, eventually, produce more women judges.

Epstein's (1982) work in the USA has no equivalent in Britain: that is, there is no study of the lives and perspectives of women working in legal occupations. There is a need for research on women working as solicitors in private practice, as barristers on different circuits, and female lawyers in public agencies and big corporations. The material and analysis in chapter 10 is inevitably speculative because there is a lack of such data.

In contrast the role and status of women in medicine has been better documented in Britain and the USA. In the USA Morantz-Sanchez (1985) records the history of women doctors, showing how females had become 25.3 per cent of medical students by 1980. Morantz *et al.* (1982) contains a fascinating selection of oral histories collected from women doctors born between 1903 and 1953. Lorber's (1984) book is also packed with data on American women doctors. In medicine a variety of surveys is summarized for the UK by Elston (1980). The proportion of women entering medicine has been rising since 1970, so that by 1978 37.8 per cent of medical students were female. In both countries women cluster in certain specialties (women surgeons are rare), and the most successful women are single and childfree.

The data available on women in other professions such as architecture (Wigfall 1980; Fogarty *et al.* 1981) are similarly sparse. Architecture has shown a rise in women entrants from 9 per cent in the 1960s to 18 per cent in 1980. At the same time few women reached the top of the occupation in status or earnings. Fogarty *et al.* (1981: 226-7) report that very few women become principals in large practices or earn the top salaries paid to male architects. As in the other top jobs studied by Fogarty *et al.* (the civil service, BBC, and industrial management) single women are more successful than the married.

These three occupations, and those of university teaching and scientific research are all jobs which ambitious women must enter to replace the lost career paths in teaching, nursing, social work and librarianship. There are two important issues for the sociology of education here which the researchers have not yet begun to consider.

## The new middle class?

Bernstein's (1973a) original statement was that the middle- and upper-middle classes in Britain were increasingly divided between those (the old middle class) who had material capital and aimed to reproduce the social order and those (the new middle class) who had cultural capital and aimed to interrupt the social order. Bernstein suggested that the two sectors placed different demands on the school system, and expected childrearing to be done by contrasting people. He stressed the importance of the role of the mother in childrearing in the new middle class as opposed to the delegation of childrearing to *au-pairs*, nannies, and other surrogates. What Bernstein did not analyse, and what needs analysis, is the role of the sexual division of labour within elite occupations. There are two important social changes associated with the increasing proportion of women entering elite occupations. First, the daughters of the new middle class are entering the same occupations as their brothers – using their share of the family's cultural capital as entry credentials. This is making these occupations heavily self- recruited, because there is less room in the professional schools for the children of other social classes. At the same time, there are signs of sexual divisions within these elite occupations, where males and females in the law, or science or architecture work in different specialisms or sectors. It is plausible that the female professionals are more heavily engaged in those sectors of the professions that deal with symbolic and cultural capital, rather than material wealth. Women lawyers deal with domestic disputes, women doctors with general practice, psychiatry (especially child psychiatry), and women architects work in teaching and research or town planning. Rather than search for certain occupations which form the new middle class, it seems more profitable to examine the possibility that women work in those sectors of the elite occupations which deal with the manipulation of cultural capital and symbolic property, while men are predominant in the sectors where material property is handled.

If this insight is pursued, an explanation for male and female performance differentials in the elite occupations may be found. Men and women lawyers, university teachers, scientists, and doctors may not actually be members of the 'same' occupation at all but be engaged in quite different social roles while holding the same occupational title. Some men will be functioning in the 'women's' sphere, and vice versa; single childfree women will be most common in the male sector of the elite, men married to women who are also professionally qualified and practising most common in the 'female' or rather the symbolic sector. If this hypothesis has a basis of fact the male doctor who told Epstein (1983: 335) 'If you want to spend an evening with an interesting, attractive woman these days, chances are she will be a lawyer. No one really bright anymore will become a school teacher or go into social work', will be in a different segment of medicine from the man who told a woman resident that being pregnant was 'presumptuous and a disservice to oneself and one's colleagues' (Morantz-Sanchez 1985: 360).

These issues need research attention, as part of the wider refocusing of the sociology of science and of the professions suggested in chapter 10.

# 9
## Mobile or nubile?
## Social stratification, mobility, marriage, and education

On the face of it the question of gender and occupational classifications is not one to quicken the pulse with the prospect of intellectual stimulation.

(Prandy 1986)

Women's conception of their world of work, and of the occupational world of the menfolk, remain virtually uninvestigated.

(Coxon, Davies, and Jones 1986: 4)

### Introduction

This chapter applies the theoretical perspective of Mary Douglas to the writings of the British authors on gender and stratification. It treats these scholars as a group whose cosmology can be located in terms of the group/grid system. The conventional work on stratification from other English-speaking countries could be located in the same way, but for simplicity only that from the British Isles is included here. Applying Douglas's schema to the British stratification theorists explains why their work has several peculiar features, including androcentrism and ethnocentrism. When those peculiarities are examined in the light of the group/grid analysis, several issues concerning the educational and marital factors affecting female social mobility, especially in elite strata, are clarified.

*Figure 9.1 Pollution beliefs in various cosmologies*

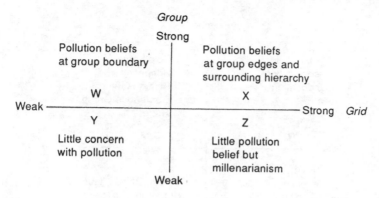

## Group/grid and stratification

Douglas's schema of group and grid allows us to predict where pollution beliefs will occur and how strong they will be. Figure 9.1 shows the four possibilities. We can locate the British stratification work in these terms, and the positions in which the authorities are found predicts their response to the theoretical and empirical challenge of feminist sociology. Since Acker (1973) there have been repeated arguments that the exclusive focus on males in stratification work cannot be justified either theoretically or in terms of empirical reality. While some of the scholars have seen these arguments as interesting and become engaged with them, a large number of authorities have reacted as if the feminist arguments were a dead mouse in their after-dinner brandy or a streaker in their college chapel or a dirty nappy on their breakfast table. That is, they have either become hysterical and abusive, or turned away from the issues in pained silence hoping it will go away.

Figure 9.2 locates the leading British stratification theorists according to their position on the group/grid matrix. The authors in quartile X have reacted to criticisms of conventional approaches exactly as if they were mice in claret: by violent anger or cold disdain and boycott. The authors in quartile Z are offering radical challenges to conventional accounts, which are utopian or millenarian in that their aims are probably unobtainable. The authors in quartile Y are those who are attempting a reworking of conventional theories by incorporating gender, and those in W are

Figure 9.2 British stratification researchers located on the group/grid schema

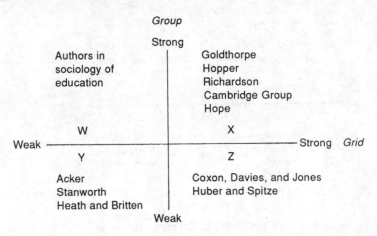

writers who have used the extant material in an unquestioning way in the sociology of education.

These four groups of writers are categorized following Douglas's schema of scholarly roles, shown in figure 9.3. Coxon, Davies, and Jones (1986) are classified as utopian because their data collection methods and their underlying theories involve such complex and time-consuming procedures they are unlikely to appeal to the traditionalists. Huber and Spitze (1983) have a radical theory of stratification that has been largely ignored because of its emphasis on ecology and housework. The classification of both approaches as outside the mainstream discourse is supported by the fact that neither set of authors is cited in Heath (1981) or Crompton and Mann (1986). They are outside the boundaries of the discourse.

## Women and the stratification system

Joan Acker (1973) was probably the first feminist sociologist to challenge the male-dominated, androcentric theories and methods of American stratification theories in the high-status *American Journal of Sociology*. Acker argued that American stratification theories, focused on white males, were losing touch with the reality of the American labour market. By ignoring women, the

*Figure 9.3 Styles within a learned discipline*

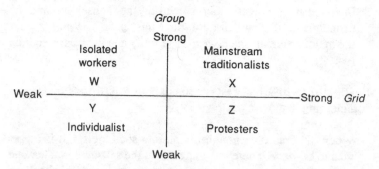

stratification theorists were developing elaborate theories that only applied to half the workers in the labour market. Marie Haug (1973, 1977) took a similar position, and in the USA a vigorous debate took place in the academic journals. When Joan Acker (1980) returned to the topic of women and stratification she was able to identify a large body of literature, and she found three different positions being argued in the debate that she had started. These three positions were:

1. that sex stratification is a separate phenomenon from class stratification, and sex stratification can either
   (a) be ignored by sociologists, or
   (b) be treated quite separately in data collection and theorizing:
2. that although existing theories ignored women, both sexes can be incorporated into those theories without any need to modify them;
3. that a major rethinking of what stratification means in modern society is necessary to produce a theory which includes both sexes and their labour.

Acker is primarily concerned with American material, and did not consider several British works which were already available. Since 1980 further data on stratification have appeared, and the debate has finally begun in the UK. However Acker's three basic positions have not been overtaken, for the material published since 1980 has fallen into one of her three categories.

As Heath (1981: 107-9) pointed out, most British stratification theorists took Acker's first position, arguing that:

in Western capitalist societies married women are primarily involved in domestic labour within the household and are economically dependent upon their husbands. The man's job is the major articulation between the family and the class structure. (p.107)

Heath (1981: 109) had reservations about this British consensus, commenting that:

Where there is such unanimity among sociologists, it is a good idea to be wary. There is a danger that the self-evident character of the premises will distract us from the need to check the conclusions...*a priori* arguments are no substitute for evidence. (pp.109-10)

More forcefully, Britten and Heath (1983) later wrote: 'The treatment of women in classifications of social class has become something of a scandal' (p.46). Their remedy for the scandal was to adopt Acker's (1980) second position, incorporating sex inequalities into existing theory. Acker refers to several American books which have 'added' sex inequalities on to their class stratification systems without reconceptualizing their basic tenets. The best-known British work in this tradition is Westergaard and Resler (1975) now followed by Britten and Heath (1983), and Heath and Britten (1984). The main result of adopting approaches of this kind seems to be that Britain appears as a more fluid and less rigid society than studies based on class only ever revealed. Goldthorpe has remained unimpressed by such arguments. However before examining the stages of the controversy that has developed, there is an important point to be made about it. Goldthorpe's theories about the class structure, the categories of occupations sociologists should use, and other related matters have been controversial for 20 years. Normally Goldthorpe does not deign to debate his position with his critics. Thus he has never addressed the issues raised by other male researchers studying social mobility in the UK, but ignored them and their work. Indeed the disinterested outsider reading all the studies of occupations and stratification in Britain finds several strange features in addition to the neglect of gender.

The available data on stratification, social mobility, and education in the UK are predominantly about males, yet that is not the only oddity about the research area which is obvious to any newcomer to the field. Equally noticeable to any outsider to the topic of stratification are the authors' failures to come to terms with their whole of the UK, to discuss each others findings, and to address serious criticisms from knowledgeable scholars. These four problems with the data on the class system of the UK have not, so far, been properly recognized in the sociology of education, where one study of men is used in an uncritical way by most writers. Before this volume can deal with the issue of women's mobility and elite reproduction, the weaknesses of the data base must be briefly exposed.

## The oddities of the stratification literature

To any disinterested observer, Britain in the last 20 years has seen four major English and Welsh surveys (Hopper 1981; Richardson 1977; the Oxford Mobility Study – Halsey, Heath, and Ridge 1980, Goldthorpe 1980 and 1987; the Cambridge Study – Stewart, Prandy, and Blackburn 1980), four Scottish projects (the Cambridge Group, the Scottish Mobility Study – Payne, 1987a and 1987b; the Coxon and Jones project, 1978, 1979a, 1979b; and the Hope (1984) follow-up of the Scottish Mental Survey), and one Irish project, all of which leave out women as respondents, are unclear as to whether their findings apply to the whole of the UK or only to one or two of its constituent nations, and all of whose authors are selective in their citation of the others' and fail to compare and contrast their instruments, methods, findings or theories systematically. It is time that a commentator who has a proper grasp of the mathematical techniques and the sociological issues produced a synthesis of all these projects and gave a full picture of social mobility in Britain since 1945. Here I want only to address the failure of all the studies to treat women seriously, point out some of the ways in which they fail to relate to each other, and give space to the fundamental challenge of the POOC approach (Coxon, Davies and Jones 1986).

Heath (1981) is the first sociologist in Britain to treat female social mobility as an academic topic and bring to its discussion both a scholarly attitude and the statistical expertise essential for reading the literature. Taking women's social mobility seriously is difficult, however, because most of the data available on mobility and education in capitalist societies are drawn from all-male samples and populations. As Heath points out Sorokin (1929), Lipset and Bendix (1959), Blau and Duncan (1967), the Oxford Mobility

221

Group (Halsey, Heath, and Ridge 1980, and Goldthorpe 1980) and the Scottish and Northern Ireland Mobility Projects (Payne, Payne, and Chapman 1983; Jackson) all used all-male samples. Glass (1954) did collect data on women in 1949, but they were not published until 1959 by Kelsall and Mitchell. Heath's list of all-male samples does not include those of Richardson (1977) and Hopper (1981) done in England or the Cambridge group (Stewart, Prandy, and Blackburn 1980), and since 1981 Hope (1984) has published an analysis of Scottish men drawn from the mixed Scottish Mental Survey of 1947.

The all-male sample is sometimes explained and justified by the authors but frequently the reader finds no discussion at all of the sexual basis of the sampling, although topics such as residence, age, schooling, and nationality are rehearsed. K. Hope (1984) for example, has written an important book on education and social mobility in Scotland, comparing it to the USA. He reanalysed the data from the Scottish Mental Survey of 1947 as part of the SSRC/DHSS programme on the 'cycle of disadvantage'. The Scottish Mental Survey gathered data on 1,208 representative 11-year olds, of whom 590 were boys. Hope addresses only the males, looked at mobility and adult occupation only for the males, and never spares a sentence to explain, justify or defend that action. Worse, at one point he asks 'What did it feel like to be *a child* in the Scottish system?' in 1947 (K. Hope 1984: 19) (emphasis mine), and answers his own question by suggesting that his experience in Newcastle will serve as a model. Perhaps he has not noticed that not all children experience schooling in the same way. Worse, Gray, McPherson, and Raffe (1983: 343) compound the error by stating that Hope's sample 'is representative of eleven year olds in Scotland in 1947'. However, as Gray *et al.*, while having a mixed sample themselves, mention none of the research on sex inequalities and discuss none of the issues, perhaps they consider that boys are representative of both sexes. Hopper (1981) drew a sample of 500 and had 183 of them interviewed by a team of men in 1965. Nowhere in his book does he explain or justify choosing an all-male sample to test his hypotheses about the 'subjective effects' of social mobility. A scrutiny of his text and his interview schedule reveals that his whole research project is built on sexist lines which are nowhere justified, and make assumptions about his respondents' social worlds that may not even be accurate. Hopper claims (1981: 2) that he became interested in the 'subjective effects' of social mobility when lecturing at Leicester University.

He claims that male students from working-class homes told him that 'middle class girls did not consider them seriously as potential mates' and, if such young men met the mothers of these middle-class girls they could not establish good relationships with them. Hopper therefore designed an investigation into 'the personal and interpersonal consequences of social mobility' (p.13).

His respondents were men in their thirties in 1965-6 from different educational backgrounds who were asked about their careers, health, and their personal, familial, and social lives. Hopper's assumptions about their lives are permeated with unexamined sexism. For example, when enquiring about reference groups, his sample are expected to have 'friends' who are all men, with 'wives' (p.125). When asked about their schooldays, the respondents were expected to have had 'mates' and 'girl friends', and at college a 'group of friends' (all males) different from the 'girls' they had 'gone out with' (p.255). There was no possibility of having women friends, at school, at college or in adulthood, and a man's reference group was assumed to be other men. Similarly when Hopper enquired about his sample's relations to see how far they formed a reference group, he focused on 'their brothers and brothers-in-law' (p.118) because that produced 'the clearest illustration of the hypotheses' (p.301). No-one is gay in Hopper's world, and all a man's friends are males.

Hopper's work is flawed in two ways. First, he never explains whether his hypotheses about the personal consequences of social mobility are meant to be applied to both men and women or not. It is not clear if he drew an all-male sample because his ideas only apply to men, or because he forgot that some women in Britain are mobile too. Second, he is guilty of poor methodology. Men aged 30-7 in 1965 may well have had all-male reference groups and all-male friendship groups, but this should have been investigated, not assumed. Indeed Hopper may have missed some interesting differences between his sub-samples in the matter of relationships with women because he did not design his instruments carefully enough.

Richardson (1977) worked with data from the Institute of Community Studies 1970 survey on leisure and labour. He used the survey data on 854 males aged 17 or more in the London area, and then interviewed 117 of them. Glass (1977) in his preface actually points out that 'the analysis has a ... limitation – it is concerned solely with the status and mobility of men. Women enter as mothers ...' (p.iv). Richardson admits that his research:

shares with most other studies of social stratification the weakness that women are left out .... Economically independent women are largely ignored .... It reflects the social fact that women do not 'fit', cannot be incorporated adequately into existing theories and measures of social stratification. (p.15)

Not only does Richardson leave out women from his sample, although the survey data included women and he could have studied both sexes, but in his interviews he fell into similar traps to Hopper. For example he discounts his respondents' opinions when they claim their wives are their friends (p.218)! If a man said his best friend was his wife, he was recorded as lacking a best friend. When he dealt with his sample's ambitions for their children, several of his questions referred to sons only, yet he felt able to conclude that men do not seem to have any ambitions for their daughters (p.315).

Stewart, Prandy, and Blackburn (1980) use two main samples for their discussion of social mobility. The first was a group of 1,918 male non-manual workers employed in establishments of over 500 employees within 60 miles of Cambridge. The second contained 5,000 respondents around York, Leicester, Cambridge, and Glasgow, half urban and half rural, in manual and non-manual jobs (Stewart *et al.* 1980: 12). The authors do not state that this was another all-male sample in the text, only on page 208 where they mention 'usable' data on 4,942 'men'. They do not mention marital mobility at all, and include no discussion on wives or daughters, or brothers-in-law. Theirs is an all-male world, where the maleness is so taken-for-granted it is not even mentioned. In short, as Payne, Payne and Chapman (1983) put it: 'The sociology of social mobility has virtually no female dimension.'

Another Scottish project needs mentioning here: that of Andrew McPherson and his colleagues (Gray, McPherson, and Raffe 1983). This research group in Edinburgh have data on nearly 20,000 Scottish school leavers in 1975-6, and surveys of 'qualified' leavers done in 1962-3, 1971 and 1973, plus a smaller group of adolescents who left school in 1979. Combining these with the Scottish Mental Survey of the cohort born in 1936, the Douglas cohort of 1946, and the National Children's Bureau one of 1958, they are able to examine pertinent issues of class, schooling, and occupational entry across a 40-year period in Scotland's history. They used the Registrar General's occupational classification, eschewing either the Hope-Goldthorpe or the Cambridge group's scales.

Additionally they have ignored all the debates about women and mobility, and treat their mixed sample as a whole for most of their argument; that is they have not used their precious data on girls to join the sociological debates on women and stratification or social mobility. Hutchison and McPherson (1976) did make one foray into the public discussion of sex and class inequalities but that is not followed up in the 1983 book.

In the absence of statements from the authors about sex differences in education and social mobility, the reader has to assume that their conclusions apply to both sexes. These are that 'overall class inequality in secondary school attainment or university entrance' was not

> substantially different between the 1948 and 1970-2 transfer [to secondary school] cohorts. (Gray *et al.* 1983: 225)

> The folk image of the lad o' pairts, and the accompanying notion of equality receive a sharp knock. Scottish education has been neither meritocratic nor equal. (p.226)

> Educational expansion has been accompanied by only very small gains in educational equality. (p.227)

Gray, McPherson, and Raffe are quite uninterested in elite recruitment and educational credentials, failing to refer to either John Scott's research on capital ownership in Scotland (Scott 1979; Scott and Hughes 1980) or my St Luke's data, as I have pointed out elsewhere (Delamont 1984c). While their book is of interest for many debates within the sociology of education, it has nothing to say about the education and training of elite women.

Before examining the data on women's roles in the reproduction of elites, there is one further complication in relying on these class and mobility data which must be scrutinized: the POOC (Project on Occupational Cognitions) *caveat.*

## The challenge of POOC

The Oxford and Cambridge groups have differences about the prestige scales that should be used as the basis of occupational classification. Both groups, however, have been challenged by the Edinburgh-based study conducted by Coxon and Jones (1978, 1979a, 1979b) reported in an accessible form in Coxon, Davies, and Jones (1986). Underlying all the work discussed so far on class lie classifications of occupational titles – whether produced by government agencies or social scientists. There are several severe problems with these scales or classifications of occupations. The most outspoken, high-profile, and even foolhardy defence of these systems is probably Donald Treiman's (1977). Treiman argues that his task was to examine 'the nature of inequality in human society' (1977: xv) and set out to produce an international comparison of all schemes of occupational prestige. Boldly striding out where no person has gone before, Treiman announces that 'men are known by their work' (p.1), and that in all societies with a division of labour, occupations can be scaled. Among the criteria that are used to judge the ranking of occupations – and 'people in all walks of life share understandings' – are (i) the skills needed to do the jobs, (ii) the physical demands of the jobs, and (iii) 'whether they are considered men's work or women's work' (p.1). However the most salient criterion, used by 'every adult member of society' is prestige. Treiman's book consists of comparing and combining eighty-five studies from sixty countries into one international prestige scale. He rarely mentions sexual divisions, but feels confident that 'the sex of the incumbent ordinarily has no effect on the prestige accorded occupations' (p.51), and that 'women perceive the same hierarchy as men' (p.59). Coxon, Davies, and Jones (1986) present a devastating historical critique of the origins and arbitrary development of occupational scales, although they pay little attention to the issue of whether women do perceive the same hierarchy as men.

There is one piece of empirical research, on the desirability of a set of seven jobs which all appear at the top of the occupational heap in everyone's schemes, which suggests that neither the sex of job holder nor that of the rater can be ignored. More than 20 years ago Rossi (1965) gathered responses from 3,500 women graduates on the desirability of women working in seven elite jobs. The seven occupations were architect, business executive, college professor, doctor, engineer, lawyer and research scientist, all of which are located in the top sector of all the occupational prestige scales, and rated as fairly similar when held by men. The female respondents were asked to give both their own rating, and that of their husband/boyfriend, mother, father, 'most women' of their age, and 'most men' of their age. While the respondents felt that these different groups would vary in their disapproval of women occupying these roles, the rank order of the jobs varied hardly at all. The seven jobs were seen as ranging from undesirable for women to highly approved for women in the following order: the least acceptable job for a women was that of business executive, then engineer, then architect, lawyer, doctor, research scientist, with college professor the most approved female occupation. The engineer and the business executive were seen as particularly unsuitable jobs for women, while the research scientist and college professor were felt to be very appropriate. It was, however, believed that men and women would see these least suitable jobs slightly differently: women were expected to be particularly hostile to engineering for women, men to business executive.

If we ignore women's jobs and women's perceptions of the occupational hierarchy, and concentrate on the POOC team's central critique of social mobility studies, they argue that *all* the conventional research projects begin by evacuating the data of 'subjective meaning' and then make 'unsubstantiated inferences' about those meanings when the data are interpreted. The respondents' cognitive processes are ignored and the complexities of those processes, together with their accompanying folk models and belief systems, simply left out of the research design and the theories.

Goldthorpe and the Oxford team have either never taken the POOC challenge seriously, or have taken it so seriously that they dare not debate it in public. The various authors of all-male studies relying on what Coxon, Davies, and Jones (1986) have revealed to be inadequately developed classification systems have avoided debating with each other, and especially with the POOC team. As the sociologists of science (e.g. Collins 1985) have consistently demonstrated, ignoring counter-arguments is the best way of destroying their scientific credibility altogether. Debating with opponents actually gives credibility to their arguments. Such a background makes the vigour and acrimony of Goldthorpe's attacks on those who have queried the treatment of women in conventional work particularly interesting. The arguments are given publicity and credibility by his attacks on them, and the very bitterness which fuels his writings suggests that there is more going on than a scholarly debate about the relationship of women to the class system.

The acrimony of the debate on women and the UK class structure is striking to outsiders. The emergence of Goldthorpe into public debate on the topic of women and the class structure in itself gives greater credence to the criticisms of stratification theory as sexist than to the challenges from Hopper, Coxon, and Jones, or the

Cambridge group. As Harry Collins (1985) points out, engaging in a debate in any academic area automatically gives greater prominence and credence to the ideas one tries to discredit.

Goldthorpe (1983) emerged from his habitual silence to attack Acker (1973, 1980), Allen (1982) and other critics of 'the conventional view' of stratification theory and research. He first argued that there was not one conventional view but two: one Parsonian, functional, and based on ideas about the needs of society, the other more European, starting from the division of labour, and associated with Goldthorpe himself, Parkin, Giddens, and Westergaard and Resler. This distinction was pointed out by Middleton (1974) earlier, and Goldthorpe is right to remind his audience that the two schools are rather different, and distance himself from the Parsonian approach. Parsons took his ideas about American society needing, for stability, women to remain confined to expressive roles, from Catharine Beecher who had adapted them from de Tocqueville, and while the vision of American women sacrificing all economic independence to stabilize the body politic has rhetorical possibilities, the majority of American women (especially Black women) have never had the luxury of experimenting with the expressive role.

For the purposes of the sociology of education, however, a different issue arises. Goldthorpe argues that European class analysis is interested in 'establishing how far classes have formed as relatively stable collectivities ... over time' and in understanding 'the class structure itself' (1983). That is a minority concern, and an esoteric one. Most sociologists are more concerned to use class as a variable in studies of smoking, domestic violence, housing, crime, suicide, race relations or educational achievement. Any sociologist of education who turns to the debates on women and the class structure at present will be unable to find an up to date, dispassionate account of where women 'fit' in the various class schema of the Oxford, Cambridge and Scottish groups, or in the Hopper (1981) approach.

Goldthorpe's differentiation of his own school from the Parsonian is couched in terms of an approach based on the facts of the work-place rather than the subjective evaluations of status in communities. In the European tradition different classes have different interests and class conflict is to be expected; in the Parsonian, the variety of status groups is a factor strengthening an organic whole: America. Goldthorpe also argues that while the functionalists did disregard women (because society's needs were not met if they competed in the labour market) the European class theorists treated the family as the unit of analysis because of sexual inequalities in the labour market. That is, because women's wages are so low, their fringe benefits so poor, and their chances of promotion so bad compared to their husbands', the finances, health, politics, housing, and other aspects of family life-style will be more dependent on what the man does than on anything women earn.

With this argument, Goldthorpe manages to do three clever things. First he rids himself of the American writers such as Acker (1980) because they have focused primarily on the Parsonian school from which he has dissociated himself. Then he ridicules any other critics who have not 'seen' the difference between the two schools. Then he shows that the European school was correct to collect data on all-male samples and write about men 95 per cent of the time, because of the inequality in the sexual divisions of the labour market. That is, feminists do not need to tell him that there is sex inequality in Britain: he built that into his theory.

The remainder of Goldthorpe's article is devoted to discussing the two changes in the social structure of advanced societies which have led some critics of earlier work to argue that it no longer represented the society it purported to analyse. These trends are the rising proportion of female headed, one parent, households; and the increasing proportion of dual-earner households. In 1985, less than 45 per cent of UK households were of the Parsonian archetype, and only 69 per cent of children were being reared in such a home. The single-parent household, Goldthorpe claims, does not create 'serious problems' for class analysis. The class analyst classifies the family according to the member who has the greatest 'commitment to, and continuity in' the labour market. If that is a lone mother, then the family can be allocated to a class. The dual-earner family would only be a problem if both adults were equally committed to, and continuously in, the labour market, a situation Goldthorpe is confident Britain rarely sees. He then attacks the work of Britten and Heath (1983) which attempted to analyse the importance of dual-earner families on family income and politics, and presents data from a 1974 follow-up to the 1972 survey to support his overall case.

Stanworth (1984) wrote a reply to this article by Goldthorpe which suggested there were logical and empirical flaws in his argument. Then Heath and Britten (1984) defended their 1983 paper against Goldthorpe, presenting more complex and detailed analyses to substantiate their earlier work. Goldthorpe (1984) then replied to both critiques, pointing out that it was 'congenial' to find that Stanworth did not altogether agree with Britten and Heath. (Hopper and the Cambridge group do not agree with each other either, of course, though both have criticisms of Goldthorpe to which he has not deigned to respond.) The detail of these arguments is not relevant here, though I have used some of the Britten and Heath material later in the chapter. What is interesting is Goldthorpe's violent reaction to the Britten and Heath material, and what it reveals about the cosmologies of British mobility research.

In the Britten and Heath research, the authors have classified families by one occupation if only one adult is employed, and by two if both are. Doing this means that families may 'move' from category to category quite frequently in their life cycle. Goldthorpe (1983) caricatures their approach in the following example: a man is a manual wage worker. The woman works for the first two years of their marriage in a shop, stays home to rear two children for eight years, works for one year in a factory, has a third child and leaves the labour market for five years, then goes back to the factory for one year, then gets another shop job. Goldthorpe jeers: 'An everyday story of working-class folk? But according to the Britten-Heath schema, the family has been class mobile five times in less than twenty years.' Goldthorpe holds this up as ridiculous, at least in part because such a fluid scheme makes the classifying and measuring tasks of the researcher so difficult. However sociologists must face the complexities of social reality, and perhaps that family has in all the important senses been 'mobile' five times in twenty years.

Essentially Goldthorpe is, from his elite position, reacting to the contamination of his neat model exactly as if he found a streaker in his college chapel, or menstrual blood on his study floor. He is an archetypal occupant of Douglas's X quartile where an ascribed hierarchy of mainstream traditionalist scholars have strong fears of pollution both at their boundaries and supporting the hierarchy. Once this is recognized, and the fears of the twin challenges from those who wish to take gender seriously and from the POOC perspective are seen as irrational reactions to 'contamination', the way is clear for true scholars to treat the ideas on their merits.

In that disinterested scholarly spirit, we can examine dispassionately what is known about the social mobility and cultural reproduction of elite women.

## Social mobility and elite recruitment of women

Richardson's (1977) argument that women do not fit into existing theories is important. Heath (1981) makes strenuous efforts to examine the data on women in Britain and see how their social mobility patterns differ from men's, and his conclusions are summarized later in the section. Researchers in the USA (Tyree and Treas 1974; Hauser and Featherman 1977) and in Canada (Tepperman 1975) have conducted more research on the social mobility of women than has been done in the UK and this needs brief discussion.

Acker (1980) argues that the American research on social mobility has been carried forward more by enthusiasm for new statistical, computing, and methodological techniques than by theoretical or political concerns. As soon as women were spotted as a legitimate focus for research, their potential as another population on which the methods could be tested led to a variety of studies. These investigations focused on the relative importance of marital and occupational factors in assessing women's mobility and compared the mobility patterns of men and women. Leaving aside for the moment the difficulties attached to all research based on scales of occupational prestige – discussed in the next section – the American researchers came to the following conclusion. The research of Tyree and Treas (1974) and Hauser and Featherman (1977) suggests that the marital and occupational mobility patterns of men and women in the USA are not significantly different, and the effects of educational credentials and family background on mobility are broadly similar for males and females. This does not mean that the destinations of men and women are the same; merely that they travel similar distances up and down the class system.

In Britain, Heath (1981) argues that there are three questions which deserve attention:

1. How do women's marital and occupational mobility chances compare with the social mobility of men?
2. How great are the inequalities of opportunity that divide women themselves? (i.e. the liberal issue of equality of opportunity.)
3. What is the significance for class action and class formation of women's occupational and marital mobility? (p.110)

It is noticeable that Heath does not treat women's mobility as a norm and ask how much males deviate from them! The data he was able to borrow to address his three questions are not of the same quality as those gathered on men by the Oxford Mobility Group, but are worth examining.

## *Marital mobility*

Men and women can both marry into a higher social class (hypergamy) or a lower one (hypogamy). A man may gain status by an hypergamous marriage: hence 'the son-in-law also rises'. The Oxford Mobility Group gathered data on the class position of their sample's fathers-in-law, and so can compare the marital and occupational mobility of their 10,000 men – or at least the 7,377 who had ever married. Heath (1981: table 4.1, p.112) offers a table of marriage patterns analogous to the occupational mobility table (table 2.1, p.54). Heath's comparison leads him to conclude that:

> The typical father from Class 1 is more likely to see his daughter downwardly mobile than his son, or, to be more precise, to have a son-in-law of lower social class [origin] than his son....A man's class position is likely to be more similar to his father's than his father-in-law's. There is both more downward and more upward mobility through marriage for women than there is through the labour market for men. (pp.113-4)

However, not all women marry – and the major thrust of the nineteenth-century feminist campaigners was to provide careers for single women. While single people are in a minority in contemporary Britain, there are class differences in how staying single is related to sex. There are women from the top social classes who remain single, whereas among men it is those of low origin who do not marry. The numbers, and the class differences are small, so 'the problem of high-status spinsters' (Heath 1981: 113) is not 'a major one'. However, the mobility of single women is greater than that of single men. Heath (1981: 121) adapting data analysed by Psacharopoulos from the GHS in 1975, presents the picture shown in table 9.1, which indicates that 37 per cent of single women are upwardly mobile while only 27 per cent of single men are, while 25 per cent of single men are downwardly mobile compared to 17 per cent of single women. The single women who are upwardly mobile are likely to 'enter a small range

Table 9.1 Origins and destinations of single people

|  | Father's class | | Respondent's class | |
| --- | --- | --- | --- | --- |
|  | Men | Women | Men | Women |
| I |  |  | 10.2 | 13.1 |
|  | 17.5 | 23.5 |  |  |
| II |  |  | 12.1 | 24.9 |
| III | 9.8 | 12.2 | 16.5 | 40.3 |
| Other | 72.8 | 64.2 | 61.3 | 31.7 |
| N | 315 | 221 | 315 | 221 |

of "women's jobs" – school teaching, nursing and social work' (p.120). These 'semi-professions' are, of course, among those opened by, or created by the feminist pioneers in the last century to enable women who did not marry to live respectably. As Heath points out, these traditionally female jobs may well have sex discrimination within their internal labour markets – in that the top jobs and high-paying posts are predominantly held by men – but they also 'provide a definite channel of upward mobility for career-oriented women' (p.120). It is precisely because teaching is a channel for the upward mobility of women that the loss of senior positions with the coming of co-education outlined in the previous chapter is such a serious matter. There is also a striking difference in the downward mobility of men and of single women which deserves attention. Among English and Welsh men some born into white-collar classes 'fall' into manual work, as both the national survey (Goldthorpe 1980) and smaller studies (Richardson 1977) show. This is almost unheard of for women. As Heath puts it (p.127) 'in the case of single women, those from non-manual origins almost without exception find non-manual work to do themselves.'

The majority of women in Britain marry. If we examine their occupational destinations we find a large concentration of women in lower white-collar work and in semi-skilled and unskilled manual work. That is if we divide the occupational hierarchy into two halves – manual and non-manual – we find women at the base of each half: absent from the top management and professional jobs, and from skilled manual work. This concentration of women produces more downward mobility for women, as the daughters of architects and top managers drop into secretarial work, and the daughters of craftsmen drop into semi-skilled manual labour.

Heath concludes that 'women have inferior chances of occupational mobility than men.... The concentration of women in lower white-collar work of intermediate status works to the disadvantage ... of women as a whole' (1981: 118).

If women as a whole have worse chances of mobility than men, it is important to disentangle the relative effects of class and sex in social mobility. It is generally agreed that opportunities for males are significantly affected by their class of origin. Heath (1981: 126) calculated the chances of women from different classes of origin (using the GHS data) reaching various destinations compared to men. It transpires that women have *less* chance of reaching top jobs, and less chance of sinking into bottom ones, than their 'class brothers', but because of the great concentration of women in clerical and service jobs there is a measure of equality in which women end up there. In other words the few women who do reach top jobs are more likely to have high-status fathers than the equivalent males.

From Heath's analysis, in so far as the top jobs demand credentials, educational success may be more crucial for girls than boys if they are to be mobile (or stable in the top class). However Payne, Payne, and Chapman (1983), using the 1975 Scottish Mobility Study (SMS), offer a rather different account. The SMS sampled men aged 20-64 domiciled in Scotland, and gathered data on the women those men were married to (or lived with). Thus material was available on women in Scotland who had entered the labour market between 1930-70. Payne *et al.* found that 'white blouse' work had expanded in Scotland, so that there had been room for working-class girls to 'rise' into the lowest non-manual category, and Scottish women had shown greater rates of 'mobility' than men. They also found, however, that the changing industrial base of Scotland was affecting male and female employment differently. Their overall conclusions were that among women there was little sign of the 'tightening link, between educational qualifications, occupational attainment and mobility' which has been postulated for men. (Their data are not sufficiently numerous or detailed on the daughters of Class I to see if that is true of elite recruitment.) Their conclusion is that once women are included the interrelations of origin, education, and destination become even more complex than they were for single-sex samples. 'Mobility analysis is a good example of a paradigm which worked quite well in a world where women did not work.' (By which they mean take paid employment!)

Heath's (1981: 135-6) overall remarks are particularly interesting as far as the subject of this book is concerned. He concludes that single women are 'more likely to be upwardly mobile' than unmarried men, and single middle-class women are unlikely to fall into manual work. These women are successful because they monopolize the few 'good' jobs in 'women's occupations', and, Heath summizes, may be more committed to their occupations than men or married women. That conclusion leads us neatly into the area of elite recruitment.

## Elite recruitment

Both Glass (1954) and Westergaard and Resler (1975) regarded the extent to which the top social class in Britain was self-recruited as evidence of British stability and lack of meritocracy. Heath's (1981) discussion of this issue is interesting and, for the purposes of this book, focuses on one especially pertinent issue: that of recruitment into different *sectors* of the top social class. Within the Oxford Group's Class I there are five different types of person as follows:

1. Self-employed professionals such as architects and barristers in private practice.
2. Salaried professionals such as university lecturers and scientists.
3. Senior bureaucrats in public service and commerce such as the gas industry, the civil service and banks.
4. Industrial managers in large enterprises.
5. Proprietors of large enterprises – that is owner-managers.

When one examines the Oxford Mobility Group's data on recruitment to these groups it is clear that categories 3 and 4, particularly 4, are the most open to upwardly-mobile men, while groups 1 and 5 only admitted a quarter of their number from the working class. Whereas the large proprietors self-recruit at least in part by transferring actual property (the firm itself, shares, stocks and bonds, money), the self-employed professionals give their sons educational and cultural capital. Not only are they the best-educated sector within Social Class 1, but their self-recruited successors are better-educated than the 'newcomers' (Heath, 1981: 66-7). As Heath summarizes it: 'children from privileged backgrounds have substantial, indeed grotesque, advantages in the competition for elite positions' (p.76). Heath must actually mean sons from privileged homes, for as his own data show, many daughters from privileged backgrounds fall into clerical occupations rather than following their fathers into Class 1 jobs.

Before discussing the material on women, a brief outline of the extent to which other British studies of men have found self-recruitment in Social Class 1 is a useful corrective to the neglect of Scottish studies by everyone in England, and of the Cambridge group by the Oxford one. Stewart, Prandy and Blackburn (1980) had a larger proportion (18 per cent) of their samples in Social Class 1 than the UK population as a whole (6 per cent). They had sampled 468 men with a degree, and 242 with membership of a major professional association. They found that 80 per cent of these respondents had started work in Social Class 1 (i.e. it was their first job). Having a father in Class 1, and attending a selective school, was highly correlated with a longer than average education (i.e. in school till 18, and/or entry to HE). Their Class 1 was self-recruited to a similar extent to the Oxford Mobility Survey's sample. Richardson (1977) reports a similar pattern in so far as no man in his sample with selective schooling and higher education had been downwardly mobile, and nearly all those who had had that type of education had been 'born' to it. There are, however, two issues that arise from the Oxford study's data that deserve attention. One is, do the differences in elite self-recruitment between sectors of Class 1 which hold for men also apply to women? The second is, if cultural capital is the explanation for the high degree of self-recruitment in Sector 1 of Class 1, what role do women play in accumulating and passing on that cultural capital? The first of these questions is examined here, the second forms the subject of chapter 10, and is also considered in chapter 9.

The access of women to the five sectors of the top social class is a fascinating topic on which the data are simply not available. Yet if cultural capital from the families of salaried and self-employed professionals is the best passport for entry to those sectors of RG1 and if daughters in those families have equal access to that cultural capital, then those women should have a better chance of becoming members of those occupations than men born outside them. This spectre was raised by Hutchison and McPherson (1976), who suggested that middle-class girls had 'displaced' working-class boys in the Scottish universities when entry standards rose, but can also be apposite to the self-employed and salaried professionals. If women born into professional families decide to use their cultural capital to have careers of their own, rather than to be new middle-class mothers only, then their natal inheritance of cultural capital should gain them entry to the professional schools and occupations, ahead of men without that inheritance. Crompton (1986) has begun to discuss how the increasing level of qualifications found among women in white-collar jobs may be heralding radical changes in the 'service class', and the issues in the professional segments of the highest social class are essentially similar, yet no one appears to be working on them. The sociology of education needs both to examine the relative standing of the different schools of thought in terms of the classification given in figure 9.2, and recognize the role of pollution beliefs in the debate. Then sociologists of education can begin to examine the implications for their discipline of scholars from quartiles X and Z rather than relying on the inadequate arguments rehearsed by those in quartile X. Once free to examine the ideas of the individualist scholars and the protestors, the sociology of education can use those insights to look at the relations between family, education, and achievement in a novel way.

# 10

## Professions and powerlessness: the inadequacy of the sociology and the chauvinism of the professionals

Sometimes I go to look at the deer at Magdalen and think that they brought them there to make the boys from large estates feel at home, and that probably the descendents of those boys think that women ought to be kept in more or less the same attractive and confined way.

(Cross, *The Question of Max*, p.119)

There has never been any question but that the women of the poor should toil alongside their men. No angry, and no compassionate, voice has been raised to say that women should not break their backs with harvest work, or soil their hands with blacking grates and peeling potatoes. The objection is only to work that is pleasant, exciting or profitable.

(Sayers 1946: 119)

The way to the top is still much clearer for women who, in terms of family responsibilities, travel light.

(Fogarty *et al.* 1981: 10)

The theme of this chapter is the sociological literature on those occupations which can loosely be termed the professions. There are three reasons for devoting a whole chapter in a sociology of education text to that sector of the occupational hierarchy.

1. The sociology of education has become dislocated from the sociology of work and occupations in general, and that of 'the professions' in particular, and that dislocation is damaging both fields (Atkinson 1981a, 1981b, 1983; Atkinson and Delamont 1985b).

2. Those occupations which can loosely be termed 'professions and semi-professions' are those which make up most of Bernstein's new middle class (if it exists), which demand the highest educational qualifications, whose stock in trade is knowledge, and in whose reproduction cultural capital is most central. They are, *de facto*, central to any sociological analysis of education, even if most of its practitioners have chosen to ignore the fact.

3. Despite a liberal ideology the professions and semi-professions have managed to marginalize and exclude women, or confine them like the deer at Magdalen, to pretty parks (chapter 8). This exclusiveness casts doubts both on how 'liberal' they are, and how limited most analyses of these occupations have been.

Chapter 9 presented criticisms of conventional research on social stratification which are important for a discipline which uses that material to relate to educational achievement. This chapter focuses in detail on the occupations in Social Class 1 which were particularly characterized by self-recruitment of males: the self-employed professions and the salaried professions. Powerful and highly-paid men and women in managerial and business careers are not covered here, but a parallel analysis of those sectors which are most open to the upwardly-mobile man and particularly hostile to women, is a necessary task for the future.

The chapter is concerned with two main arguments. It begins by examining the variety of sociological approaches to professional work which have been developed, with a focus on how each approach has handled gender divisions in those occupations. Then there is a section on women who work in science, pulling together what is known about them. They serve as a test case for the sociology of the professions, for the sociology of education and for the approach of this book. Throughout the chapter there will be material on medicine, law and science, though the analysis applies equally to architecture, university teaching, dentistry, and other professions. These are not, of course, all the occupations that would be categorized into the two sectors of Social Class 1 that Heath showed to be self-recruiting, but are both a reasonable cross section of them and occupations where data on women are available.

## The sociology of the professions and of scientists

The sociological literature on those occupations termed 'learned professions', that on scientists, and on the 'semi-professions', lacks any overall coherence or integration. There are several different traditions of research, and authors rarely utilize findings from other traditions. If a reader wishes to discover how sociologists of occupations or of science have researched or commented on gender divisions within the field of study, it is necessary to scan several different bodies of literature from various traditions. There is no book on 'top jobs' which examines gender divisions utilizing all the literature from all the scholarly schools of thought; nor is there even an overview of women in top jobs which has been informed by more than one theoretical perspective. Thus Richard Hall's (1975) student text on occupations in American society includes a balanced review of the literature on women and work, including work in 'top jobs', has a detailed chapter on 'the professions', but only uses literature from the structural-functional or trait theorists. Similarly Cynthia Epstein's (1970, 1981) writings on women in professional work only cites work by Merton, Parsons, Goode and like-minded authors; she fails to refer to anything by either the Chicago School writers, or Eliot Freidson and his colleagues. Books which show greater balance between traditions of sociology (e.g. Johnson 1972) have neglected gender divisions within the occupations that they discuss, and failed to accommodate the evidence about sex discrimination within these occupations to their explanatory frameworks. Thus Dingwall and Lewis (1983) contains not a single reference to Epstein's work on women lawyers, from sixteen authors in twelve papers.

In other words, this chapter is forced to do two things which should not, 15 years after Epstein, need doing: consider the implications of gender divisions for theories of 'the professions' and provide an account of women in professional jobs that does not limit itself to work from one theoretical school. Both tasks are undertaken in this chapter, complicated by the necessity of linking the analysis to the sociology of education which has allowed itself to become detached from the sociology of work and occupations (Atkinson and Delamont 1985).

The sociological literature on 'the professions' contains programmatic statements about them and their place in society created out of whole cloth, and empirical research on established practitioners (e.g. Freidson 1970; Thomas and Mungham 1983;

Professions and powerlessness

Cole and Cole 1973) and on socialization into the occupation in, for example, medical schools (e.g. Merton *et al.* 1957; Becker *et al.* 1961; Atkinson 1981b), or law schools (e.g. Phillips 1982). Throughout all three types of writing one can trace the influence of different traditions of sociological thought, at least two of which – the functionalist and the symbolic interactionist – have American origins.

## The functional and trait theorists

Those occupations commonly designated 'professions' were taken as particularly apt exemplars in functionalist theorizing: Parsons's (1951) remarks on medicine are a notable case in point. His characterization of professional roles as achieved, universalistic, functionally specific, affectively neutral and collectivity-oriented (Parsons 1951: 434) has been widely accepted by subsequent authors in this tradition, such as Epstein (1970, 1981) and Hall (1975). From the functionalist perspective occupations such as medicine and the law were marked by a high degree of homogeneity and consensus constituting, in Goode's (1957) famous formulation

> 'communities within the community', whose members share identity, values, definitions or roles, and interests. There is room in this conception for some variation, some differentiation, some out-of-line members, even some conflict; but, by and large, there is a steadfast core which defines that profession, deviations from which are but temporary dislocations.

This rather reverential view of law and medicine can also be found in the Columbia School of writers work on scientists (Cole and Cole 1973; Gaston 1978a). These authors have proved to their own satisfaction that science is 'a remarkably self-regulating social system, honouring great cognitive breakthroughs with extraordinary rewards and largely ignoring those scientists who make no mark with their research discoveries' (Cole 1979: 4).

Cole and Cole (1973), Zuckerman (1977), Gaston (1978a) and Cole (1979) have produced a body of work which argues that science is a social system which is meritocratic, universalistic, characterized by a disinterested search for knowledge, rational, and achievement-oriented. Just as Parsons used such adjectives to justify the autonomy, economic security, and organizational structure of American science so too the Columbia School are eloquent apologists for the American scientific establishment. Although the sociology of science does not cross-refer to work on professions to any great extent, the functional writers on both topics share a similar world view. The main American tradition which challenged the functionalists' view of 'the professions' was that of symbolic interactionism.

## The symbolic interactionists

While the functionalists had tended to reproduce the 'professionals' own claims, suggesting such high-flown ideals as 'service' and 'collectivity' orientations, the interactionists focused on more mundane aspects of 'professional' work. Writers in the Chicago vein have studied how members of occupations operate pragmatically and survive amid conflicting pressures in everyday performance of their work. The moral concerns of this latter school lead them to celebrate the 'underdog' (Becker 1961) while debunking the rhetoric of superordinates.

Whereas the functionalists tended to see 'professions' as a special category of occupations, the latter saw them as essentially similar to other jobs. Gouldner summarized the difference between the two 'schools' in this way:

the former [functionalists] are more respectful of the medical establishment ... they are more prone to view it as a noble profession. [Chicago sociologists] however, tend to be uneasy about the very idea of a profession as a goal for study, believing instead that the notion of an 'occupation' provides more basic guidelines for study, and arguing that occupations as diverse as the nun and the prostitute, or the plumber and the physician, reveal instructive sociological similarities.

(Gouldner 1962)

Consequent upon this desire to treat all types of occupation as potentially similar in sociologically interesting respects, Becker and Geer followed their studies of medical students with liberal arts undergraduates, and then turned their attention to occupational learning in different contexts. Rather than mounting yet another study of a single institution, they directed a number of small, related projects (mostly undertaken single-handed by junior colleagues).

These were deliberately focused on topics other than 'professions': a barber school; apprentice high steel workers; learning door-to-door selling; a county jail school; workers learning new jobs in an electronic plant (Geer 1972). Glaser's (1964) study of the working lives of scientists in a large organization is a symbolic interactionist equivalent to the Columbia-based work on science. In his Foreword to Glaser's book, Anselm Strauss writes (1964: vii) that the book

> can be read as if it were about scientists, but also as if it were about ... men and their work. The sociologists who study work and occupations are beginning to look closely at scientists as if they were not only innovators and culture heroes, rather than merely mortal, but also men who are subject to specifiable and consequential conditions of work.

This captures the flavour of the interactionist work – with its desire to see scientific work as similar to other occupations rather than separated from them, to focus on everyday life and career management, and to concern itself with men.

There are few citations of the functionalist research in that of the symbolic interactionists and vice versa, and to an outsider it appears that each school has failed to notice the research of the other. For example, Epstein (1970), a student of Goode's, cites one paper of Everett Hughes's (from 1945!), and makes one reference to Becker, one to Strauss and two to Oleson. Blanche Geer, Rue Bucher, Barny Glaser, Len Schatzman and Julius Roth are ignored. Similarly, Coombs (1978) and Haas and Shaffir (1977) follow the well-trodden path of *Boys in White* without deviation into functional work. Susan Leigh Star's (1985) work bridges medicine and science, and aligns itself to the Hughes/Strauss tradition. An examination of Star reveals that few symbolic interactionists have studied scientific work, that science is conceptualized as part of sociology of work, that gender divisions are invisible, and that the Columbia School is ignored as sociologists of science. In the same year Susan Cozzens (1985) published a piece of pure 'Columbia' sociology of science, untouched by other traditions of research.

In summary then, while these two traditions in scholarship about the professions were carried on in mutual isolation, they set the tone for research on both the working lives of qualified members of occupational groups and the aspiring students learning the role. The functionalists were over-reverent in their comments on the professions, and generally accepted the occupations' own self evaluations with their rhetoric of 'service' and 'colleagiality' (Gouldner 1962). The interactionists were more sceptical about such rhetoric, and focused on the everyday working lives of members of so-called professional occupations. The great strength of the Chicago School has been their analyses of survival strategies in complex organizations, and members' perspectives on the organization of their work.

## Other authors and a rapprochement

While most of the sociological work on 'the professions' in the 1950s and 1960s was dominated by one or other of the two approaches outlined above, there were voices being raised that neither group was moving the sociological enterprise forward. Johnson (1972) set out to show deficiencies in both approaches, and refocus the debate onto issues of power, control, and knowledge, while Freidson (1970a, 1970b, 1975, 1983) made the debate focus on the power professional organizations have to ensure the autonomy of the occupations. Jamous and Peloille (1970) made an attempt to re-organize sociological thinking about occupations by focusing attention on each job's location in a two-dimensional space of 'indeterminacy' and 'technicality'. Indeterminacy is their term for the 'hidden curriculum' of job performance: all the tacit, implicit, unexamined ways of being a member of any occupational group; for rules of thumb, genius, flair, and other unspecifiable aspects of being a chef, nurse, or streetsweeper. Technicality is the explicit, rule-governed, codified part of a job. Thus for a London taxi driver, 'the knowledge' and ability to pass the driving test are the technical parts of the job; being able to deal with drunks, rich Americans, bewildered Arabs, and other cabbies the indeterminate. For a lawyer, the legal knowledge is the technical part of the job; dealing with clerks, colleagues, and clients the indeterminate. (For a more detailed discussion of this work, see Atkinson, Reid, and Sheldrake 1977.)

Unfortunately none of the recent writing on women in the professions has drawn on these developments in theorizing about them, and the authors of the new approaches have signally failed to consider gender division within the occupations they discuss. Here I have tried to extrapolate from one of the fruitful analyses of the last decade to include gender divisions in my discussion of it.

Murray, Dingwall, and Eekelaar (1983) have offered a useful rapprochement between the functional and interactionist work, as follows. Murray *et al.* see tension between the claims made by professions that are directed outwards, i.e. made publicly in the wider society where occupations compete for esteem, power and status, and those which are made about the private sphere, where an individual client is the focus of the claim. For Dingwall and his co-authors, Parsons's (1951) idealistic and reverential statements are not simply an uncritical reiteration of "professionals'" own statements of pious hopes and self-interests, as Roth (1974) pointed out. Instead they are:

> telling us no more than what the professionals might tell us themselves, which may bear little relation to the realities of their everyday practice. Nevertheless, this account still has value as an induction from these public assertions. It tells us how professionals justify to a wide audience their claim to a peculiar measure of functional autonomy, the organizational forms and economic security which are said to enable them to adopt a dispassionate view of the general good.

As a contrast to this public claim – being disinterested, universalistic, altruistic, and on so – there is the 'private face' of a profession. Dingwall *et al.* characterize this as follows:

> a service uniquely tailored to its recipient, based on the personal experience of its provider, who is, in turn, entitled to offer the service not merely because of his technical competence but because of his social and moral rectitude.

These contrasting rhetorical claims are made visible when one examines the ways in which the professions are organized. Here, as Murray *et al.* point out, we find:

> Professions tend to form occupational communities with strong collective organizations. These articulate the public dimension of professional life. At the level of everyday practice, however, the organisational forms tend to be collegial, loose federations of practitioners in their own right rather than formal bureaucracies with clear, hierarchical lines of authority. This collegial model enshrines the individual discretion of the professional and this is further buttressed by the assumption of a

fee-for-service relationship with a client as the 'natural' mode of practice.

Murray and her colleagues argue that the tension between these two dynamics at rhetorical and organizational levels makes sense of many of the findings of research into the training and work practices of professionals. Among the 'shortcomings' (that is lapses from the idealized behaviour patterns eulogized by Parsons and Goode) which Murray *et al.* seek to explain are the 'strong suggestions that ascribed characteristics are as important as achieved in gaining entry to, and graduating successfully from, professional schools'. Also explicable are the reports of 'generalized universalistic judgements' being overthrown for decisions based on experience, 'and personal experience defeating formal rationality'. Dingwall and his colleagues summarize their position as follows:

> We have, then, identified the Janus character of professions. On the one hand, it is publicly asserted that they offer an impartial, objective and freely available way of resolving problems of social or natural order. On the other, a private promise is given of a service that is personal, individualized and oriented to the resolution of private problems to the satisfaction of particular rather than general interests.

In the tensions between these positions, at national level, at local level, and in the life of any individual member of the occupational group, it is possible both to assimilate the functionalists and the symbolic interactionists, and to appreciate where gender divisions may be included in our analysis. Also, while Murray *et al.* were not considering science as an occupation, the same tension is apparent there.

The public rhetoric of science is strikingly similar to that of the professions, and the Columbia School have celebrated the claims to impartiality, objectivity, and universality. The professional's promise of personal service is paralleled in science by the individualistic nature of scientific practice, where single scientists or small teams struggle to wrest novel meanings from experimental results, and build individual careers via their publications, honours, and communication networks. Here we found the work of the scholars who have grouped themselves under the label of 'New Historians and Sociologists of Science'. Harry Collins (1985), Latour and Woolgar (1979), Barnes and Mackenzie (1979) and Wynne (1979) all produce empirical work on the 'individual' level of scientific work, which parallels material on law and medicine cited by Murray and her co-workers. If we take both the Columbia School research and that of the NHSS seriously, we can see that science, like the professions, is Janus-like.

If we accept that both science and the professions are characterized by a tension between their rhetorical public face and their individualistic private world or everyday practice, we can begin to accommodate the data on gender divisions. As Huber and Spitze (1983: 5) point out, in nineteenth-century America the professions were only open to white males: '"Headwork" was the prerogative of a small group of elite men.' Since the 1850s women have campaigned for the right to enter these occupations, and gradually won. They have become a minority presence in all those top jobs, and a muted group within each occupation. As the Ardeners argued for anthropological research, listening to a muted group may reveal things about the society as a whole which are ignored, or misunderstood by a social science based on the dominant group's perspective.

For women to gain access to the professions they needed three separate things. First they needed access to the type of schooling which would qualify them to enter professional training, to certain kinds of knowledge and particular types of school. Then they needed to start professional schools equivalent to the men's ones (as was done with the Royal Free in London and the Philadelphia Women's Medical School) and/or gain entry to the men's professional schools (as was done with law). Once qualified they then had to find some way of practising as a professional; and here they needed to deploy the indeterminate skills of the occupation as well as the technocratic ones (Jamous and Peloille 1970; Atkinson, Reid, and Sheldrake 1977). Although women had succeeded in the first by 1880, and the second by 1920 for some occupations, and by 1980 for all of them, the third stage has proved a struggle for a century. It is the indeterminacy of the professions – their *habitus* – that women are seen as lacking.

The history of the first two phases has been documented elsewhere (Bell 1953; Harris 1978; Rossiter 1982; Morantz-Sanchez 1985) and needs only a brief reprise here, with a focus on the knowledge and the *habitus* of the relevant occupations.

## Knowledge and the professional training institutions

Freidson (1983) summarizes the history of the interrelationship between particular kinds of knowledge and professional training institutions, making the following points: 'the medieval universities of Europe spawned the three original learned professions of medicine, law and the clergy (of which university teaching was a part)'. These can usefully be termed, in the late Philip Elliot's phrase, 'status professions' (1972: 32) because

> The performance of the professional function seems to have been a less important aspect of the professional role than the ability to live a suitable leisured and cultured life. The professional's acquaintance with the knowledge available in society was symbolic of his status position rather than useful as a practical expertise.

As pointed out in chapter 5, classics formed the basis of the school and university curriculum for these occupations, and that was why the uncompromising feminist pioneers laid such stress on teaching Latin and Greek in their schools and colleges. During the nineteenth century in both Britain and the USA several 'newly reorganized or newly formed middle-class occupations' began to claim the label of profession 'because it was connected with the gentlemanly status of the traditional learned professions' (Freidson 1983).

Reader (1967) and Larson (1977) both describe this movement. Gaining the status of a profession gave an occupation a protected position in the market-place: only licensed practitioners could legitimately earn money, and the 'professional' controlled the licensing. Each occupation campaigned for recognition as a profession and for its protected economic position. Part of the campaign often involved excluding women who were earning a living from the occupation and/or defining the occupation as men's work. Thus women were, when the Buss, Beale and Davies generation began their lifework, excluded from the 'status professions' by lack of a classical schooling and a university to attend, at the same time as the newer middle-class occupations had closed against them. The uncompromising group set out to provide a classical – and hence vocational-professional – education for girls, but at the same time the classical domination of the curriculum was being challenged by reforming men.

At the beginning of the nineteenth century classics dominated the colleges and hence the schools on both sides of the Atlantic, but it was in America that this supremacy was first challenged. Boas (1935: 166) says:

> Latin and Greek were the backbone of a 'liberal education' ... the study of modern languages was thought seductive; such studies led students away from the ancient languages which provided the true discipline of the mind. Mathematics was included ... for the clergyman, Hebrew was added.

However, by the 1830s

> Latin and Greek were sacrosanct; but there was felt a growing doubt as to their absolute value. If only the professional men needed education, then Latin and Greek were the only branches of the tree of knowledge.

But if education was for a wider audience then 'a broader curriculum was called for'. Classics were 'of doubtful use to the ordinary citizen'. Thus, as Newcomer (1959: 56) has made clear: 'even for men ... the classical tradition was being challenged by the time that higher education of women was seriously considered'. Gradually during the century, the college curricula changed, and at the same time the college stranglehold on school curricula began to relax. Science education began to grow with that relaxation and Rossiter argues that 'the rapid development of secondary and then higher education for women' (1982: 313) in the USA meant that:

> by the 1880s and 1890s educated women ... began to encroach upon men's former monopoly of the nation's intellectual life. To head off this impending feminization of science, new barriers and restrictions, unnecessary earlier, quickly arose. (p.313)

One of the most formidable barriers was the doctorate, which few women's colleges offered, yet was soon essential in order to hold a post in the universities. It took until 1910 for women to convince the presidents of the doctorate-granting universities to award Ph.Ds to women. However getting a Ph.D did not gain employment for women scientists because 'at the same time that the universities were showing themselves to be liberal educators, they were also proving to be highly discriminatory employers' (Rossiter 1982:

314). Sex-segregated faculties persisted through the 1920s and 1930s. Women scientists therefore gained access to the education and the vocational training (the undergraduate and then the Ph.D degrees) but did not get the jobs.

Thus there were at least four campaigns about the curriculum going on at once; each being waged by different coalitions:

1. uncompromising women fixated on classics and maths, distrusting science, English, modern languages, and social science;
2. curriculum reformers pressing for science in schools and colleges, mostly men, but with some women scientists sharing their vision of the potential of the new subjects;
3. separatist women's educationalists who wanted a feminine, home-centred education for future mothers, and therefore desired both home economics and the newer subjects of modern languages, English, and so on to be allowed into the curriculum;
4. traditionalist men, defending the classical curriculum against both women and science.

Rossiter (1982) is especially good on why in America the male scientists did not want women feminizing, and lowering the status of, their fledgling disciplines. A woman wanting to be a scientist could face the hostility of male classical traditionalists, male scientists, the uncompromising females, and the women separatists.

The resultant complications, of the uncompromising feminists struggling against both male curriculum reformers and traditionalist men who did not want women to have an academic education at all, have been covered in chapter 4. The legacy of the struggles for curriculum reform in the boys' schools and the universities can be seen in the hierarchy of prestige and difficulty of subjects found today. Gray, McPherson and Raffe (1983: 89-90) report the hierarchy of subjects in Scottish schools:

The ordering of classical languages, modern languages and sciences, and social subjects corresponds to the chronological ordering of these subjects' emergence in the Scottish university curriculum and in the school. New subjects have had to compete for able pupils and for prestige against established subjects that opened the gates to the university.

Proving that women could learn Latin and Greek, mathematics, and later science, did not hamper women's claims for entry to the professions for long. Once they had the opportunity, the material was mastered. When medical schools were hostile to women, they founded their own, and although it took both the Sex Disqualification (Removal) Act of 1919 and the Sex Discrimination Act of 1975 to provide equal opportunities in all professional schools in Britain, learning the technical knowledge of these occupations was, eventually, made possible (except for Anglican ordination in Great Britain). However women have not managed to achieve equality either in numbers or in power and prestige within these occupations. The problem has shifted from the technical knowledge to the indeterminate, to the 'aura' of professional style that successful doctors, vets, architects, lawyers, and scientists have, the *habitus* of the elite occupations.

Atkinson (1983) has argued that research on professional socialization, done by both major traditions, has neglected to apply the insights offered by Bourdieu's work, especially the concepts outlined in chapter 2. For Atkinson symbolic violence, a cultural code, and the notion of *habitus*, offer analytic potential for studying professional socialization, to enable research on the topic to find a route out of stagnation. He develops this argument for medical students, and we have also proposed it to revitalize research on teacher training (Atkinson and Delamont 1985a). Of course, a profession, or its socialization, or its training schools, are not characterized by one single *habitus*. However: 'one very common component of the habitus can be indicated. That is, the emphasis on "personal knowledge", "personal experience" and "personal judgement"' (Atkinson 1983: 237).

These components are recognizably Jamous and Peloille's (1970) indeterminacy, and are akin to Freidson's (1970a) 'clinical mentality'. Fox (1957), as Atkinson (1984) has pointed out, has treated the indeterminacy of medical education as 'training for uncertainty' as if it were an individualized problem for the novice, who must make psychological adjustments. In reality, as Atkinson (1983: 238) points out 'The definition of "indeterminate" knowledge and its preservation is part and parcel of the politics of professional knowledge and professional power. It is a crucial claim in the quest for autonomy.' Indeterminacy is not the *habitus* of any particular profession, for there is always tension between the indeterminate and the technocratic, and always disputes, within occupations and between them, about whose indeterminacy is relevant and valid for particular client groups (see Atkinson *et al.* 1977). For the purposes of understanding the position of women in the professions, however, that part of the *habitus* of the occupation which rests on indeterminacy is crucial.

Bourdieu's whole argument about the power of the *habitus*, and about symbolic violence, is that mastery of the *habitus* is treated by the initiates as a matter of natural talent, of personality, of the 'virtuality' of practitioners. That is, a central part of the essential performance skills of the occupation is never explicitly taught but is believed to be innate, natural, inborn, and personal. Bourdieu used this to argue that the French secondary and higher-education systems *de facto* examined qualities that were never explicitly taught, which middle- and upper middle-class children had from their families but working-class pupils did not, and thus he explained inequalities in educational outcomes. Atkinson (1983) has suggested that 'the notorious propensity of [professional] occupational groups to self-recruit' (p.238) may be explained in the same way. That is practitioners of a profession and those in its training schools share 'a sort of "mythical charter"', that the sons (and daughters?) of practitioners 'have already assimilated much of the profession's oral tradition and habitus' (p.238).

It is plausible to look at the marginal status which women have held in the professions and in science as being due not to their lack of the technical skills needed for the jobs, but to their perceived failure to behave in ways which reveal their mastery of the indeterminate: that is their failure to share the *habitus*. Mary Rowe (1977) has called the subtle barriers that operate against women in the learned professions and in science Saturn's Rings. She argues that just as Saturn is partially obscured from us by its rings – whirling particles of dust and ice – so the real nature of much professional work is obscured from many marginal recruits (such as women and ethnic minorities). I prefer to use the powerful metaphor to suggest that the rings are obscuring the *habitus*, while leaving the purely technical skills of the job visible.

Before a more detailed explanation of what I mean here, it is necessary to substantiate the marginality of women in science and the learned professions, and examine the explanations put forward by other commentators, which seem to me inadequate because of their failure to address issues raised by sociological writing from schools other than their own.

Richard Hall's (1975) textbook on occupations is a piece of undiluted functionalism, in that research from other traditions is never discussed. He has, however, been influenced by feminist sociology and says that 'the women's movement has led to new data and new interpretations of old data in regard to the place of women in the occupational setting' (p.xi). When he considers the place of the professions in the American occupational structure, he concludes that:

> The evidence on women in the professions also suggests that the professions are not as universalistic and fair as their proponents and many analysts have suggested. There is both official and unofficial discrimination against half of their potential membership. (p.122)

This position is supported by Epstein (1970, 1983), Lorber (1984), Kennedy (1978) and many other commentators. For science the position is more complex. Hence, this discussion of how the ideas of *habitus*, indeterminacy, and Saturn's Rings can illuminate the position of women in contemporary science, and resolve problems which neither the Mertonian nor the 'new' sociology of science have dealt with. The argument which follows can be applied equally well to architecture, medicine, law, dentistry, or lecturing in French in a university, but science illustrates it well. The sociology of science is shown to be full of unexamined assumptions about women, and an alternative account based on separating the indeterminate aspects of scientific work from the technical is sociologically more plausible and less sexist.

## Saturn's Rings and the woman scientist

Many practising scientists, male and female, believe that the position of women is little better today than when Rossiter's (1982) history ends in 1940, at which point 'Women in all areas of science had reached an impasse. They could be educated to the doctoral level but would encounter great restrictions on their employment' (p.315). As Rossiter's book shows in great detail

> By 1940, women had been participating in American science for over a century, though in a variety of carefully circumscribed and camouflaged ways .... The essential structure of women's place in ... science had been set in 1910; thereafter sexual segregation not only persisted but even spread into other newly emerging areas of science. (p.314)

The careers of women who entered science in the 1930s, 1940s and 1950s were still being constrained by the sex segregation of science which Rossiter documents. Thus three senior male scientists who wrote a book aimed at the student wanting to do postgraduate research in science (Calvert, Pitts, and Dorian 1972) specifically warn women that their job prospects are poor. 'In the past, it has been almost unheard of that a woman would be elected to the faculty of a major university in the United States' (p.221). In 1971 60 per cent of chemistry faculties in universities had all-male staff. Women are unlikely to earn equal salaries (in 1970 a woman with a Ph.D in chemistry who had been in full-time work for 5 to 9 years was earning an average 73 per cent of the salary of the equivalent man). The authors say there will never be jobs for women in scientific administration because neither men nor women will work for a woman. All in all, they paint a gloomy picture of the future for a woman who completes a Ph.D in a physical science.

Jonathan Cole (1979), a scion of the Columbia tradition of sociology of science, will have none of this, however. He set out to answer the question 'could an institution [American science] that so nearly approximates the ideals of a meritocracy fail to approximate such high standards in dealing with women of science?' (p.9) Cole sets out ten widely-held beliefs about biological, attitudinal, structural, and behavioural barriers to women in science and then devotes a long book to demolishing all of them. His title, *Fair Science*, is his conclusion that science does operate universalistically and meritocratically: women who produce the same amounts of quality work receive the same jobs, honours, and recognition from their peers as equivalent men. (He had no data on salaries.) For Cole, the biggest problem facing women scientists is that they do not publish as much as men, and what they do publish cannot be as good as men's work because it gets cited less frequently. The rare women who publish a lot, and get cited a lot, are honoured as much as men.

Subsequent research (Cole and Zuckerman 1984) based on a re-analysis of fifty studies into gender differences in scientific productivity reveals that 'some important changes may be under way' (p.245). Cole and Zuckerman found that among younger prolific scientists there was a larger proportion of women than in earlier generations. The authors are now convinced that women scientists do *not* fail to publish collaboratively, and are just as frequently the first author. Cole remains convinced of science's meritocratic and gender-fair nature.

Irvine and Martin (1986) have contributed to this debate with data on British radio astronomers. They conclude that there is no evidence that women scientists perform less well than equivalent men at science, but clear indications that women scientists are sacrificing their careers to their husbands'. They conclude that 'only when work becomes less dominant in the lives of men can it become more dominant in the lives of women' (p.99).

Interestingly Cole (1979) says that his data and conclusions are received everywhere with scepticism and disbelief. Men and women, scientists and non-scientists, all tell him that he must be mistaken (1979: 81). A typical response to his work comes from Anne Briscoe (1984: 151), a biochemist at Columbia. She writes angrily: 'The scientific establishment, with a little help from sociologists like Jonathan Cole (1979), contend that women get their fair share of the jobs.' Briscoe objects to claims that the pool of qualified women is small, and then goes on: 'There is another spurious argument that women are less productive, publish fewer papers, papers of lesser quality ... of lesser quality because they are cited less often by other authors.' Briscoe implies that relying on citation counts is mistaken because Cole himself fails to cite her work (Briscoe and Pfafflin 1978) or that of Kundsin (1974). While Briscoe's anger is understandable, it can hardly be used to dismiss a serious work of scholarship. Cole says that most of his sceptical readers have personal experience of women being refused posts, which leads them to doubt his conclusions. Briscoe's autobiography is precisely the type of example Cole's critics use. She was born in 1919, and of her childhood says: 'you knew where you were then – girls were girls and men were men and all the standards were double' (1984: 147).

She received her Ph.D in biochemistry from Yale in 1949, and did a year's 'post-doc' at Pennsylvania. When she went job-hunting, her male coevals got an average of twenty-five offers of tenure-track jobs; she got three, none doing what she wanted, which was to teach biochemistry to medical students and postgraduate biochemists. She took a post in the psychiatry department at Cornell, an elite school, but she was isolated from other biochemists. She wrote to the chairmen of biochemistry departments and two told her explicitly that her 'credentials were very good; but each said he didn't want a woman' (p.153). She became an assistant professor at Cornell, and also taught at night at Hunter College. After marriage she 'relocated' to Columbia in 1957 and 'the chairman of the biochemistry department said he could not possibly make me an assistant professor' (p.154).

Briscoe spent sixteen years doing clinical research in the medical school, without a promotion. She says that: 'I was publishing, but I felt invisible .... I really thought there was something wrong with me: I had not worked hard enough; I was not smart enough.' After she became active in American Women in Science, Briscoe says she became visible. In 1972 Columbia promoted her to the assistant professor grade (the same level she had held at Cornell), and in 1976 she finally got tenure, after twenty-five years as a full-time scientist. Lest the reader feel this means that Briscoe was not a good biochemist, three women who won Nobel prizes have similar career patterns. M.G. Mayer 'never had a regular academic appointment until 1960, when she was 53' (Zuckerman 1977: 192). She got a tenured post nine years after the research for which she won the Nobel prize was done. Gerty Corti was 'a research associate' for sixteen years, did her Nobel prize-winning work at the age of 40, but only became a full professor at 51, the year she shared the prize (Zuckerman 1977: 192). Barbara McClintock did not have a secure post until 1942, when she was 40, and had struggled for twenty years on fellowships and grants (Keller 1985: 158-9). So while I cannot judge Briscoe's competence as a biochemist, the lack of a tenured job means nothing: she could be another Corti.

Given this case history, it is not surprising that Briscoe feels that Cole's findings and conclusions are wrong. Cole himself is not insensitive to the disquiet and disbelief that his conclusions engender. He spends a considerable time discussing why very few women manage to perform the role of scientist in a qualitatively and quantitatively similar way to men who start off with doctorates from equivalent graduate schools. Because Cole does not recognize any sociological literature outside the functional, Mertonian tradition, he does not cite any of the work on occupations, or on cultural reproduction, that would offer a way forward for him. A career in scientific research in an academic or research institutional setting is a professional one, characterized by indeterminacy and technicality. It has its own *habitus*. The work of the post-Kuhnian 'new historians and sociologists of science' is addressed to describing and analysing the indeterminate parts of scientific discovery, and it is to that part of the role performance that researchers must look to understand the lives of women scientists.

Barbara Reskin (1978), although herself an associate of the Columbia School, has produced a paper which looks at gender divisions in the social organization of science. Reskin's particular concern is the importance of collegial relations for the everyday practice of science, and the difficulties that many women scientists have in establishing networks that function as effectively as those among men. Male scientists rely on their colleagues to maintain their surveillance of the literature, as a reference group, for technical help, and for friendship. Reskin argues that because people learn sex-role behaviours long before they learn scientific collegial ones, and because the two systems of interpersonal relations do not fit well together, problems arise when the two systems have to be merged into one. She points out that male scientists can ignore the sex-role system and relate to women scientists as scientists or forget the science and relate only as men to women. More frequently they chose an intermediate position where 'they adapt conventional sex roles to the scientific setting to create a hybrid of gender and collegial roles that systematically introduces sex-role differentiation into the scientific community' (1978: 10).

Reskin argues that American society offers several models for male-female relations which are all antithetical to the truly egalitarian collegiality of scientists. These models include those based on kinship (father-daughter), on marriage, on romance (where the woman is reduced to the status of wife, girlfriend or mistress), or on quasi-scientific roles (where the woman scientist is seen as lab technician or assistant). All these models, where the man is in the dominant role, impede the development of egalitarian colleagueship for women – instead the woman is left in a position of structural dependence.

Reskin then argues that being relegated to a position of dependence excludes women from a variety of scientific processes. These include informal communication, collaborative work, and co-authorship. Informal communication, for Reskin, includes both scientific knowledge and professional information. She says:

> this information is sometimes available through formal channels ... [but] some professional gossip may never become available outside informal networks. Missing out on stories about a colleague's squash game or prodigious drinking capacity will not hamper a scientist's performance, but careers can suffer if a scientist does not hear gossip about who is helpful and who is not to be trusted.
>
> (Reskin 1978: 21)

Reskin thinks that lower levels of collegial interaction partially explain the lower patterns of co-authorship found among women social scientists. Sayre (1975: 96-7) argued that one reason why Rosalind Franklin's social relationships with her colleagues at King's College, London, were so bad was the barriers to informal contacts. Sayre writes that King's was 'not distinguished for the welcome that it offered women'. It had been built as a theological college, and even in 1951 women were kept

> in a kind of purdah ... male staff at King's lunched in a large, comfortable, rather clubby dining room, though the female staff – of any age or degree of distinction whatever – lunched either in the students' hall, or off the premises .... The lunching arrangements ... virtually ensured that, for women staff, encounters with their male counterparts were formal...

In Jonathan Cole's theoretical schema, the woman scientist is less well-rewarded because her productivity is lower both in quantity and in quality (by which he means citations). David Edge (1979) has produced a thoroughgoing critique of citation analysis as practised by the Columbia School because its proponents 'make implicit assumptions about the nature of science'. Edge sees Cole and his colleagues as glossing over the areas of science that other sociologists see as most problematic, and says they 'may be perpetuating a "rationalized" account of the scientific processes they are attempting to measure ... [which] systematically ... excludes key features'. In short, the Columbia School are using 'an inappropriately positivist and realist approach'. Edge argued for a sociological approach to science that gave precedence to the participants' perspectives, and emphasized the tacit and informal dimension of science.

As far as using citations as a measure of quality is concerned, there is a body of research which makes that part of Cole's model look dubious. Moravcsik and Murugesan (1975) examined a leading physics journal and concluded that one-third of the references in papers were redundant, and two-fifths were perfunctory. Edge uses these findings to argue that the object of a scientific papers is 'to persuade and convince' the audience (other scientists in the sub-specialty) to accept the line taken in the paper as a contribution to 'valid knowledge'. In other words, citing the other papers that the audience will recognize is a way of demonstrating that the authors 'belong' in the right circles. Nigel

Gilbert (1977) took up the same point in a paper arguing that citations are part of a rhetoric of persuasion. He goes on to say that some papers are seen as particularly useful legitimating citations and 'once a paper has begun to acquire such a favourable reputation' this snowballs, and its use increases.

Law and Williams (1972) actually observed a group of research scientists composing an article reporting a set of results. The scientists were trying to ensure that their discovery reached the right audience in an acceptable and assimilatable form as quickly as possible. Law and Williams say that the scientists were aiming to 'present their product to maximum effect' and so they '*package* and *place* it carefully'. That is, it must go into a journal read by their intended audience, and be written in a manner that that same audience will recognize as authoritative. Attention was paid to the title which had to be 'snappy' and to the opening paragraph. The citations were discussed into two main ways. Some references were included to papers that would enable the audience to locate the new work in the context of previous efforts; that is, they were cited so the readers 'have something they can look up'. However, there were also citations made on the grounds of friendships, justice, and charity, so that one senior team-member spoke of referencing as follows: (i) we must try to get C into the game; (ii) unfair to the C group not to cite them; (iii) must put B in, and so on. Citation here is not at all the rational, universalistic, idealized behaviour that is assumed in the Columbia School work. Instead it is part of a complex social process which is the subject of Collins (1985) and other work in the NHSS. Collins sees citations as one of the ways in which new knowledge, when offered to the core set that legitimate it in any sub-specialty, is packaged in taken-for-granted reality.

Core sets are small networks of scientists involved in particular lines of research, who legitimate the new knowledge in that line. They are private and informal, and their existence is only apparent to those involved in any particular dispute about new areas. Few scientists experience being part of one, but they are responsible not only for legitimating the new knowledge, but for producing an account of it along Popperian lines and laundering out the social and political interests that characterize all disputes and research lines, before the knowledge is offered outside the core set to the wider scientific community. Thus, citing work by core-set members is an important way of bringing new work to their attention, and claiming their legitimacy for it. Zuckerman (1977: 183-4) includes a perfect example of such a core set in her description of the reception of Maria Goeppert Mayer's research on the shell model of the nucleus. Mayer said that once she and her colleague had convinced Heisenberg, Bohr, and Fermi their ideas were accepted because 'the others don't mean anything'. Heisenberg, Bohr, and Fermi, with their close colleagues, were the core set in disputing the model of the nucleus at this period.

Citations then are not a simple measure of quality. Rather they are one token to be played in a game of getting recognition by a core set. The position of women scientists is more complex, and less under their own control, than Cole's (1979) simple argument would suggest. He believes that if women scientists published more, and did better work, they would get tenured posts, promotion, better pay, more Ph.D students, more esteem, visibility, and honours. In short, the remedy is in the hands of the women themselves.

However, an alternative view is possible and more plausible. If women scientists are in marginal jobs and low-status places, their work will have little rhetorical weight or persuasive power. Publishing more will not help, and in the NHSS perspective, the 'quality' of the work is a meaningless notion. Women scientists need to be visible to core-set members and/or members of core sets themselves, so that citation of their work has rhetorical power. M.G. Mayer achieved this, with her colleague, when Heisenberg paid attention to her shell model. Most women, however, trapped as instructors or assistant professors, are not visible to core-set members, so citing their publications has no payoff for other authors. There is no easy way – and perhaps no way at all – for a scholar to make her own work rhetorically weighty for others in the field. If it is possible to do so, the route is probably not through publishing more, or even through doing 'better' research, but through personal contacts: friendships, correspondence, visits, conferences, seminars, and co-operative work with core-set members.

R.S. Yalow gained core-set membership via Berenson, M.G. Mayer and G.S. Corti via their husbands; several British women gained it via J.D. Bernal. Cole's implicit advice to women is deeply flawed, because the way to visibility is through a variety of indeterminate behaviours such as demeanour at conferences, not through massive increases in publication. When Anne Beloff-Chain, a Reader at London University, told an interviewer (Wheeler-Bennett 1977: 55) that 'There is no prejudice in experimental science, you just have to do good work. The administration and politics of science is another matter', she is wrong. Good work has not only to be done, but be seen to be done. Briscoe (1984) argues that only when she became active in the American 'Women in Science' pressure group did anyone take her scientific work seriously. She had, though she seems not to be aware of the process herself, made her work visible. Once read, it was presumably acceptable to the relevant core-set in biochemistry.

Few scientists, men or women, actually see and understand the crucial role of the indeterminate skills whereby one's work is made visible to the relevant core set and accepted by them. Successful scientists understand the processes but, as members of core sets, launder them out of the public histories of how new knowledge came to be 'discovered' (i.e. how it came to be accepted as legitimate). Core sets are only characteristic of controversial areas in science, and include the adherents of both sides of the controversy. As Collins (1985) successfully demonstrates, one way of legitimating scientific work is to have vocal, powerful enemies (cf. the argument on stratification rehearsed in the previous chapter). Many women scientists are apparently not taken seriously enough to be disagreed with.

## Overview

The argument of this section, which can be made about other professional occupations such as law, medicine and architecture as well as science, is that women's failure to be accepted as full members of the occupation is due to the fact that many aspects of the occupation's *habitus*, especially the indeterminate aspects of job performance, are hidden from a substantial proportion of the members, including the women and the ethnic minorities, by Saturn's Rings. Sociologists have been equally blinded by the social equivalent of whirling particles of dust and ice, leading to inadequate analyses such as that offered by Cole.

Just as the Columbia School have provided a limited analysis of science, ignoring all those aspects of the occupation which are the central concern of the NHSS (e.g. Collins 1985), so too Mertonian analyses of law (e.g. Epstein 1981) and of medicine are inadequate. The interactionist accounts of these elite occupations are lacking in other ways, and both approaches would be improved by paying more attention to the analytic power of Bourdieu's thought.

# Part IV
## Conclusions

# 11
## The old middle class strikes back

The concepts, methods, relevances, and topics of sociology are accomplished in the social organization of the discourse.... The discourse is maintained by practices that determine who can participate in it as fully competent members.... To be recognized as a proper participant, the member must produce work that conforms to appropriate styles and terminologies, makes the appropriate deferences, and is locatable...in the traditions...whose themes it elaborates...and by whose criteria it is to be evaluated.

(Smith 1979: 147)

Dorothy Smith's account of how academic work has to be presented in order to be treated seriously is a good point from which to start the conclusion of this volume. Smith's analysis comes from an essay in which she discusses women as a muted group in sociology, whose perspective is not heard in academic theorizing. This book has deliberately focused on a range of issues which are currently as far outside the conventional discourse of the sociology of education as the work of Coxon and his collaborators (1986) is outside the discourse of social-mobility studies. In the conclusion some of the themes from the book are related to current events in British education because, as the chapter title suggests, the old middle class are striking back.

Since the election of the first Thatcher Government in 1979 there have been two sets of changes which suggest that the old middle class are fighting back against the new. There has been a series of measures designed explicitly to reduce the numbers, limit the power, and ignore the expertise of the new middle class and especially the liberal professions. Health policies which the

265

medical profession objects to, the abolition of restrictive practices in legal work, and the cuts in higher education are all clear signals that those who manipulate symbolic capital are under attack. As the attractiveness of jobs in finance and banking has been fostered, the balance of the division of labour by sex in elite occupations is shifting. Evidence outlined from Australia (Connell *et al.* 1981), the USA (Rossi 1965), and Britain suggests the upper and middle classes are enthusiastic about professional careers for their daughters, but not commercial and entrepreneurial ones. As the 'best' male graduates are recruited into the city, the professions become increasingly feminized. It is not a coincidence that these occupations should be attractive to young women even while they lose ground financially and in terms of power and influence. As the new middle class increasingly becomes characterized by dual-career households, and equal educational credentials for daughters and sons, the interests of that sector of the elite are under sustained attack.

The educational policies of the Thatcher government have also been those most likely to appeal to the old middle class. All those educational developments espoused by Hargreaves (1982) in *The Challenge for the Comprehensive School*, characteristic of an invisible pedagogy, are being legislated out of existence. A national curriculum which explicitly excludes the integrated subjects and all these concerned with personal development (e.g. careers or health education), is an extreme form of a visible pedagogy. Only one of the educational campaigns of the new middle class has been assimilated: a sex-blind curriculum. The insistence on science and maths in the core, for girls as well as boys, is the only issue on which old and new middle class agree. In all other respects the fears of pollution, and maintenance of strong boundaries between subjects and people, which characterized the old middle class are evident in government policy.

Throughout this volume the emphasis has been on using structuralist theorists to re-examine certain themes from the sociology of education. Bernstein and Bourdieu are the two theorists who can illuminate the disputes over the form and content of the British education system. As Bernstein (1973a) argued, that debate and policy change in education were a matter for the middle- and upper middle-class, who held different symbolic systems to be 'natural'. The main consumers/receivers of education, the working-class majority of the population, are powerless to influence or even participate in these ideological/symbolic disputes. For both Bernstein and Bourdieu their national education systems had shifted from ones of rigid, clear boundaries, sharply marked, towards ones where 'fuzzy classifications and blurred edges' (Bourdieu 1986: 154), and indeterminacy are celebrated. The Thatcher government is currently attempting to reinforce the sharp boundaries.

Sociologists need to understand that educational change is often not change at all, but shifts in the rhetoric about who does symbolic violence to whom under what justifications. It is crucial for sociologists to understand the symbolic systems which the two factions of the middle- and upper middle-class are ruled by and which they attempt to reproduce through the schools. A crucial aspect of these symbolic systems is that of pollution beliefs, and here Mary Douglas's group and grid theory becomes relevant. The old and new middle class (the bourgeoisie and intelligentsia) occupy different quartiles in Douglas's schema, and sociologists need to appreciate that.

This book has illustrated these arguments with a variety of educational material – but with a crucial extra twist. Throughout the work of Bernstein, Bourdieu and Douglas there is no indication that male and female members of any class segment might see the world differently. If the work of the Ardeners is added to that list it is clear that the sociology of education has neglected the perspective of muted groups, such as women, in the intelligentsia and in the bourgeoisie. Feminists have stressed the importance of studying the intersection of class and gender in the working class; it is equally important to examine that intersection in the 'privileged' classes.

Throughout this volume emphasis has been placed on how the emerging and changing intelligentsia have developed an education system to produce a new kind of woman. The changes in the nature of the product of the girls' schools are interrelated with changes in the sexual division of labour and the gender makeup of elite occupations. These changes have not been properly studied by sociologists, who have failed to appreciate that fundamental aspects of occupational recruitment, career structures, knowledge, and power are thrown into relief and made visible to enquiry by recognizing those changes.

There are then four main lessons that the analyses in this book could teach sociologists of education. The discipline needs a structuralist perspective, and attention to muted groups, a focus on elites and their educational ideologies, and a concern with the findings of the sociologies of science and occupations. This book

# Conclusions

has not been comfortable, and it does not easily fit into existing discourse. Structuralist analyses never are. The volume can end fittingly, with Mary Douglas (1975: 173-4):

> Basil Bernstein is an inveterate critic of sanctuaries in sociology and in education. For this reason his work is disturbing and uncomfortable...when we see reality it is not consoling. But it is invigorating to have the veil drawn aside.

# Appendix 1:
# The impact of feminism in the sociology of education

This appendix shows the ways in which the rise of feminist scholarship has influenced the sociology of education in general, and two specific empirical areas. Acker (1981) analysed the educational articles in British sociology journals from 1960-79 and compared the four best-selling introductory textbooks. Her article 'No-woman's-land' has a self-explanatory title and her argument is discussed in more detail in chapter 7. Acker (1983) also highlights the peculiarly sexist bias of the literature on teaching as an occupation where women have been either ignored or stereotyped in an unscholarly way. The treatment of women in the sociological research on teaching is, to say the least, bizarre. Many articles and books on teachers use 'he' and 'him' when 75 per cent of American teachers are women, and 60 per cent of British ones. One can even find studies of primary- and elementary-school teachers using masculine pronouns when teachers in that sector are overwhelmingly female. Developments in the 1970s within the sociology of education exemplified by Young (1971) and Sharp and Green (1975) and criticized by Bernbaum (1977) did not reduce sexism. That movement attempted to centre the sociology of education on the content of education, on the knowledge which is transmitted, and the social control exerted over cultural reproduction. That shift made the area much more theoretical – and so probably frightening to women students – yet failed to provide any analyses of sexual inequalities in the content of education.

Thus feminist sociology of education has to rethink not only the traditional work, but also the output of the 'new' sociologists of education. The resurgence of Marxist work in the sociology of education has not led to the incorporation of women, and in Britain these authors have paid little or no attention to gender inequalities under capitalism. The chapters in current books on women are written by women, and form little ghettoes. Despite the serious nature of criticisms of the male bias in the sociology of education (e.g. Lightfoot 1975; Acker 1980) the mainstream of the research area has flowed on largely indifferent and unimpressed. Work on women has been 'ghettoised' – given a separate chapter which is isolated from the rest of the contents.

For example Hartnett's (1982) *The Social Sciences in Educational Studies: A Guide to the Literature* contains a comprehensive chapter on women and education by Sandra Acker (1982). This shows the success that authors like Acker have had in getting feminist scholarship accepted. However, the succeeding chapter on adolescence and youth by David Marsland shows that the impact has been very limited. Marsland takes it for granted that adolescents are male, only discusses research on males, fails to list any criticisms of the area which have mentioned its male bias, and never hints to the reader that 'adolescence and youth' might include females. Sandra Acker (1982: 48) has commented that: 'Considerable research on women and education is now taking place' but she points out that it is not being incorporated into the mainstream academic disciplines and warns that 'some of the research results need careful replication'.

If as a typical empirical area we take either classroom interaction, or the pupil careers of adolescents, we find two things which characterize the sociology of education as a whole. These are: generalizations made by feminists on a shaky database which scholars with a detailed knowledge of the literature cannot accept, and a considerable imbalance in both the available data and in published studies. The two together go some way to explain the 'ghetto' that is women's studies in education.

The rise in women's studies has led to new journals, new conferences, new caucuses, new courses, but it has not yet produced any impact on the mainstream subjects. Some of the blame for this lack of impact has to be placed on the scholars in the new field, for as the next section shows, the claims made for the new research have sometimes outrun the data they draw on.

## The shaky database

The relative novelty of research on girls' schooling and the role of the school in reproducing sex-roles has meant that we still lack a large database on all the important questions. Because the reproduction of sex-roles and sex-inequalities in outcome have not been seen as national problems in Britain or the USA they have not received the research attention focused on class or race. This has allowed some authors to make startling claims on shaky foundations. The best-known claim about adolescents in British schools is that of Dale Spender (1982) who claims that, in co-educational, secondary, comprehensive schools, there is an extremely unjust division of classroom talk. She maintains that teachers devote a disproportionate share of their talk, time, and attention to boys and that the boys, in their turn, take an unfair share of the available pupil talk. Boys, Spender argues, make 70 per cent of the pupil contributions to the classroom discourse and, if the teacher attempts to redress this imbalance to give girls more of the talk, boys react violently to what they feel as bias. Spender (1982) says:

> it would seem that in a sexist society boys assume that two thirds of the teacher's attention constitutes a fair deal and if this ratio is altered so that they receive less than two thirds of the teacher's attention they feel they are being discriminated against. (p.57)

Spender has made these claims on the basis of some unspecified number of lessons, sometimes described as 'many' and sometimes as 'ten'. No serious classroom researcher would dream of making sweeping claims about teacher or pupil behaviour on the basis of such an inadequate and badly-selected sample of lessons. Flanders (1970) proposed that any generalization about a teacher should be based on at least 6 hours of observation. Croll (1980) points out that the ORACLE project is based on 47,000 observations of fifty-eight teachers and 84,000 observations of 489 pupils. Spender's own research is clearly not based on an adequate number of classrooms nor did it take place across a long-enough time period and range of subjects. The research she cites by others (Stanworth 1981; Clarricoates 1980) is also small-scale and cannot be used as a basis for sweeping generalizations.

It is perfectly possible that Spender's claims are true, but it is definitely true that her data are inadequate, her methods left so unspecific that her work cannot be replicated, and sex-equality not advanced by such polemical and unsubstantiated claims. There is a body of research in America on sex differences in classroom experiences which has been summarized by Bossert (1982). He reviews a number of studies and concludes:

> These results leave us in a muddle. Teachers do treat girls and boys differently, but the extensiveness of this differential treatment, whether it is perceived by students and how it might affect their sex-role behaviour and attitudes is unknown.

Bossert stresses that interaction may differ from one activity to another and across the various subjects, and we lack comparative data on this range of teacher-pupil interactions. He feels that teachers should monitor their own behaviour in this area, and that a systematic research programme needs to be undertaken. The verdict on sex-inequalities in teacher-pupil interaction has to be 'not proven' despite Spender's claims.

The inequalities of teacher-pupil contacts between boys and girls are one important topic where research is needed in Britain. I have argued elsewhere (Delamont 1983a) that such research should be done by sceptical males. We need to know whether there are inequalities in any subject areas, whether participants have any accurate knowledge of them, and also whether males and females think the common pattern of contributions found – whatever it turns out to be – is just and equitable.

## An imbalance in published work

One interesting topic in the sociology of education that shows the imbalance in published work is that on teenagers' careers as school pupils. Table A1.1 shows the British ethnographic work on this topic available, with the sex of the sample, whether the material is publicly available as a monograph or articles, and the type of school in which the data were gathered. (Full details of the works listed are given at the end of this appendix.) Two things are immediately apparent: fewer of the studies of girls have resulted in monographs, and as co-education has become commoner more studies do include both sexes. While there are enough data to make some generalizations about male pupil careers (though there is no published ethnography of Scots boys at school, and only one of Welsh males), there is next to nothing on female careers.

Table A1.1 Publicly available research on adolescent pupil careers

| Author | School type | Sex of sample | Book | Articles |
|---|---|---|---|---|
| Ball | Comprehensive | Both | Yes | Yes |
| Beynon | Comprehensive | Boys | Yes | Yes |
| Bird | Comprehensive | Girls | No | Yes |
| Burgess | RC comprehensive | Both | Yes | Yes |
| Chessum | Comprehensive | Girls | No | Yes |
| Corrigan | Comprehensive | Boys | Yes | Yes |
| Davies | Comprehensive | Girls | Yes | Yes |
| Delamont | Public | Girls | No | Yes |
| Denscombe | Comprehensive | Both | Yes | Yes |
| Fuller | Comprehensive | Girls | No | Yes |
| Furlong (1) | Comprehensive | Girls | Yes | Yes |
| Furlong (2) | Comprehensive | Boys | Yes | Yes |
| Gannaway | Comprehensive | Both | No | Yes |
| Griffin | Comprehensive | Girls | Yes | Yes |
| Hammersley | Sec. modern | Both | No | Yes |
| Hargreaves, A | Middle | Both | Yes | Yes |
| Hargreaves, D. (1) | Sec. modern | Boys | Yes | Yes |
| Hargreaves, D. (2) | Comprehensive | Both | Yes | Yes |
| Lacey | Grammar | Boys | Yes | Yes |
| Lambart | Grammar | Girls | No | Yes |
| Lees | Comprehensive | Girls | Yes | Yes |
| Llewellyn | Grammar & sec. modern | Girls | No | Yes |
| Measor and Woods | Middle & comprehensive | Both | Yes | No |
| Meyenn | Middle | Both | No | Yes |
| Pollard | Middle | Both | Yes | Yes |
| Tattum | Sin bins | Boys? | Yes | Yes |
| Turner | Comprehensive | Both | Yes | Yes |
| Willis | Sec. modern | Boys | Yes | Yes |
| Woods | Sec. modern | Both | Yes | Yes |

# The introductory texts

Because the database is so shaky there may be some excuse for the shabby treatment of gender-related issues in the textbooks which are used to introduce students to the field. An examination of the contents of introductory texts and readers presents a changing picture, but one that reveals there is a long way to go! Table A1.2 shows the coverage of gender in introductory textbooks in the sociology of education, table A1.3 that in collections of papers.

## Appendix 1

### Table A1.2 Coverage of sex-inequalities in introductory textbooks

| Date | Author(s) | Country | Table of contents Sex mentioned? | Women | Girls | Sex diffs. | Feminism or sexism |
|------|-----------|---------|------|-------|-------|------|----------|
| | | | | | | Index mentions | |
| 1960 | Cook and Cook | USA | No | None | None | None | None |
| 1965 | Corwin | USA | No | None | None | None | None |
| 1966 | Brembeck | USA | No | None | None | None | None |
| 1971 | Brembeck | USA | No | None | None | None | None |
| 1967 | Havighurst and Neugarten | USA | No | None | None | None | None |
| 1975 | Havighurst and Neugarten | USA | Yes | 8 | None | None | None |
| 1968 | Stalcup | USA | No | None | None | None | None |
| 1969 | Graham | USA | No | None | None | None | None |
| 1971 | Guthrie | USA | No | None | None | None | None |
| 1972 | Boocock | USA | Yes | 2 | None | 13 | None |
| 1975 | Brookover and Erickson | USA | No | 3 | None | 1 | None |
| 1978 | Parelius and Parelius | USA | No | 34 | None | None | None |
| 1965 | Musgrave | UK | No | None | None | None | None |
| 1972 | Musgrave | Australia | No | 3 | 4 | 10 | None |
| 1979 | Musgrave | Australia | No | None | None | 4 | None |
| 1969 | Swift | UK | No | No Index | | | |
| 1971 | Banks | UK | No | 4 | None | None | None |
| 1976 | Banks | UK | Yes | None | None | None | None |
| 1969 | Ashley et al. | UK | No | None | None | None | None |
| 1972 | Morrish | UK | No | None | None | None | None |
| 1972 | Hargreaves | UK | No | None | None | None | None |
| 1973 | Evetts | UK | No | None | None | None | None |
| 1974 | Levitas | UK | No | None | None | None | None |
| 1969 | King | UK | No | None | None | 2 | None |
| 1977 | King | UK | No | None | None | 7 | None |
| 1978 | Reid | UK | No | None | 4 | 8 | None |
| 1979 | Murphy and Denis | Canada | No | 9 | None | None | 1 |
| 1980 | Blakemore and Cooksey | Africa | No | 8 | None | 6 | None |
| 1981 | Robinson | UK | No | None | None | None | 1 |
| 1981 | Shaw | UK | Yes | 2 | None | 2 | None |
| 1984 | Fletcher | UK | No | 2 | None | None | None |
| 1985 | Burgess | UK | No | None | 10 | 7 | None |
| 1985 | Blackledge and Hunt | UK | No | None | None | 1 | None |
| 1986 | Burgess | UK | Yes | 1 | None | 19 | 2 |

274

*Table A1.3 Coverage of sex-inequalities in introductory 'readers' on sociology of education*

| Date | Compiler(s) | Country | No. of readings | No. on sex/gender |
|------|-------------|---------|-----------------|-------------------|
| 1963 | Kallenbach and Hodges | USA | 38 | Nil |
| 1965 | Raths and Grambs | USA | 31 | 2 |
| 1967 | Sexton | USA | 35 | Nil |
| 1968 | Pavalko | USA | 34 | 1 |
| 1968 | Stub | USA | 23 | Nil |
| 1970 | Cordasco | USA | 26 | Nil |
| 1973 | Sieber and Wilder | USA | 31 | Nil |
| 1974 | Cave and Chester | USA | 36 | 2 |
| 1975 | Stub | USA | 24 | Nil |
| 1976 | Figueroa and Persuad | Caribbean | 14 | Nil |
| 1965 | Halsey *et al.* | UK | 42 | Nil |
| 1970 | Craft | UK | 14 | Nil |
| 1970 | Swift | UK | 18 | Nil |
| 1971 | Cosin *et al.* | UK | 40 | Nil |
| 1971 | Hopper | UK | 12 | Nil |
| 1972 | Cosin | UK | 15 | Nil |
| 1973 | Silver | UK | 34 | Nil |
| 1973 | Raynor and Harden | UK | 49 | Nil |
| 1974 | Eggleston | UK | 22 | Nil |
| 1974 | Fludo and Ahior | UK | 10 | 1 |
| 1977 | Karabel and Halsey | USA | 38 | Nil |

Between 1976-85 I have examined thirty-three books in the sociology of education from Britain and the USA. There were fifteen introductory texts and eighteen collections of readings. Where two substantially different editions of a book existed I examined both. In each case the table of contents and the index were scrutinized for mentions of women, girls, or sex differences, sexism or feminism. Any references which existed were examined, books without such references were skimmed. In most cases these preliminary inspections were not encouraging. For example, opening Havighurst and Neugarten (1967) one is confronted by cameos of classrooms, one of which is meant to be a portrayal of an outstandingly good teacher in the slums. Three pupils are mentioned as excellent products of the teacher's work: a boy taught many years earlier who has won a fellowship to do graduate work in chemistry, and two currently in the class. One of these, a negro boy, is described as having the potential to be a scientist or doctor. The other, Maria, a Puerto Rican girl, has 'looks', 'talent' and could be a 'great dancer'. The teacher is instructing her in 'manners' so that she will 'be accepted by the people she would have to work with' (p.5). The lesson is clear – boys can use academic success and brains to master science and escape the ghetto. Girls have a better chance of escape if their bodies are supple and pretty.

A more systematic survey of the sexism in these introductory texts is given below. The full list of texts examined is given at the end of the appendix. Tables A1.2 and A1.3 demonstrate the neglect of women in conventional sociology of education texts and readers. Only four texts (Shaw, Parelius and Parelius, Boocock, and Banks) mention a section on women in their table of contents and only four readers have papers on women. A survey of the indexes is equally dispiriting. Only twelve of the text books consider any aspect of women and education important enough to index. The bias of these works is even more apparent when one examines what they do consider worth indexing and hence discussing. Havighurst and Neugarten (1967) ignored women but covered feral children (those reared by wild animals like Romulus and Remus). Cordasco indexes Eskimos but not women. Stub has two references to Richard Nixon and Morrish five on cybernetics. However, there is a clear trend towards including something on women, girls or sex-inequalities in the more recent books. Thus the fourth (1975) edition of Havighurst and Neugarten adds the topic, while Parelius and Parelius (1978) cover it quite extensively. In more recent volumes, the omission of sex and gender causes comment, so that reviews of Fletcher (1984) and Blackledge and Hunt (1985) specifically mentioned that they omitted sex-inequalities as a criticism of them.

It would be all too easy, however, to relax in the light of the coverage given to women and education in a text such as Burgess (1985) or a Reader such as that accompanying the Open University E205 Course (Purvis and Hales 1983) and feel that the point has been established. One glance at Hope (1984) will dispel any complacency. Hope, as chapter 9 reveals, is still locked into the paradigm of men defining male experience as universal on the basis of an all-male sample.

## Data sources for appendix 1

*Part 1: Adolescent careers (table A1.1)*

This list refers the reader to the most easily available source on the research. Full details of one publication per author are given, unless the work is already cited in the main bibliography.

Ball, S. (1981) – see main bibliography
Beynon, J. (1985) *Initial Encounters in the Secondary School,* London: Falmer
Bird, C. *et al.* (1980) *Disaffected Pupils,* Uxbridge, Middx.: Brunel University
Burgess, R.G. (1983) *Experiencing Comprehensive Education,* London: Methuen
Chessum, R. (1980) in Bird *et al., Disaffected Pupils*
Corrigan, P. (1979) *Schooling the Smash Street Kids,* London: Macmillan
Davies, L. (1984) *Pupil Power,* London: Falmer
Delamont, S. (1984c) – see main bibliography
Denscombe, M. (1984) 'Keeping'em quiet'. in S.Delamont (ed.) *Readings on Interaction in the Classroom,* London: Methuen
Fuller, M. (1980) 'Black girls in a London comprehensive'. in R.Deem (ed.) – see main bibliography
Furlong, V.J. (1976) 'Interaction sets in the classroom' in M.Stubbs and S.Delamont (eds) *Explorations in Classroom Observation,* Chichester: Wiley
Furlong, V.J. (1980) in Bird *et al., Disaffected Pupils*
Gannaway, H. (1976) 'Making sense of school'. in M.Stubbs and S.Delamont (eds) *Explorations in Classroom Observation,* Chichester: Wiley
Griffin, C. (1985) *Typical Girls?,* London: Routledge
Hammersley, M. (1974) 'The organization of pupil participation', *Sociological Review* 22, 3: 355-68
Hargreaves, A. (1986) *The Two Cultures of Schooling,* London: Falmer
Hargreaves, D. (1967) – see main bibliography
Hargreaves, D. *et al.* (1975) *Deviance in Classrooms,* London: Routledge
Lacey, C. (1970) – see main bibliography
Lambart, A. (1982) 'The expulsion'. in R.Frankenberg (ed.) *Custom and Conflict in Britain,* Manchester: The University Press
Llewellyn, M. (1980) 'Studying girls at school', in R.Deem (ed.) – see main bibloigraphy
Measor, L. and Woods, P. (1984) – see main bibliography
Mayenn, R. (1980) 'Schoolgirls' peer groups', in A.Hargreaves and L.Tickle (eds) *Middle Schools,* London: Harper and Row
Pollard, A. (1985) *The Social World of the Primary School,* London: Holt Saunders
Tattum, D. (1982) *Disruptive Pupils in Schools and Units,* Chichester: Wiley

## Appendix 1

Turner, G. (1983) *The Social World of the Comprehensive School*, London: Croom Helm
Willis, P. (1977) – see main bibliography
Woods, P. (1979) *The Divided School*, London: Routledge

## Part 2: Sociology of education books (table A1.2)

Books listed in the main bibliography are not included here. Books are listed in the order in which they appear in the table (chronological order).

Cook, L.A. and Cook, E.F. (1960) *A Sociological Approach to Education* (3rd ed.), New York: McGraw Hill
Corwin, R.G. (1965) *A Sociology of Education*, New York: Appleton, Century, Crofts
Brembeck, Cole S. (1966) *The Social Foundations of Education*, New York: Wiley (2nd ed. 1971)
Havighurst, R.J. and Neugarten, B. (1967) *Society and Education*, Boston: Allyn & Bacon (4th ed. 1975)
Stalcup, R. (1968) *Sociology and Education*, Columbus: Merrill Pub. Co.
Graham, Grace (1969) *The Public School in the New Society*, New York: Harper and Row
Boocock, S.S. (1972) *An Introduction to the Sociology of Learning*, New York: Houghton Mifflin
Brookover, W.B. and Erickson, E.L. (1975) *Sociology of Education*, Illinois: The Dorsey Press
Parelius, A. and Parelius, R.J. (1978) *The Sociology of Education*, Englewood Cliffs, NJ: Prentice Hall
Swift, D. (1969) *The Sociology of Education*, London: Routledge and Kegan Paul
Ashley, B.J., Cohen, H., and Slatter, R. (1969) *An Introduction to the Sociology of Education*, London: Macmillan
Morrish, I. (1972) *The Sociology of Education*, London: Allen and Unwin
Hargreaves, D. (1972) *Interpersonal Relations and Education*, London: Routledge and Kegan Paul
Evetts, J. (1973) *The Sociology of Educational Ideas*, London: Routledge
Levitas, M. (1974) *Marxist Perspectives in the Sociology of Education*, London: Routledge and Kegan Paul
King, R. (1969) *Education*, London: Longmans (2nd ed. 1977)
Reid, I. (1978) *Sociological Perspectives on School and Education*, London: Open Books
Murphy, R. and Denis, A. (1979) *Sociological Themes in Education*, Toronto: McGraw Hill Ryerson
Blakemore, K. and Cooksey, B. (1980) *A Sociology of Education for Africa*, London: Allen and Unwin
Robinson, P. (1981) *Perspectives on the Sociology of Education*, London: Routledge

278

Shaw, B. (1981) *Educational Practice and Sociology*, Oxford: Martin Robertson
Fletcher, R. (1964) *Education in Society*, Harmondsworth, Middx: Penguin
Burgess, R.G. (1985) *Education, Schools and Schooling*, London: Macmillan
Blackledge, D. and Hunt, B. (1985) *Sociological Interpretations of Education*, London: Croom Helm
Burgess, R.G. (1986) *Sociology, Education and Schools*, London: Batsford

## Part 3: Readings on sociology of education (table A1.3)

These are also listed in chronological order and exclude those in the main bibliography.

Kallenbach, W.W. and Hodges, H.M. (eds) (1963) *Education and Society*, Columbus: Merrill Books
Raths, J. and Grambs, J.D. (eds) (1965) *Society and Education*, New York: Prentice Hall
Sexton, P. (ed.) (1967) *Readings on the School in Society*, New York: Prentice Hall
Pavalko, R.M. (ed.) (1968) *Sociology of Education*, Itasca, Illinois: Peacock
Stub, H.R. (ed.) (1968) *The Sociology of Education* (3rd ed. 1975)
Cordasco, F. (ed.) (1970) *The School and the Social Order*, Scranton, Pa: Intext
Sieber, S.D. and Wilder, D.E. (eds) (1973) *The School in Society*, New York: The Free Press
Cave, W. and Chester, M. (eds) (1974) *Sociology of Education*, London: Collier-Macmillan
Figueroa, P.M.E. and Persuad, G. (eds) (1976) *Sociology of Education*, London: OUP
Halsey, A.H. *et al.* (eds) (1965) *Education, Economy and Society*, London: Collier-Macmillan
Craft, M. (ed.) (1970) *Family, Class and Education*, London: Longmans
Swift, D. (ed.) (1970) *Basic Readings in the Sociology of Education*, London: Routledge
Cosin, B *et al.* (eds) (1971) *School and Society*, London: Routledge
Hopper, E. (ed.) (1971) *Readings in the Theory of Education Systems*, London: Hutchinson
Cosin, B. (ed.) (1972) *Education: Structure and Society*, Harmondsworth, Middx: Penguin
Silver, H. (ed.) (1973) *Equal Opportunity in Education*, London: Methuen
Raynor, J. and Harden, J. (eds) (1973) *Readings in Urban Education (2 vols)*, London: Routledge and Kegan Paul
Eggleston, S.J. (ed.) (1974) *Contemporary Research in the Sociology of Education*

# Appendix 1

Flude, M. and Ahier, J. (eds) (1974) *Educability, Schools, and Ideology*, London: Croom Helm

Karabel, J. and Halsey, A.H. (eds) (1977) *Power and Ideology in Education*, New York: OUP

Purvis, J. and Hales, M. (eds) (1983) *Achievement and Inequality in Education*, London: Routledge and Kegan Paul

# Appendix 2:
# A note on the history of education

There are three main perspectives on the history of education in nineteenth-century Britain and America. One tradition sees the development of mass education as a 'good' thing, which a benevolent upper class provided for the workers despite opposition from reactionaries. In these accounts the working classes' own educational institutions are ignored, and the idea that the owners of capital deliberately introduced education to produce a docile workforce is not stressed. An example of such a 'liberal' historian is Pauline Gregg (1950). A minority of historians, notably Brian Simon (1974) and Harold Silver (1980) have offered a Marxist version of the development of mass education in which both working-class aspirations and achievements are thoroughly discussed, and the relationship between a capitalist economy and an emergent education system is explored. These historians do, however, generally regard education as potentially liberating and beneficial for the working class. Most recently a new group of Marxist historians have come to the fore, commonly called 'revisionist' historians. These writers (for example Michael Katz (1971) and Joel Spring (1976)) ignore the earlier Marxist historians, and take an essentially negative attitude towards education in America and Britain. These writers argue that mass education has always served the needs of capitalism, has been racist and class segregated, and that all the supposed liberal or benevolent pioneers of mass education were really conscious or unconscious lackeys of capitalism. Karier has, for example, spent years demonstrating that John Dewey was anti-Semitic, anti-Polish, and owned shares, which is intended to shake American faith in him as a philosopher and educational reformer.

These three kinds of history present essentially different

accounts of the development of upper-class, middle-class, and working-class education in the nineteenth century. What they all share, however, is a neglect of gender as a relevant organizing principle in nineteenth-century education. Yet, as I argue in chapters 4 – 6, the history and development of the education systems (both private and state) since the mid-nineteenth century can only be understood if the interplay of gender and class is understood, especially in the sphere of curriculum and the structure of education. Unfortunately, examining the class and gender divisions in the structure and content of education in Britain and the USA in the nineteenth century is not an easy task. Histories of education in both Britain and the USA have neglected women, or issues of gender differentiation, whether they worked in the liberal tradition, the classical Marxist one, or are adherents of the new revisionist history. Histories of women and feminism have little data on education, while histories of women's education have not been written by distinguished historians but by journalists with little historical training, so that the theories and explanations utilized in recent works on history of education are not applied to the campaigns for women's education. In Britain there are three modern histories of women's education – Kamm (1965), Turner (1974) and Borer (1976) – but none is theoretically exciting. Histories of education are infuriating because they usually omit any discussion of sex and gender. For example, Rothblatt's (1968) history of the radical changes at Cambridge during the nineteenth century does not even mention the admission of women. Brian Simon's (1974) *magnum opus* on class conflict in the last 150 years of British education does not discuss gender at all. Women and girls are dismissed from the history of education with assumptions such as those from Middleton and Weitzman (1976: 21) who say: 'Girls' education remained centred on the home and domestic round, so it is the development of the education of boys that is significant...' and then do not mention women for 100 years until, when discussing the 1943-4 period, the reader is told: 'Working class views on education were conditioned by personal experience....They saw women's place as in the home which meant little support for nursery schools. They favoured training in domestic skills for girls' (p.268). No evidence is offered for this statement.

The growth of women's studies and the rise of the new feminism have produced a range of scholarly histories which are beginning to dispel our ignorance. Carol Dyhouse (1981), Joan Burstyn (1980),

William Ellsworth (1979), and Sheila Fletcher (1980) are examples of serious scholarship applied to women's education in the period covered by part III. The History of Education Society in Britain had its first conference devoted to women's education in 1984, and the proceedings (Purvis 1985) contain references to the research done up to that date.

In the USA there do not seem to be equivalent texts to Kamm's (1965), so that Woody (1929, reprinted 1966) is still the best source. Woody set out to write 'a History of Education in the United States' but discovered that among the many gaps in the available research was one major one:

> Particularly impressive was the comparative silence – in some educational histories, almost complete – on the subject of women's education; and equally striking, the scant attention given her emancipation and education in general histories of the country. (p.vii)

Woody turned to and wrote a massive two-volume history of women's history in the USA which has not been superseded. Today there are several good histories of higher education for women (Horowltz 1984; Solomon 1985), but no good account of the struggle for schooling. Farello (1970) and Stock (1978) are both derivative, dull and add nothing to Woody.

One important source for the history of women's education is the published memoirs and recollections of life in the schools and colleges. Many girls' schools and colleges have produced histories or collections of memories. Barbara Barr (1984) has produced a bibliography of the histories of girls' schools held in UK education libraries, which is one record of an invaluable historical source. The American source material on higher education can be traced from Beach (1976) and Wilkins (1979), but there is no complete bibliography of the histories of the girls' schools in the USA. I have been unable to trace a history of women's education in New Zealand or Australia, and have relied on the histories of individual schools listed below.

In the absence of comprehensive bibliographies of school histories, college histories, and biographies and autobiographies of female education pioneers I have listed all those used for the background reading that informed this volume. The main purpose of these lists is to show that the small number of schools, colleges, and pioneers usually cited (Cheltenham and North London

Collegiate, Vassar and Girton, Buss, Beale and Davies) is only a small part of the whole which could be researched. Constance Jones and Eleanor Lord are just as interesting, and deserve modern biographies.

## Institutional histories used in the research

The following schools and colleges have produced histories which were used in the research for this volume. The institutions are listed by country, and then by town. If a volume is listed in Barr (1984), no location is given. Volumes not listed by Barr are given a location (e.g. Sussex University library) or shown to be in my private collection (SD)

*Scotland*

*Edinburgh*
Mary Erskine School by Sommerville (1970)
The Merchant Company Schools by Harrison (1920) (SD)
St George's by Welsh (1939)
Edinburgh Ladies' College by Pryde (1893)
St Trinnean's by Lee (1962)

*Glasgow*
Laurel Bank School by Anon (1953)
Park School by Anon (1930)

*St Andrews*
St Leonards by Grant *et al.* (1927)
St Leonards by Macauley (1978) (SD)

*Wales*

*Cardiff*
Cardiff High School by Carr (1955)
Cardiff High School by Leech (1986) (SD)
Howell's School by McCann (1972)

*Newport, Gwent*
Newport High School by Anon (1946)

*Pontypool*
County High School by Hughes (1947)

*Northern Ireland*

*Belfast*
Richmond Lodge School by Robb (1967)

*Enniskillen*
Enniskillen Collegiate School by Malone (1981)

*Eire*

*Dublin*
Alexandra College by O'Connor and Parkes (n.d.) (SD)

*North America*

*Boston*
Boston Girls' High School by Woods (1904) (SD)

*Andover, Mass.*
Abbot Academy by Phillips (1979) (UC, Cardiff)

*Waterbury, Conn.*
St Margaret's by Ohmann (1965) (SD)

*Australia*

*Melbourne*
Melbourne Church of England Girls' School by Anon (1953) (SD)
Presbyterian Ladies' College by Fitzpatrick (1975) (SD)

*New Zealand*

*Otago*
Otago Girls' High School by Wallis (1972) (SD)

*England*

*Abbots Bromley*
St Anne's by McPherson (1924)
St Mary's by Rice (1947)
St Mary's and St Anne's by Wells and Mead (1961)
Biography of Marcia Rice by Hall and MacPherson (1961)

*Ashford, Middx*
Welsh Girls' School by Leighton (1950)

*Bath*
The Royal School by Osborne and Manistry (1966)

*Batley*
Batley Girls Grammar School by Fleming (1955) (SD)

*Bedford*
Bedford High School by Westaway (1932)
Old Girls' in New Times by Westaway (1945)
Bedford High School by Westaway (1957)
Bedford High School by Gobber and Hutchins (1983)
Bedford Girls' Modern School and Dame Alice Harpur by Broadway and Buss (1982)

*Bideford*
Edgehill College by Pyke (1934) (SD)
Edgehill College by Pyke (1957)
Edgehill College by Shaw (1984) (SD)

*Birmingham*
King Edward VI High School by Vardy (1928)
Edgbaston High School by Whitcut (1976)

*Bolton*
Bolton School and Bolton Girls' High School by Brown and Poskitt (1976)

*Bradford*
Bradford Girls' Grammar School by Ellison (1965) (SD)

*Brentwood*
Brentwood County High School by McKerness (1964)

*Brighton*
Roedean by Cornford and Yerbury (1927)
Roedean by Anon (1934)
Roedean by de Zouche (1955)

*Bristol*
Clifton High School by Anon (1927)
Clifton High School by Glenday and Price (1977)
Colston's Girls' School by Clutton (1941)
Redland High School by Shaw (1932)
Redland High School by Bungay (1982)
Redmaids by Sampson (1908) (SD)
Redmaids by Sampson and Leighton (1924) (SD)

*Burford, Oxon*
Burford School by Simpson (1979) (SD)

*Chelmsford*
Chelmsford High School by Kenyon (1982)

*Cheltenham*
Cheltenham Ladies' College by Beale (1904)
*In the days of Miss Beale* by Steadman (1931)
Cheltenham Ladies' College by Clarke (1963)
Cheltenham Ladies' College by Clarke (1979) (SD)

*Chester*
Queen's School by Phillips (1978)

*Chorleywood*
Chorleywood College by Monk (1944) (SD)

*Croydon*
Croydon GPDST School by Anon (1954) (Sussex UL)

*Darlington*
Polam Hall by Davies (1981)

*Eastbourne*
Queenswood by Carew (1967)

*Exeter*
Maynards/Exeter High School by Bradbeer (1973)

*Farnborough*
Farnborough Hill by Mostyn (1967?) (SD)

*Gateshead*
Gateshead and Newcastle GPDST by Carter (1956)

*Guildford*
Tormead School by Clark (1982) (SD)

*Harrogate*
Queen Ethelburga's by Anon (1930) (SD)

*Hertford*
Christ's Hospital by Lempriere (1929)
Christ's Hospital by Page (1953)
*Blue Skirts to Blue Stockings* by Angus (1981)

*High Wycombe*
Wycombe Abbey by Bowerman (1965)

*Ipswich*
Northgate Grammar School by Atkinson (1980)

*Knutsford*
Brook House by Herford (1907)

*Lancaster*
Schools in Lancaster by Gregg (1982)

*Leeds*
Leeds Girls' High School by Jewell (1976)

*London*
Blackheath High School by Malim and Escreet (1927)
Burlington School by Burgess (1924)
Burlington School by Burgess (1948)
Camden School by Burchell (1971)
Channing School by Saunders (1984) (SD)
Francis Holland School by Dunning (1931)
Francis Holland School by Hicklin (1978) (SD)
Francis Holland School by Moberly Bell (1939) (SD)
Grey Coat Hospital School by Day (1902)
Mary Datchelor School by Anon (1957)
Mary Datchelor School by Anon (1977)
North London Collegiate by Scrimgeour (1950)
Northwood College by Anon (1978) (SD)
Notting Hill and Ealing High School by Sayers (1973)
Putney High School by Pike (1960)
Queen's College by Grylls (1948)
Queen's College by Kaye (1972)
Roan School by Kirby (1929)
St Martin in the Fields Girls' School by Thomas (1929)
St Martin in the Fields Girls' School by Thomas (1949)
St Olave's and St Saviours by Carrington (1971)
St Paul's Girls' School by Hardy (1925)
St Paul's Girls' School by Hirschfeld (1954)
South Hampstead GPDST by Bodington (1976)

*Luton*
Christchurch School by Bennett (1984) (SD)

*Malvern*
Malvern Girls' College by Phillips (1980)
Elleslie by Anon (1972) (SD)

*Manchester*
Manchester High School by Burstall (1911)

*Newcastle upon Tyne*
Newcastle upon Tyne Church High School by Anon (1935)
Rutherford Schools by Horsley (1981)

*Oxford*
Oxford High School by Stack (1963)
Central and Cheyney by Spackman (1974)

*Plymouth*
St Dunstan's Abbey School by Sister Margaret Teresa (1924) (SD)

*Rickmansworth*
Royal Masonic Girls' School by Anon (1954)
Royal Masonic Girls' School by Anon (1966)
Royal Masonic Girls' School 1934-1984 by Anon (1984)

*Rugby*
Rubgy High School by Randall (1969) (SD)

*Salisbury*
Godophin School by Douglas and Ash (1928)

*Sevenoaks*
Walthamstow Hall by Pike and Curryer (1973)

*Sherborne*
Sherborne School for Girls by Anon (1949)

*Shrewsbury*
Shrewsbury High School by Bates and Wells (1962)

*Southwold*
St Felix School by Watson and Brown (1923)

*Sunderland*
Sunderland High School by Bowling (1964) (SD)

*Sutton*
Sutton High School GPDST by James (1984) (SD)

*Teeside*
Teeside High School GPDST by Scott (1970)

*Truro*
Truro High School by Clarke (1979)

*Watford*
Watford Boys' and Girls' Grammar Schools by Hughes and Sweeney (1954)

*West Malvern*
St James's by Baird (1956)

*Weybridge*
The Hall School by Anon (1949)

*Worcester*
Worcester Girls' High School by James (1914)
Alice Ottley School by Noake (1952)

*York*
Mount School by Sturge and Clarke (1931)
Mount School Register 1931-2

*Higher Educational Institutions*

Bedford College, London, by Tuke (1939)
Barnard College, New York, by Anon (1964)
Bennington College, Vermont, by Brockway (1981)
Bedford PE College, Bedford, by Fletcher (1984)
Cambridge by Tullberg (1975)
Cornell by Conable (1977)
Girton by Stephen (1927)
Girton by Stephen (1933)
Girton by Jones (1913)
Girton Register by Butler and McMorran (1948)
Girton by Bradbrook (1969)
Goldsmiths, London, by Dymond (1955)
Mills College, USA, by Keep (1946)
Newnham by Hamilton (1936)
Newnham by Phillips (1979)
Oxford by Brittain (1960)
Radcliffe by the college (1938)
Radcliffe by Baker (1976)
Randolph-Macon by Cornelius (1951)
Ripon College, Yorks, by Wilkinson (1963)
St Anne's, Oxford, by Butler and Prichard (1930)
St Anne's, Oxford, by Butler (1949)
Smith College, by Seelye (1923)
Somerville College Register 1879-1959
Somerville by Farnel (1948)
St Hilda's, Durham, by Lawrence (1958)
St Hugh's by Griffin (1986)
Truro Training College by Brown (1938)
Vassar by Plum (1961)
Wellesley by Converse (1915)
Westfield College, London, by Wilson (1932)

## Biographies and autobiographies consulted

(This list only contains material from before the re-awakening of feminism. Recent works are all listed in the main bibliography.)

Hertha Ayrton by Sharp (1926)
Vera Brittain, 3 vols (Testaments of Youth, Experience and Friendship)
Sara Burstall's autobiography
Dorothea Beale and Frances Mary Buss by Kamm (1958)
Dorothea Beale by Raikes (1908)
Buss's notebook's edited by Topliss (1896)
Catharine Beecher by Sklar (1973)
Autobiography of Miss Bentick-Smith (1927)
Elizabeth Cadbury by Scott (1955)
Mary Clarke autobiography (1973)
Dora Dalglish autobiography (1938)
C.I. Dodd by Wilson (1936)
Millicent Fawcett autobiography (1925)
Lillian Faithful sermons (1927)
Virginia Gildersleeve autobiography (1953)
Frances Gray autobiography (1931)
Caroline Haslett by Messenger (1967)
Mary Agnes Hamilton autobiography (1944)
Grace Hadow by Deneke (1946)
Winifred Holtby by White (1938)
Winifred Holtby by Brittain (1940)
Molly Hughes, 3 vols of autobiography (1978)
Constance Jones autobiography (1922)
Eglantyne Jebb by Wilson (1967)
E.E. Lawrence's letters 1896-1926 (1933)
The Lawrence sisters by Anon (1935)
E. Lodge autobiography (1938)
Lonsdale by Martineau (1936)
Louisa Lumsden autobiography (1933)
Hilda Martindale autobiography (1944)
Hilda Martindale portraits (1948)
C.L. Maynard by Firth (1949)
Winifred Mercier by Grier (1937)
Alice Freeman Palmer by Palmer (1908)
Winifred Peck autobiography (1952)
M. Popham autobiography (1968)

Naomi Mitchison, 3 vols of autobiography
Kathleen Raine autobiography (1975)
Roberts memoirs (1934)
Gwen Raverat autobiography (1954)
Mrs Henry Sidgwick by Sidgwick (1939)
Edith Summerskill autobiography (1967)
Marion Talbot autobiography (1948)
Elizabeth Wordsworth autobiography (1912)
E.A. Willey by Evans (1971)

# Appendix 3:
# Direct-grant and independent schools aided by the IFASES 1955-63

*Building and Equipment Grants – (total fourteen schools in England and Wales)*

Ashford School, Kent
Bradford Girls' Grammar School
Cheltenham Ladies College
Croydon High School for Girls
Howell's School, Llandaff
Leeds Girls' High School
Malvern Girls' College
Manchester High School for Girls
Mary Erskine School for Girls (Scotland)
Monmouth Girls' School
North London Collegiate School
Sherborne School for Girls
St Leonard's School, St Andrew's (Scotland)
Walthamstow Hall School, Sevenoaks (Girls)
Withington Girls' School
Wycombe Abbey School

*Equipment Grants only – (total fifty-three schools in England and Wales)*

Abbey School, Reading
Badminton School, Bristol
Bath High School
Benenden School
Berkhamsted School for Girls
Birkenhead High School
Bolton School (Girls' Division)

Bradford Girls' Grammar School
Bury Grammar School for Girls
Christ's Hospital Girls' School
City of London Girls' School
Clifton High School for Girls
Dame Allan's Girls' School, Newcastle-upon-Tyne
Derby High School
Dr William's School, Dolgelly
Downe House School, Ash
Edgbaston C of E College for Girls
Edgehill Girls' College, Bideford
Fallowfield Convent Grammar School
George Watson's Ladies' College, Edinburgh (Scotland)
Godolphin School, Salisbury
Harrogate College
King's High School for Girls, Warwick
Laurel Bank School, Glasgow (Scotland)
Loretto High School, Manchester
Loughborough High School
Maynard School, Exeter
Merchant Taylors Girls' School, Crosby
Newcastle-upon-Tyne Church High School
Notre Dame Convent School, Blackburn
Park School, Glasgow, (Scotland)
Perse Girls' School, Cambridge
Queen Anne's School, Caversham
Queen's College, Harley Street
Queen's School, Chester
Queenswood School, Hatfield
Redland High School
Roedean
Royal School, Bath
Sacred Heart Convent, Fenham
Sheffield High School
Stamford High School
St Felix School, Southwold
St George's Girls' School, Edinburgh (Scotland)
St Mary's and St Anne's, Abbots Bromley
St Mary's, Calne
St Paul's Girls' School
St Helen and St Katharine, Abingdon
Talbot Heath, Bournemouth

Truro Girls' High School
Ursuline Convent High School, Brentwood
Ursuline High School, Ilford
Victoria College, Belfast (N. Ireland)
Wakefield Girls' High School
Westbourne School for Girls
Westonbirt School
Winckley Square Convent, Preston

# Bibliography

Abel, Elizabeth and Abel, Emily, K. (1983) 'Introduction', in E.Abel and E.K.Abel (eds) *Women, Gender and Scholarship,* Chicago: The University Press, pp.1-10

Acker, Joan (1973) 'Women and social stratification', in J.Huber (ed.) *Changing Women in a Changing Society,* Chicago: The University Press

—— (1980) 'Women and stratification', *Contemporary Sociology, 9:* 25-39

Acker, Sandra (1980) 'Women, the other academics', *British Journal of Sociology of Education* 1, 1: 81-92

Acker, S. (1981) 'No woman's land', *Sociological Review* 29, 1: 77-104

—— (1982) 'Women and education', in A. Hartnett (ed.) *The Social Sciences*

—— (1983) 'Women and teaching', in S. Walker and L. Barton (eds) *Gender, Class and Education,* London: Falmer

—— *et al.* (eds) (1984) *World Yearbook of Education,* London: Kogan Page

Acker, S. and Piper, D.W. (eds.) (1984) *Is Higher Education Fair to Women?* Guildford: SRHE

Addelson, K.P. (1983) 'The man of professional wisdom', in S. Harding, and M. Hintikka (eds) *Discovering Reality,* Dortrecht, Holland: Reidel

Airlie, Mabell Countess of (1956) *Thatched with Gold: Memoirs 1866-1956,* London: Hutchinson

Allen, Grant (1895) *The Woman Who Did,* London: John Lane

—— (1889) 'Plain words on the women question', reprinted in Newman (ed.) (1985) *Men's Ideas / Women's Realities*

Allen, Sheila (1982) 'Gender inequality and class formation'. in A.Giddens and G.Mackenzie (eds) *Social Class and the Division of Labour,* Cambridge: The University Press

Anon (1953) *Nissi Dominus Frustra: The Melbourne Church of England Girls' Grammar School Jubilee History,* Melbourne: Arbuckle, Waddle Pty Ltd

Ardener, E. (1972) 'Belief and the problem of women', in J.Lafontaine (ed.) *The Interpretation of Ritual,* London: Tavistock

—— (1975) 'The "Problem" Revisited', in S.Ardener (ed.) *Perceiving Women*

Ardener, S. (ed.) (1975) *Perceiving Women,* London: Dent

—— (ed.) (1978) *Defining Females,* London: Croom Helm

—— (ed.) (1981) *Women and Space,* London: Croom Helm

—— (1985) 'The social anthropology of women and feminist anthropology', *Anthropology Today,* 1,5: 24-6

Armstrong, David (1980) 'Health care and the structure of medical education', in H. Noack, (ed.) *Medical Education and Primary Health Care,* London: Croom Helm

Aronson, S.H. (1952) 'The sociology of the bicycle', *Social Forces* xxx, pp. 305–12

Arscott, C. (1937) *The Headmistress Speaks,* London: Kegan Paul, Trench, Trubner & Co

Atkinson, E.J. (1980) *A School Remembered: an Account of the Origins and Development of the Northgate Grammar School for Girls*, Ipswich: Ancient House Pub.

Atkinson, P. (1978) 'Fitness, feminism and schooling', in S.Delamont and L.Duffin (eds) *The Nineteenth Century Woman*

—— (1981a) 'Bernstein's structuralism'. *Educational Analysis* 3,1: 85-95

—— (1981b) *The Clinical Experience*, Farnborough: Gower

—— (1983) 'The reproduction of professional community', in R.Dingwall and P.Lewis (eds) *Sociology of the Professions*

—— (1984) 'Training for certainty', *Social Science and Medicine*, 19, 9: 949-56

—— (1985a) *Language, Structure and Reproduction*, London: Methuen

—— (1985b) 'Strong minds and weak bodies', *British Journal of the History of Sport*, 2, 1: 62-71

—— (1987) 'The feminist physique', in J.A.Mangan and R.J.Park (eds) *From 'Fair Sex' to Feminism*, London: Frank Cass

Atkinson, P. and Delamont, S. (1976) 'Mock-ups and cock-ups', in M.Hammersley and P.Woods (eds) *The Process of Schooling*, London: Routledge

—— (1985a) 'Socialisation into teaching', *British Journal of Sociology of Education*, 6, 3: 307-22

—— (1985b) 'Bread and dreams or bread and circuses?', in M.Shipman (ed.) *Educational Research*, London: Falmer

Atkinson, P., Reid, M., and Sheldrake, P. (1977) 'Medical mystique', *Sociology of Work and Occupations*, 4, 3: 243-80

Auld, R. (1976) *Report on the inquiry into William Tyndale School*, London: ILEA

Bailey, Gemma (ed.) (1923) *A Short History of Lady Margaret Hall*, Oxford: privately printed

Baird, A. (ed.) (1956) *I Was There: St.James, West Malvern*, West Malvern: Littlebury

Baker, Liva (1976) *I'm Radcliffe! Fly Me!* New York: Macmillan

Ball, S. (1981) *Beachside Comprehensive*, Cambridge: The University Press

Banks, J. and Banks, O. (1964) *Feminism and Family Planning*, Liverpool: The University Press

Banks, O. (1968) *The Sociology of Education* (2nd edn, 1971; 3rd edn, 1976), London: Batsford

—— (1981) *Faces of Feminism*, Oxford: Martin Robertson

—— (1982) 'Sociology of education, 1952–82', *British Journal of Educational Studies* xxx, 1, 18–31

Banner, Lois (1974) *Women in Modern America*, New York: Harcourt, Brace Jovanovich

Barnes, B. and Mackenzie, D. (1979) 'On the role of interests in scientific change', in R.Wallis (ed.) *On the Margins of Science.*

Barnes, D. (ed.) (1971) *Language, the Learner and the School*, Harmondsworth, Middx: Penguin

Barr, B. (1984) *Histories of girls' schools and related biographical material*, Leicester: The School of Education

Bates, Hazel and Wells, Anne A.M. (1962) *A History of Shrewsbury High School 1885-1960*, Shrewsbury: Wilding and Sons

Battiscombe, Georgina (1978) *Reluctant Pioneer: The Life of Elizabeth Wordsworth*, London: Constable

298

Beach, Mark (1976) *A Bibliographic Guide to American Universities and Colleges*, Westport, Conn.: Greenwood Press

Becker, H.S. *et al.* (1961) *Boys in White*, Chicago: The University Press

Beecher, C. (1841) *A treatise on domestic economy*, Boston: T.H. Webb

Bell – See Moberly Bell

Bellack, A.A. *et al.* (1966) *The Language of the Classroom*, New York: Teachers College Press

Bennett, S.N. (1976) *Teaching Styles and Pupil Progress*, London: Open Books

Benson, T. (1934) 'Cheltenham Ladies College', in G. Greene (ed.) *The Old School*

Bernbaum, Gerald (1977) *Knowledge and Ideology in the Sociology of Education*, London: Macmillan

Bernstein, Basil (1971) 'On the classification and framing of educational knowledge', in M.F.D.Young (ed.) *Knowledge and Control*

—— (1973a) 'Class and pedagogies: visible and invisible', Paris: OECD (reprinted in *Educational Studies*, 1, 1 (1975), 23-41

—— (1977a) 'Introduction', *Class, Codes and Control*, 3 (2nd edn), London: Routledge

Blackledge, D. and Hunt, B. (1985) *Sociological Interpretations of Education*, London: Croom Helm

Blackstone, T. and Fulton, O. (1975) 'Sex discrimination among university teachers', *British Journal of Sociology*, 26: 261-75

Blau, P.M. and Duncan, O.D. (1967) *The American Occupational Structure*, New York: Wiley

Bloor, C. and Bloor, D. (1982) 'Twenty industrial scientists', in M.Douglas (ed.) (1982b) *Essays on the Sociology of Perception*

Boas, Louis Schutz (1935) *Women's Education Begins*, Norton, Mass: Wheaton College Press, (reprinted by Arno Press, New York, 1971)

Bogart, K., Wells, K., and Spencer, A. (1985) 'Improving sex equity in post secondary education', in S.S. Klein (ed.) *Handbook for Achieving Sex Equity through Education*, Baltimore: Johns Hopkins UP

Booth, Meyrick (1927) 'The present day education of girls', *The Nineteenth Century and After*, 102 (August):259-69

—— (1932) *Youth and Sex*, London: Allen and Unwin

Borer, M.C. (1976) *Willingly to School*, London: Lutterworth

Bossert, S. (1982) 'Understanding sex differences in children's classroom experiences', in W. Doyle and T.L.Good (eds) *Focus on Teaching*, Chicago: The University Press, pp.170-81

Bourdieu, Pierre (1971) 'The Berber house or the world reversed', in M.Douglas (ed.) (1973) *Rules and Meanings*

—— (1977) *Outline of a Theory of Practice*, Cambridge: The University Press

—— (1986) *Distinction*, London: Routledge

Bourdieu, P. and Passeron, J.C. (1977) *Reproduction in Education, Society and Culture*, London: Sage

Bowen, Elizabeth (1934) 'Downe House', in G.Greene (ed.) *The Old School*

—— (1967) Foreword in A. Ridley's book re Downe House

Bowerman, Elsie (1966) *Stands There a School*, Brighton: privately printed

Bradbrook, Muriel C. (1969) *That Infidel Place*, London: Chatto and Windus

Briscoe, Anne M. (1984) 'Scientific sexism', in Haas and Perrucci (eds) *Women and Scientific and Engineering Professions*

# Bibliography

Briscoe, A.M. and Pfafflin, S.N. (eds) (1978) *Expanding the Role of Women in the Sciences*, New York: New York Academy of Sciences

Brittain, Vera (1933) *Testament of Youth*, London: Gollancz

—— (1960) *The Women at Oxford*, London: Harrap

Britten, N. and Heath, A. (1983) 'Women, men and social class', in E.Gamarnikow *et al*. (eds) *Gender, Class and Work*, London: Heinemann

Broadway, C.M. and Buss, E.I. (1982) *The History of the Bedford Girls' Modern School 1882-1982 (Dame Alice Harpur School)*, Bedford: privately printed

Brown, W.E. and Poskitt, F.R. (1976) *The History of Bolton School*, Bolton: privately printed

Browne, Joan (ed.) (1979) *Teachers of Teachers*, London: Hodder & Stoughton

Bryant, M. (1979) *The Unexpected Revolution*, London: The London Institute of Education

Bucher, R. and Strauss, A.L. (1961) 'Professions in process', *American Journal of Sociology*, 60: 325-34

Bungay, Joan (ed.) (1982) *Redland High School 1882-1982*, Bristol: privately printed

Bullivant, B.M. (1978) *The Way of Tradition*, Melbourne: ACER

Burman, S. (ed.) (1979) *Fit Work for Women*, London: Croom Helm

Burrage, Hilary (1983) 'Women university teachers of natural science 1971-72', *Social Studies of Science*, 13: 147-60

Burstall, Sara (1909) *Impressions of American Education in 1908*, London: Longmans, Green and Co.

—— (1933) *Retrospect and Prospect*, London: Longmans

Burstall, Sara and Douglas, M.A. (1911) *Public Schools for Girls*, London: Longmans

Burstyn, Joan (1980) *Victorian Education and the Ideal of Womanhood*, London: Croom Helm

Butler, J.R.M. (1925) *Henry Montague Butler*, London: Longmans

Butler, R.F. and Pritchard, M.H. (eds) (1938) *The Society of Oxford Home Students*, Oxford: Oxonian Press

Byrne, E.M. (1975) 'Inequality in education – discriminal resource allocation in schools?', *Educational Review*, 27, 3: 179-91

Callan, H. and Ardener, S. (eds) (1984) *The Incorporated Wife*, London: Croom Helm

Calvert, J.G., Pitts, J.N., and Dorian, G.H. (1972) *Graduate School in the Sciences*, New York: Wiley

Caplan, P. (ed) (1987) *The cultural construction of sexuality*, London: Tavistock

Carr, Catherine (1955) *The Spinning Wheel*, Cardiff: Western Mail and Echo Ltd.

Chubin, D. (1974) 'Sociological manpower and womanpower', *American Sociologist*, 9, 2: 83-92

Clarke, Amy K. (1979) *The Story of the Truro High School*, Truro: Oscar Blackford Ltd.

Clarke, M.G. (1937) 'Feminine challenge in education', in C.Arscott (ed.) *The Headmistress Speaks*

Clarricoates, K. (1980) 'The importance of being Ernest...', in R.Deem (ed.) *Schooling for Women's Work*

Cochran-Smith, M. (1984) *The Making of a Reader*, New York: Ablex

Cohen, G. (1981) 'Culture and educational achievement', *Harvard Educational Review*, 51, 2: 270-85

# Bibliography

Cole, Arthur C. (1940) *A Hundred Years of Mount Holyoke College*, New Haven: Yale University Press

Cole, Jonathan (1979) *Fair Science: Women in the Scientific Community*, New York: The Free Press

Cole, Jonathan, R. and Cole, Stephen (1973) *Social Stratification in Science*, Chicago: The University Press

Cole, J.R. and Zuckerman, H. (1984) 'The productivity puzzle', *Advances in Motivation and Achievement*, 2: 217-58

Coleman, J.S. (1963) *The Adolescent Society*, Glencoe: The Free Press

Collins, H.F. (1985) *Changing Order*, London: Sage

Connell, R.W., Ashenden, D.J., Kessler, S., and Dowsett, G.W. (1982) *Making the Difference*, Sydney: Allen and Unwin

Connell, R.W., Dowsett, G.W., Kessler, S., and Ashenden, D.J. (1981) 'Class and gender dynamics in a ruling-class school', *Interchange*, 12, 2-3:102-17

Coombs, R. (1978) *Mastering 'Medicine'*, New York: Free Press

Coser, R.L. and Rokoff, G. (1982) 'Women in the occupational world', in R.Kahn-Hut *et al.* (eds) *Women and Work*, Chicago: The University Press

Courtney, Janet E. (1934) *The Women of My Time*, London: Lovat Dockson

Coxon, A.P.M., Davies, P.M., and Jones, C.L. (1986) *Images of Social Stratification*, London: Sage

Coxon, A.P.M. and Jones, C.L. (1978) *The Images of Occupational Prestige*, London: Macmillan

—— (1979a) *Class and Hierarchy*, London: Macmillan

—— (1979b) *Measurement and Meanings*, London: Macmillan

Cozzens, Susan E. (1985) 'Comparing the sciences', *Social Studies of Science*, 15, 1: 127-53

Croll, Paul (1980) 'Replicating the observational data', in M.Galton and B.Simon (1980) *Progress and Performance in the Primary Classroom*, London: Routledge

Crompton, R. (1986) 'Women and the "service class"', in Crompton and Mann (eds) *Gender and Stratification*

Crompton, R. and Mann, M. (eds) (1986) *Gender and Stratification*, Cambridge: Polity Press

Cross, Amanda (1972) *The Theban Mysteries*, London: Gollancz

—— (1976) *The Question of Max*, London: Gollancz

Cross, B.M. (ed.) (1965) *The Educated Woman in America*, New York: Teachers College Press

Crow, Duncan (1972) *The Victorian Woman*, New York: Stein and Day

Croydon, GPDST (1954) *Croydon High School, 1874-1954*, Croydon: privately printed

Cunningham, G. (1978) *The New Woman and the Victorian Novel*, London: Macmillan

Curti, Merle (1959) *The Social Ideas of American Educators* (2nd edn), Paterson, N.J.: Pageant Books

Cuthbert, T. (1953) *Laurel Bank School 1903-1953*, Glasgow: J.Smith

Dainton, Report (1968) *Enquiry into the flow of candidates in science and technology into higher education*, London: HMSO

Dale, R.R. (1969) *Mixed or Single Sex School? Vol. 1*, London: Routledge

—— (1971) *Mixed or Single Sex School? Vol. 2*, London: Routledge

—— (1974) *Mixed or Single Sex School? Vol. 3*, London: Routledge

Dalglish, D.N. (1938) *We Have Been Glad*, London: Macmillan

Dane, Clemence (1917) *Regiment of Women*, London: Heinemann

## Bibliography

Daner, F.J. (1974) *The American Children of Krsna*, New York: Holt, Rinehart and Winston

Davidoff, L. (1973) *The Best Circles*, London: Croom Helm

Davies, Kathleen (1981) *Polam Hall*, Darlington: Prudhoe

Davies, Muriel (1937) 'The county secondary school and its service to the community', in C.Arscott (ed.) *The Headmistress Speaks*

Davidson, Helen (1985) 'Unfriendly myths about women teachers', in J.Whyte *et al.* (eds) *Girl Friendly Schooling*

Deem, R. (1978) *Women and Schooling*, London: Routledge

—— (ed.) (1980) *Schooling for Women's Work*, London: Routledge

—— (ed.) (1984) *Co-education Reconsidered*, Milton Keynes: The Open University Press

Delamont, S. (1972) 'Fallen Engels', *New Edinburgh Review*, 18: 16-19

—— (1973) 'Academic conformity observed', unpublished Ph.D. Thesis, University of Edinburgh

—— (1976a) 'The girls most likely to', *Scottish Journal of Sociology*, 1,1: 29-43 (reprinted in R.Parsler (ed.) *Capitalism, Class and Politics in Scotland*, Farnborough: Gower 1980)

—— (1976b) 'Beyond Flanders Fields', in M.Stubbs and S.Delamont (eds) *Explorations in Classroom Observation*, Chichester: Wiley

—— (1976c) *Interaction in the Classroom*, London: Methuen

—— (1978a) 'The contradictions in ladies education', in S.Delamont and L.Duffin (eds) *The Nineteenth Century Woman*

—— (1978b) 'The domestic ideology and women's education', in S.Delamont and L.Duffin (eds) *The Nineteenth Century Woman*

—— (1980a) *Sex Roles and the School*, London: Methuen

—— (1980b) *The Sociology of Women*, London: Allen and Unwin

—— (1981) 'All too familiar? A decade of classroom research', *Educational Analysis*, 3,1: 69-84

—— (1983a) 'A woman's place in education: myths, monsters and misapprehensions', (Presidential Address to BERA), *Research Intelligence*, 14: 2-4

—— (1983b) 'Salmon, chicken, cake and tears', in A.Murcott (ed.) *The Sociology of Food and Eating*, Farnborough: Gower

—— (1983c) 'The conservative school', in S.Walker and L.Barton (eds) *Gender, Class and Education*, London: Falmer

—— (1983d) *Interaction in the Classroom* (2nd edn), London: Methuen

—— (1984a) 'The old girl network', in R.Bugess (ed.) *The Research Process in Educational Settings*, London: Falmer

—— (1984b) 'Debs, dollies, swots and weeds', in G.Walford (ed.) *British Public Schools*, London: Falmer

—— (1984c) 'Lessons from St.Luke's', in W.Dockrell (ed.) *An Attitude of Mind*, Edinburgh: SCRE

—— (1984d) 'Sex roles and schooling or "See Janet suffer, see John suffer too"', *Journal of Adolescence*, 7: 329-35

—— (1985) 'The observation and classification of classroom behaviours', in D.Fontana (ed.) *Behaviourism and Learning Theory in Education*, Edinburgh: Scottish Academic Press

—— (1986) 'From lettuces to lasers', *Journal of Curriculum Studies*, 18, 4: 457-61

—— (1987a) 'Three blind spots?', *Social Studies of Science*, 17, 1: 163-70

—— (1987b) 'Clean baths and dirty women', in N. McKeganey and S. Cunningham-Burley (eds) *Enter the Sociologist*, Aldershot: Avebury

# Bibliography

Delamont, S. and Duffin, L. (eds) (1978) *The Nineteenth Century Woman*, London: Croom Helm

Delamont S. and Galton, M. (1986) *Inside the Secondary Classroom*, London: Routledge

Dingwall, R. and Lewis, P. (eds) (1983) *Sociology of the Professions*, London: Macmillan

Dobkin, M.H. (ed.) (1979) *The Making of a Feminist*, Kent, Ohio: Kent State University Press

Douglas, Mary (1966) *Purity and Danger*, London: Routledge

—— (1970) *Natural Symbols*, London: Barrie and Rockliff

—— (ed.) (1973) *Rules and Meanings*, Harmondsworth: Penguin

—— (ed.) (1975) *Implicit Meanings*, London: Routledge

—— (1980) *Evans Pritchard*, London: Fontana

—— (ed.) (1982a) *In the Active Voice*, London: Routledge

—— (ed.) (1982b) *Essays on the Sociology of Perception*, London: Routledge

—— (ed.) (1984) *Food in the Social Order*, New York: Russell Sage Foundation

—— (1986) *Risk Acceptability According to the Social Sciences*, London: Routledge

—— (1987) *How Institutions Think*, London: Routledge

Douglas, M. and Isherwood, Baron (1978) *The World of Goods*, New York: Basic Books

Douglas, M. and Wildavsky, A. (1982) *Risk and Culture*, Berkeley: University of California Press

Dresslehaus, M.S. (1974) 'Electrical engineer', in R.B.Kundsin (ed.) *Women and Success*

Duffin, Lorna (1978a) 'The conspicuous consumptive', in S.Delamont and L.Duffin (eds) *The Nineteenth Century Woman*

—— (1978b) 'Prisoners of progress', in S.Delamont and L.Duffin (eds) *The Nineteenth Century Woman*

Dyhouse, Carol (1976) 'Social – Darwinist ideas and the development of women's education in England 1880-1920', *History of Education*, 5, 1: 41-58

—— (1977) 'Good wives and little mothers', *Oxford Review of Education*, 3, 1: 21-35

—— (1981) *Girls Growing Up in Late Victorian and Edwardian England*, London: Routledge

—— (1985) 'Feminism and the debate over co-education/single sex schooling', in J.Purvis (ed.) *The Education of Girls and Women*, Leicester: History of Education Society

—— (1987) 'Miss Buss and Miss Beale', in F.Hunt (ed.) *Lessons for Life*, Oxford: Basil Blackwell

Edge, David (1979) 'Quantitative measures of communication in science', *History of Science*, 17: 102-34

Eggleston, J.F., Galton M. and Jones, M. (1976) *Processes and Products of Science Teaching*, London: Macmillan

Eggleston, S.J. (1974) 'Sex and the single schools', *Times Educational Supplement*, 10.6.1974

Elliot, P. (1972) *The Sociology of the Professions*, London: Macmillan

Ellsworth, Edward W. (1979) *Liberators of the Female Mind*, Westport, Conn.: Greenwood Press

Elston, Mary Ann (1980) 'Medicine', in R.Silverstone and A.Ward (eds) *Careers of Professional Women*

# Bibliography

EOC (1982) *Women in Universities*, Manchester: The Equal Opportunities Commission

Epstein, C. (1970) *A Woman's Place*, Berkeley: University of California Press

—— (1981) 'Women in Sociological Analysis', in E. Langland and W. Gove (eds) *A Feminist Perspective in the Academy*, Chicago: The University Press

—— (1983) *Women in Law*, New York: Doubleday

Farello, E.W. (1970) *A history of the education of women in the United States*, New York: Vantage Press

Fass, Paula S. (1977) *The Damned and the Beautiful*, Oxford: The University Press

Ferry, Abby Farwell (1931) *When I was at Farmington*, Chicago: Fletcher Seymour

Finch, E. (1947) *Carey Thomas of Bryn Mawr*, New York: Harper Bros

Finch, J. (1984) 'Working class playgroups', British Educational Research Journal 10, 1, 3–17

Firth, C.B. (1949) *Constance Louisa Maynard*, London: Allen and Unwin

Fitzpatrick, K. (1975) *Presbyterian Ladies College Melbourne: The First Century*, Clayton, Australia: Wilke & Co

Flanders, N.A. (1970) *Analysing Teaching Behaviour*, New York: Addison-Wesley

Fletcher, Sheila (1980) *Feminists and Bureaucrats*, Cambridge: The University Press

—— (1984) *Women First*, London; Athlone Press

Fogarty, M., Allen, A.J., Allen, I. and Walters, P. (1981) *Women in Top Jobs, 1968-1970*, London: Heinemann

Fogelman, K. (1976) *Britain's Sixteen Year Olds*, London: National Children's Bureau

Fox, Renee (1957) 'Training for uncertainty', in R.K.Merton *et al. The Student Physician*

Frankfort, Roberta (1977) *Collegiate Women*, New York: University Press

Freidson, E. (1970a) *Professional Dominance*, New York: Atherton Press

—— (1970b) *Profession of Medicine*, New York: Dodd, Mead & Co.

—— (1975) *Doctoring Together*, New York: Elsevier

—— (1983) 'The theory of professions', in R.Dingwall and P.Lewis (eds) *Sociology of the Professions*

—— (1986) *Professional Powers*, Chicago: The University Press

Gadesden, F. (1901) 'Secondary education of girls', in R.D. Roberts (ed) *Education in the Nineteenth Century*, Cambridge: The University Press

Galloway, H. Margo (1973) 'Female students and their aspirations', unpublished M.Phil. thesis, University of Edinburgh

Galton, M. (1981) 'Differential treatment of boy and girl pupils', in A. Kelly (ed) *The Missing Half*, Manchester: The University Press

Gaston, Jerry (1978a) *The Reward System in British and American Science*, New York: Wiley

—— (ed.) (1978b) *The Sociology of Science*, San Francisco: Jossey-Bass

Gathorne-Hardy, J. (1977) *The Public School Phenomenon 1957- 1977* London: Hodder and Stoughton

Geer, B. (ed.) (1972) *Learning to work*, Beverly Hills: Sage

Gibson, R. (1984) *Structuralism and Education*, London: Hodder & Stoughton

Giddens, A.G. (1978) *Durkheim*, London: Fontana

# Bibliography

—— (1980) *The Class Structure of the Advanced Societies.* (2nd edn), London: Hutchinson

Gilbert, G.N. and Mulkay, M. (1984) *Opening Pandora's Box,* Cambridge: The University Press

Gilbert, Nigel (1977) 'Referencing as persuasion', *Social Studies of Science,* 7:pp.113-120

Gildersleeve, Virginia C. (1954) *Many a Good Crusade,* New York: Macmillan

Gissing, George (1980) *The Odd Women,* London: Virago (originally published 1893)

Glaser, B.G. (1964) *Organizational Scientists,* Indianapolis: Bobbs-Merrill

Glass, D.V. (ed.) (1954) *Social Mobility in Britain,* London: Routledge

—— (1977) Introduction to Richardson (1977) *Contemporary Social Mobility*

Glenday, Nonita and Price, Mary (1974) *Reluctant Revolutionaries,* London: Pitman

Goffman, E. (1961) *Asylums,* Harmondsworth: Penguin

Goldthorpe, J.H. (1980) *Social Mobility and Class Structure in Modern Britain,* (2nd edn, 1987) Oxford: Clarendon Press

—— (1983) 'Women and class analysis', *Sociology,* 17, 4: 465-88

—— (1984) 'Women and class analysis: a reply to the replies', *Sociology,* 18, 4: 491-9

Goode, W.J. (1957) 'Community within a community', *American Sociological Review,* 22: 194-200

Goodsell, Willystine (1923) *The Education of Women,* New York: Macmillan

—— (1931) *Pioneers of Women's Education in the United States,* New York: McGraw Hill

Gordon, L.D. (1979) 'Co-education on two campuses', in Kelley (ed.) *Woman's Being, Woman's Place*

Gouldner, A.W. (1962) 'Anti-minotaur', *Social Problems,* 9: 199-212

GPDST (1972) *The Girls' Public Day School Trust 1872-1982: A Centenary Review,* London: GPDST

Graves, R. (1966) *Collected Poems,* Harmondsworth: Penguin

Gray, Frances R. (n.d.) *And Gladly Teach,* London: Sampson, Law, Marston & Co. (circa 1930-2)

Gray, J., McPherson, A.F., and Raffe, D. (1983) *Reconstructions of Secondary Education,* London: Routledge

Green, E.A. (1979) *Mary Lyon and Mount Holyoke,* Hanover, NH: University Press of New England

Greene, Graham (ed.) (1934) *The Old School,* London: Cape

Gregg, P. (1950) *A Social and Economic History of England,* London: Harrap

Grylls, Rosalie G. (1948) *Queens College 1848-1948,* London: Routledge

Haas, J. and Shaffir, W. (1977) 'The professionalization of medical students', *Symbolic Interaction* 1: 187–203

Haas, V.B. and Perrucci C.C. (eds) (1984) *Women and Scientific and Engineering Professions,* Ann Arbor: University of Michigan Press

Hall, Richard (1975) *Occupations and Social Structure* (2nd edn), Englewood Cliffs, NJ: Prentice Hall

Haller, John and Haller, Robin (1974) *The Physician and Sexuality in Victorian America,* Urbana: University of Illinois Press

Halsey, A.H. (1982) 'Professionals and provincials', *European Journal of Sociology* 23, 1, 150–75

# Bibliography

Halsey, A.H. and Trow, M. (1971) *The British Academics*, London: Faber

Halsey, A.H., Heath, A., and Ridge, J.M (1980) *Origins and Destinations*, Oxford: Clarendon Press

Hamilton, Mary Agnes (1944) *Newnham: an Informal Biography*, London: Faber

Hammersley, M. (1981) 'Origins and destinations', *British Journal of the Sociology of Education* 2, 1: 91-5

—— (1982) 'The sociology of classrooms', in A. Hartnett (ed.) *The Social Sciences*

Hammersley, M. and Atkinson, P, (1983) *Ethnography*, London: Tavistock

Hannam Watson, M.A. (1953) 'Reminiscences', in T.Cuthbert (ed.) *Laurel Bank School*

Harding, J. (ed.) (1986) *Perspectives on Gender and Science*, London: Falmer

Hargreaves, D.H. (1967) *Social Relations in Secondary School*, London: Routledge

—— (1982) *The Challenge for the Comprehensive School*, London: Routledge

Harris, B. (1978) *Beyond Her Sphere*, Westport, Conn.: Greenwood Press

Hartnett, Anthony (ed.) (1982) *The Social Sciences in Educational Studies*, London: Heinemann

Haug, Marie R. (1973) 'Social class measurement and women's occupational roles', *Social Forces*, 52, 1: 86-98

—— (1977) 'Measurement in social stratification', *Annual Review of Sociology*, 3: 51-77

Hauser, R.M. and Featherman, D.L. (1977) *The Process of Stratification*, New York: Academic Press

Heath, A. (1981) *Social Mobility*, London: Fontana

Heath, A. and Britten, N. (1984) 'Women's jobs do make a difference', *Sociology*, 18, 4: 475-90

Heath, A.F. *et al.* (1982) 'Cultural capital and political arithmetic', *British Journal of the Sociology of Education*, 3, 1: 87-91

HMI (1979) *Aspects of Secondary Education*, London: HMSO

Hirschon, R. (ed.) (1984) *Women and Property: Women as Property*, London: Croom Helm

Hoffman, N. (ed.) (1981) *Women's 'True' Profession: Voices from the History of Teaching*, New York: Feminist Press

Holcombe, Lee (1983) *Victorian Ladies at Work*, Newton Abbot: David and Charles

Holden, Pat (ed.) (1983) *Women's Religious Experience*, London: Croom Helm

Holtby, W. (1934) *Woman and a Changing Civilisation*, London: Bodley Head

—— (1936) *South Riding* (reprinted 1974), Glasgow: Fontana

Hope, K. (1984) *As Others See Us*, Cambridge: The University Press

Hope, Valerie (1984) *The First Hundred Years of the Church Schools Company*, Hull: Queen Print Ltd

Hopper, E. (1981) *Social Mobility*, London: Blackwell

Horowitz, Helen Lefkowitz (1984) *Alma Mater*, New York: Knopf

Howarth, Janet (1985) 'Public Schools, safety nets and educational ladders', *Oxford Review of Education*, 11, 1: 59-71

Howson, Geoffrey (1982) *A History of Mathematical Education in England*, Cambridge: The University Press

Huber, J. and Spitze, G. (1983) *Sex Stratification*, New York: Academic Press

Hughes, Everett, (1971) *The Sociological Eye*, Chicago: Aldine

Hughes, M.V. (1978a) *A London Child of the 1870s*, London: OUP (originally 1946)

—— (1978b) *A London Girl of the 1880s*, London: OUP

Hunt, F. (1985) 'Social class and the grading of schools', in J. Purvis (ed) *The education of girls and women*, Leicester: History of Education Society

Hunter, G.T. (1974) 'Pediatrician', in R.B.Kundsin (ed.) *Women and Success*

Hurn, C.J. (1978) *The Limits and Possibilities of Schooling*, Boston: Allyn and Bacon

Hutchins, I. and Godber, J. (eds) (1982) *A Century of Challenge*, Bedford: privately printed

Hutchison, G. and McPherson, A.F. (1976) 'Competing inequalities', *Sociology*, 10 (1): 111-16

Hutter, B. and Williams, G. (eds) (1981) *Controlling Women*, London: Croom Helm

Hymes, Dell (ed.) (1974) *Reinventing Anthropology*, New York: Random House

IFASES (1963) 'Report on the Industrial Fund for the Advancement of Scientific Education in Schools', London: The Fund

Irvine, J. and Martin, B. (1986) *Foresight in Science*, London: Frances Pinter

Jacobus, M. (ed) (1979) *Women writing and writing about women*, London: Croom Helm

Jamous, H. and Peloille, B. (1970) 'Professions or self perpetuating system', in J.A.Jackson (ed.) *Professions and Professionalization*, Cambridge: The University Press

Jeffreys, Sheila (1985) *The Spinster and her Enemies*, London: Pandora

Jencks, C. and Riesman, D. (1968) *The Academic Revolution*, New York: Doubleday

Jenkins, E.W. (1979) *From Armstrong to Nuffield*, London: John Murray

Johnson, Terence (1972) *Professions and Power*, London: Macmillan

Kamm, J. (1958) *How Different from Us*, London: Bodley Head

—— (1965) *Hope Deferred*, London: Methuen

Katz, M. (1971) *The irony of early school reform*, Boston: Beacon Press

Keep, R. (1946) *Fourscore and Ten Years*, privately printed by Mills College: California

Keller, E.F. (1985) *Reflections on Gender and Science*, New Haven: Yale University Press

Kelley, Mary (ed.) (1979) *Woman's Being, Woman's Place,* Boston: G.K. Hall

Kenealy, Arabella (1899) 'Woman as an athlete', *Nineteenth Century* 45: 635-45

—— (1920) *Feminism and Sex-Extinction*, London: Fisher Unwin

Kennedy, H. (1978) 'Women at the Bar', in R. Hazell (ed) *The Bar on Trial*, London: Quartet Books

Kennett, John (1974) 'The sociology of Pierre Bourdieu', *Educational Review*, 25, 3: 237-49

Keohane, N., Rosaldo, M.Z., and Gelpi, B.C. (eds) (1982) *Feminist Theory*, Brighton: Harvester Press

King, R. (1971) 'Unequal access in education', *Social and Economic Administration*, 5, 3: 167-74

—— (1978) *All Things Bright and Beautiful*, Chichester: Wiley
Kirk, K.E. (1937) *The Story of the Woodard Schools*, London: Hodder & Stoughton
Knorr-Cetina, K. and Mulkay, M. (eds) (1983) *Science Observed*, London: Sage
Kraditor, Aileen S. (ed.) (1968) *Up from the Pedestal*, New York: Quadrangle
Kroll, U. (1975) *Flesh of My Flesh*, London: Darton, Longman and Todd
Krug, E.A. (1964) *The Shaping of the American High School*, New York: Harper and Row
Kundsin, R.B. (ed.) (1974) *Women and Success*, New York: Morrow
Lacey, C. (1970) *Hightown Grammar*, Manchester: The University Press
Lakomski, Gabrielle (1984) 'On agency and structure: Pierre Bourdieu and Jean Claude Passeron's theory of symbolic violence', *Curriculum Inquiry*, 14, 2: 151-63
Larkin, R.W. (1979) *Suburban Youth and Cultural Crisis*, New York: OUP
Larson, M.S. (1977) *The Rise of Professionalism*, Berkeley: University of California Press
Latour, B. and Woolgar, S. (1979) *Laboratory Life*, London: Sage
Law, John and Williams, R.J. (1972) 'Putting facts together', *Social Studies of Science*, 12: 535-58
Layton, David (1984) *Interpreters of Science*, London: John Murray
Layton, D. (1986) Personal communication
Leach, E.R. (1954) *Political Systems of Highland Burma*, London: Athlone Press
—— (1961) *Pul Eliya*, Cambridge: The University Press
—— (1968) *Culture and Nature or La Femme Sauvage*, London: privately printed for Bedford College
—— (1970) *Levi-Strauss*, London: Fontana
—— (1976) *Culture and Communication*, Cambridge: The University Press
Leavis, Q.D. (1968) 'Henry Sidgwick's Cambridge', reprinted in F.R.Leavis (ed.) *A Selection from Scrutiny, Vol.1*, Cambridge: The University Press
Lees, Sue (1986) *Losing Out*, London: Heinemann
Lemert, Charles C. (ed.) (1981) *French Sociology*, New York: Columbia University Press
Lightfoot, Sara L. (1975) 'Sociology of education', in M. Millman and R.M.Kanter (eds) *Another Voice*, New York: Anchor Books
—— (1983) *The Good High School*, New York: Basic Books
Lipset, S.M. and Bendix, R. (1959) *Social Mobility and Industrial Society*, Berkeley: University of California Press
Lloyd, Susan McIntosh (1979) *A Singular School: Abbot Academy 1828-1973*, Hanover, NH: University of New England Press
Lorber, J. (1984) *Women in Medicine*, London: Tavistock
Lord, Eleanor C. (1938) *Stars over the School House*, New York: Richard R. Smith
McCormick, Kevin (1986) 'Scientific education, girls' schools, and the Industrial Fund: a research note', unpublished paper
McCullock, G., Jenkins, E., and Layton, D. (1985) *Technological Revolution*, London: Falmer
Macdonald, Gerard (1981) *Once a Week is Ample or The Intelligent Victorian's Guide to Sexuality and the Physical Passions: Quotations from Victorian Experts on Sex and Marriage*, London: Hutchinson

McGuigan, Dorothy G. (1970) *A Dangerous Experiment: 100 Years of Women at the University of Michigan*, Ann Arbor: Center for Continuing Education of Women

McGuinn, N. (1978) 'George Eliot and Mary Wollstonecraft', in S. Delamont and L. Duffin (eds) *The Nineteenth Century Woman*

McIntosh, Millicent Carey (1974) 'Educator', in R.B.Kundsin (ed.) *Women and Success*

—— (1979) Foreword to Dobkin (ed.) *The Making of a Feminist*

Mackie, M. (1977) 'Professional women's collegial relations and productivity', *Sociology and Social Research*, 61, 3: 277-93

McPherson, A.F. (1969) 'Swing from science or retreat from reason?', *Universities Quarterly* (Winter): 29-43

Macpherson, Violet M. (1924) *The Story of St. Anne's Abbot's Bromley 1874-1924*. Shrewsbury: Wilding and Sons

Magnus, Laurie (1923) *The Jubilee Book of the Girls' Public Day School Trust 1873-1923*, Cambridge: The University Press

Manthorpe, C.A. (1982) 'Men's science, women's science or science?', *Studies in Science Education*, 9: 65-80

Marsland, D. (1982) 'The sociology of adolescence and youth', in A.Hartnett (ed.) *The Social Sciences*

Martindale, Louisa (1951) *A Woman Surgeon*, London: Gollancz

Mathieson, M. (1975) *The Preachers of Culture*, London: Allen and Unwin

May, J. (1969) *Madame Bergman-Osterberg*, London: Harrap

Maynard, C.L. (1910) *Between College Terms*, London: The University Press

Measor, L and Woods, P. (1984) *Changing Schools*, Milton Keynes: The Open University Press

Megson, B. and Lindsay, J. (1960) *Girton College: 1869-1959*, Cambridge: Heffer and Sons

Meigs, Cornelia (1956) *What Makes a College? A History of Bryn Mawr*, London: Macmillan

Merton, R.K., Reader, G., and Kendall, P.L. (eds) (1957) *The Student Physician*, Cambridge, Mass: Harvard University Press

Messenger, Rosalind (1967) *The Doors of Opportunity*, London: Femina Books

Middleton, C. (1974) 'Sexual inequality and stratification theory', in . Parkin (ed) *The social analysis of class structure*, London: Methuen

Middleton, N. and Weitzman, S. (1976) *A Place for Everyone*, London: Gollancz

Miller, Ann (ed.) (1976) *A College in Dispersion: Women of Bryn Mawr 1896-1976*, Boulder, Colorado: Westview Press

Mitchison, Naomi (1975) *All Change Here*, London: Bodley Head

—— (1979) *You May Well Ask*, London: Gollancz

Moberly Bell, E. (1953) *Storming the Citadel*, London: Constable

—— (1958) *A History of the Church Schools Company 1883-1958*, London: SPCK

Morantz, R.M., Pomerleau, C.S., and Fenichel, C.H. (eds) (1982) *In Her Own Words*, New Haven: Yale UP

Morantz-Sanchez, R.M. (1985) *Sympathy and Science*, Oxford: The University Press

Moravcsik, M.J. and Murugesan, P. (1975) 'Some results on the function and quality of citations', *Social Studies of Science* v,1,: 86-92

Morgan, C., Hall, V., and Mackay, H. (1983) *The Selection of Secondary School Headteachers*, Milton Keynes: Open University Press

# Bibliography

Morrish, I. (1972) *The Sociology of Education* (2nd edn, 1978), London: Allen and Unwin

Mozans, H.J. (1913) *Women in Science*, Cambridge, Mass: MIT Press

Murdock, G. and Phelps, G. (1973) *Mass Media and the Secondary School*, London: Macmillan

Murray, T., Dingwall, R., and Eekelaar, J. (1983) 'Professionals in bureaucracies', in R.Dingwall and P.Lewis (eds) *Sociology of the Professions*

Musgrave, P.W. (1965) *The Sociology of Education*, (2nd edn, 1972; 3rd edn, 1979), London: Methuen

Nader, L. (1974) 'Up the anthropologist. Perspectives gained from studying up', in D.Hymes (eds) *Reinventing Anthropology*

Nash, R. (1973) *Classrooms Observed*, London: Routledge

Nava, Mica (1984) 'The urban, the domestic and education for girls', in G.Grace (ed.) *Education and the City*, London: Routledge

Newcomer, Mabel (1959) *A Century of Higher Education for American Women*, New York: Harper

Newman, L.M. (ed.) (1985) *Men's Ideas/Women's Realities: Popular Science 1870-1915*, Oxford: Pergamon

Newport, (1946) *The Jubilee Book of the Newport High School for Girls 1896-1946*, Newport, Mon: Johns

Noake, Valentine (1952) *History of the Alice Ottley School, Worcester*, Worcester: E. Baylis

NUT (1980) *Promotion and the Woman Teacher*, London: NUT/EOC

O'Leary, M. (1936) *Education with a Tradition*, London: The University Press

O'Neill, William (1969) *Everyone was Brave*, New York: Quadrangle

Ohman, C.B. (1965) *St. Margaret's School 1865-1965*, Waterbury, Conn: privately printed

Okely, J. (1978) 'Privileged, schooled and finished', in S. Ardener (ed.) *Defining Females*

Oldroyd, D.R. (1986) 'Grid/group analysis for historians of science', *History of Science* XXIV: 145-71

Osborne, H. and Manisty, P. (1966) *A History of the Royal School for the Daughters of Officers in the Army 1864-1965*, London: Hodder

Paley Marshall, Mary (1947) *What I Remember*, Cambridge: The University Press

Park School, (1930) *The Park School, Glasgow 1880-1930*, Glasgow: Hodge and Co.

Parker, H. (1974) *View from the Boys*, Newton Abbot: David and Charles

Parsons, Talcott (1951) *The Social System*, London: Tavistock

Partington, G. (1976) *Women Teachers in the Twentieth Century*, Slough: NFER

Patrick, J. (1972) *A Glasgow Gang Observed*, London: Methuen

Payne, G. (1978a) *Mobility and Change in Modern Society*, London: Macmillan

—— (1978b) *Employment and Opportunity*, London: Macmillan

Payne, G., Payne, J., and Chapman, T. (1983) 'Trends in female social mobility', in E. Gamarnikow *et al.* (eds) *Gender, Class and Work*, London: Heinemann

Payne, G., Ford, G., and Robertson, C. (1980) 'Changes in occupational mobility in Scotland', in R. Parsler (ed.) *Capitalism, Class and Politics in Scotland*, Aldershot: Gower

Payne, G., Ford, G., and Ulas, M. (1979) 'Education and social mobility', SIP occasional papers, no.8, Edinburgh: SIP

# Bibliography

Pedersen, Joyce S. (1975) 'Schoolmistresses and headmistresses', *Journal of British Studies*, 15: 136-62

Peterson, M. Jeanne (1972) 'The Victorian governess', in M. Vicinus (ed.) *Suffer and be Still*, Bloomington, Indiana: Indiana University Press

Philips, S.U. (1982) 'The language socialization of lawyers; acquiring the "cant" ', in G.Spindler (ed.) *Doing the Ethnography of Schooling*, New York: Holt Rinehart and Winston

Phillips, C. (1969) *Changes in Subject Choice*, London: LSE Monographs

Phillips, Grace W. (1980) *Smile, Bow and Pass on* , Malvern: St Michael's Abbey Press

Pike, E., and Curryer, C.E. (1938) *The Story of Walthamstow Hall*, London: Carey Press

Pike, E., Curryer, C.E., and Moore, U.K. (1973) *The Story of Walthamstow Hall*, London: Longmore Press

Pina-Cabral, J. de (1986) *Sons of Adam, Daughters of Eve*, London: Oxford University Press

Plum, D.A. and Dowell, G.B. (eds) (1961) *The Magnificent Enterprise*, Poughkeepsie, NY: Vassar College

Pontypool (1947) *Jubilee: The History of the County School for Girls, Pontypool*, Pontypool: The Griffin Press

Popkewitz, T.S, Tabachnick, B.R., and Wehlage, G. (1982) *The Myth of Educational Reform*, Madison: The University of Wisconsin Press

Pour-El, M.B. (1974) 'Mathematics', in R.B. Kundsin (ed.) *Women and Success*

Powell, R. and Clarke, J. (1976) 'A note on marginality', in S. Hall and T. Jefferson (eds) *Resistance through Rituals*, London: Hutchinson

Prandy, Ken (1986) 'Similarities of life style and occupations of women', in R.Crompton and M.Mann (eds) *Gender and Stratification*

Pryde, D. (1893) *Pleasant memories of a busy life*, Edinburgh: Blackwood

Punch, M. (1970) 'Who is the intellectual when he's at home?', *New Society*, 12 November: 859-62

Purvis, June (1985) 'Domestic subjects since 1870', in I.Goodson (ed.) *Social Histories of the Secondary Curriculum*, London: Falmer

Pyke, Richard (1957) *Edgehill College, 1884-1957*, London: Epworth Press

Raine, Kathleen (1975) *The Land Unknown*, London: Hamish Hamilton

Ramanathan, S. (1978) *The Novels of C.P.Snow*, London: Macmillan

Randall, G.F. (1969) *Rugby High School Golden Jubilee (1919- 1969)*, Rugby: George Over Ltd

Reader, W.J. (1967) *Professional Men*, London: Routledge

Reid, I. (1978) *Sociological Perspectives on School and Education*, London: Open Books

Reskin, B.F. (1978) 'Sex differentiation and the social organization of science', in Gaston (ed.) *The Sociology of Science*

Rice, Maria Alice (1947) *The Story of St. Mary's, Abbot's Bromley*, Shrewsbury: Wilding and Son

Richardson, C.J. (1977) *Contemporary Social Mobility*, London: Frances Pinter

Ridler, A. (1967) *Olive Willis and Downe House*, London: John Murray

Ridley, A.E. (1895) *Frances Mary Buss*, London: Longmans

Riesman, D. (1976) Preface to A.Miller (ed.) (1976) *A College in Dispersion*

Riesman, D. and Jencks, C. (1968) – see Jencks and Riesman

Robb, N.A. (1969) *A History of Richmond Lodge School, Belfast* Belfast: privately printed

Roberts, H.E. (1977) 'The exquisite slave', *Signs* 2, 3, pp. 554–69
Robertson, E. Arnot (1934) 'Sherborne', in G. Greene (ed.) *The Old School*
Robins, E. and Cohen, P. (1978) *Knuckle Sandwich*, Harmondsworth: Penguin
Robinson, P. (1981) *Sociological Perspectives on Education*, London: Routledge
Rogers, Annie, M.A.H. (1938) *Degrees by Degrees*, Oxford: The University Press
Rosenberg, Rosalind (1982) *Beyond Separate Spheres*, New Haven: Yale University Press
Rossi, Alice (1965) 'Barriers to the career choice of engineering, medicine, or science among American women', in J.A. Mattfield and C.G.van Aken (eds) *Women and the Scientific Profession*, Cambridge, Mass: MIT Press
Rossiter, Margaret W. (1982) *Women Scientists in America*, Baltimore: Johns Hopkins University Press
Roth, J. (1974) 'Professionalism', *Sociology of Work and Occupations*, 1, 1: 6-23
Rothblatt, S. (1968) *The Revolution of the Dons*, Cambridge: The University Press
Rover, C. (1970) *Love, Morals and the Feminists*, London: Routledge
Rowe, Mary (1977) 'The Saturn's Rings phenomenon', Proceedings of the Conference on Women's Leadership and Authority in the Health Professions, Santa Cruz, California, 19-21 June 1977
Ruzek, Sheryl B. (1978) *The Woman's Health Movement*, New York: Praeger
Sarup, M. (1983) *Marxism/Structuralism/Education*, London: Falmer
Sayers, D.L. (1946) *Unpopular Opinions*, London: Gollancz
Sayre, Anne (1975) *Rosalind Franklin and DNA*, New York: W.W. Norton & Co.
SCRE (1970) *A Study of Fifteen Year Olds*, London: The University Press
Scott, Anne Firor (1979) 'The ever widening circle', *History of Education Quarterly*, 19: 3-27
Scott, J. Finlay (1980) 'Sororities and the husband game', in J.P.Spradley and D.W.McCurdy (eds) *Conformity and Conflict*, Boston: Little, Brown & Co.
Scott, J.P. (1982) *The Upper Classes*, London: Macmillan
Scott, J.P. and Hughes, M.D. (1980) *The Anatomy of Scottish Capital*, London: Croom Helm
Scott, John P. (1979) *Corporations, Classes and Capitalism*, London: Hutchinson
Scribbins, K. (1977) 'Women in education', *Journal of Further and Higher Education*, 1, 3: 17-39
Scrimgeour, R.M. (ed.) (1950) *North London Collegiate School*, London: OUP
Sharp, E. (1926) *Hertha Ayrton*, London: Edward Arnold
Sharp, R. and Green, A.G. (1975) *Education and Social Control*, London: Routledge
Shaw, B. (1981) *Educational Practice and Sociology*, Oxford: Martin Robertson
Shaw, Jenny (1976) 'Finishing school', in D.L.Barker and S. Allen (eds) *Sexual Divisions and Society*, London: Tavistock
——— (1980) 'Education and the individual', in R.Deem (ed.) *Schooling for Women's Work*

# Bibliography

Shaw, M.G. (1932) *Redland High School*, Bristol: Arrowsmith
Sigsworth, E.M. and Wyke, T.J. (1972) 'A study of Victorian prostitution and venereal disease', in M.Vicinus (ed.) *Suffer and be Still*, Bloomington, Indiana: Indiana University Press
Silver, H. (1980) *Education and the Social Condition*, London: Methuen
Silverstone, R. and Ward, A. (eds) (1980) *Careers of Professional Women*, London: Croom Helm
Simon, B. (1974) *The Two Nations and the Educational Structure 1780-1870*, London: Lawrence and Wishart
—— (1985) *Does Education Matter?*, London: Lawrence and Wishart
Simpson, J. (1974) 'Meteorologist', in R.B.Kundsin (ed.) *Women and Success*
Sinclair, Andrew (1965) *The Better Half*, London: Cape
Sklar, Kathryn K. (1973) *Catharine Beecher*, New Haven: Yale University Press
Smith, B.O. and Meux, M. (1970) *A study of the logic of teaching*, Urbana, Illinois: University of Illinois
Smith, D. (1979) 'A sociology for women', in J.A. Sherman and E.T. Beck (eds) *The Prism of Sex*, Madison: University of Wisconsin Press
Smith, Lesley, S. (1978) 'Sexist assumptions and female delinquency', in S.Smart and B.Smart (eds) *Women, Sexuality and Social Control*, London: Routledge
Snow, C.P. (1934) *The Search*, London: Gollancz
—— (1951) *The Masters*, London: Macmillan
—— (1959) *The Two Cultures and the Scientific Revolution*, Cambridge: The University Press
—— (1960) *The Affair*, London: Macmillan (Penguin editions 1962, 1984)
—— (1971) *Public Affairs*, London: Macmillan
Snow, P.A. (1982) *Stranger and Brother*, London: Macmillan
Solomon, B.M. (1985) *In the Company of Educated Women*, New Haven: Yale University Press
Sorokin, P.A. (1929) *Social Mobility*, New York: Harper Bros.
Spencer, Anne and Podmore, David (eds) (1987) *In a Man's World*, London: Tavistock
Spender, D. (1982) *Invisible Women*, London: Routledge
Spring, Joel (1976) *Education and the rise of the corporate state*, Boston: Beacon Press
Stack, Violet, E. (ed.) (1963) *Oxford High School, GPDST, 1875-1960*, Oxford: privately printed
Stanworth, M. (1981) *Gender and Schooling*, London: WRRC
—— (1984) 'Women and class analysis', *Sociology*, 18, 2: 159-70
Star, S.L. (1985) 'Scientific work and uncertainty', *Social Studies of Science*, 15: 391-427
—— (1986) 'Triangulating clinical and basic research', *History of Science*, 24: 29-48
Stephen, B. (1927) *Emily Davies and Girton College*, London: Constable
—— (1933) *Girton College, 1869-1932*, Cambridge: The University Press
Stewart, A., Prandy, K., and Blackburn, R.M. (1980) *Social Stratification and Occupations*, London: Macmillan
Stimpson, C.R. (1974) 'Women at Bryn Mawr', *Change*, 6 April : 25-32
Stock, Phyllis (1978) *Better than Rubies*, New York
Sturge, H.W. (1932) Forward to M.G.Shaw (1932) *Redland High School*

Sturge, H.W. and Clarke, T. (1931) *The Mount School, York 1785-1814, 1831-1931*, London: Dent

Sutherland, M. (1985a) *Women who Teach in Universities*, Stoke on Trent: Trentham Books

—— (1985b) 'Whatever happened about Coeducation?', *British Journal of Educational Studies* xxxviii, 2, 155–63

Swann Report (1968) *The Flow into Employment of Scientists, Engineers and Technologists*, London: HMSO

Talbot, Marion (1910) *The Education of Women*, Chicago: The University Press

—— (1936) *More than Lore*, Chicago: The University Press

Talbot, Marion and Rosenberg, Lois K.M. (1931) *The History of the American Association of University Women 1881-1931*, Boston: Houghton Mifflin

Tepperman, Lorne (1975) *Social Mobility in Canada*, Toronto: McGraw Hill Ryerson

Tey, Josephine (1947) *Miss Pym Disposes*, London: Peter Davies

Thirkell, Angela (1937) *Summer Half*, London: Hamish Hamilton

Thomas, P. and Mungham, G. (1983) 'Solicitors and clients', in R.Dingwall and P.Lewis (eds) *Sociology of the Professions*

Thompson, Eleanor W. (1947) *Education for Ladies 1830-1860*, New York: Kings Cross Press

Thompson, M. (1982) 'A three-dimensional model', in M.Douglas (ed.) *In the Active Voice*

Thorp, Margaret F. (1956) *Neilson of Smith*, New York: Oxford University Press

Thrasher, F.M. (1927) *The Gang*, Chicago: The University Press

Townsend, S.B. (1959) 'The admission of women to the University of Georgia', *Georgia Historical Quarterly*, 43: 156-69

Treiman, D.J. (1977) *Occupational Prestige in Comparative Perspective*, New York: Academic Press

Tuke, M.J. (1939) *A History of Bedford College for Women*, London: OUP

Turner, Bryan (1974) *Equality for Some*, London: Ward Lock

Tylecote, Mabel (1941) *The Education of Women in Manchester University*, Manchester: The University Press

Tyree, A. and Treas, J. (1974) 'The occupational and marital mobility of women', *American Sociological Review* 39: 293–302

Vardy, W.I. (1928) *King Edward VI High School for Girls Birmingham 1883-1925*, London: Ernest Benn

Vicinus, M. (1985) *Independent Women*, London: Virago

Walford, G. (1983) 'Girls in boys' public schools', *British Journal of Sociology of Education*, 4, 1: 39-54

Walker, Michael (1983) 'Control and consciousness in the college', *British Education Research Journal*, 9, 2: 129-40

Wallis, Eileen (1972) *A Most Rare Vision: Otago Girl's High School*, Dunedin: McIndoe Ltd

Wallis, Roy (ed.) (1979) *On the Margins of Science*, Keele: Sociological Review Monograph no.27

Walters, R. (1974) *Primers for Prudery: Sexual Advice to Victorian America*, Englewood Cliffs: Prentice Hall

Ward, B.E. (1965) 'Varieties of the conscious model' in M. Banton (ed) *The relevance of models for social anthropology*, London: Tavistock

Waring, Mary (1979) *Social Pressures and Curriculum Innovations*, London: Methuen

# Bibliography

Watson, E. and Curtis Brown, B.C. (1923) *St. Felix School, Southwold 1897-1923*, London: Chelsea Pub. Co.

Weiner, R. (1974) 'Chemist and "eco-freak"', in R.B.Kundsin (ed.) *Women and Success*

Wells, J.H. (1985) 'Humberside goes neuter' in J. Whyte *et al.* (eds) *Girl – Friendly Schooling*

Westaway, K.M. (ed.) (1932) *History of Bedford High School*, Bedford: privately printed

Westergaard, J. and Resler, H. (1975) *Class in a Capitalist Society*, London: Heinemann

Wheeler-Bennett, Joan (1977) *Women at the Top*, London: Peter Owen

Whitcut, Janet (1976) *Edgbaston High School 1876-1976*, Birmingham: privately printed

White, Antonia (1934) 'Convent of the Sacred Heart', in G.Greene (ed.) *The Old School*, London: Cape

Whyte, J. (1985) *Girls into Science and Technology*, London: Routledge

Whyte, J. *et al.* (eds) (1985) *Girl Friendly Schooling*, London: Methuen

Wigfall, Valerie (1980) 'Architecture', in R.Silverstone and A.Ward (eds) *Careers of Professional Women*

Wilkins, K.S. (1979) *Women's Education in the United States*, Detroit: Gale Research Co.

Williams, G., Blackstone, T., and Metcalf, D. (1974) *The Academic Labour Market*, Amsterdam: Elsevier

Willis, P. (1977) *Learning to Labour*, Farnborough: Saxon House

Wilson, D. (1978) 'Sexual codes and conduct', in C. Smart and B. Smart (eds) *Women, Sexuality and Social Control*, London: Routledge

Wilson, Elizabeth (1980) *Only Halfway to Paradise*, London: Tavistock

Wober, M. (1971) *English Girls' Boarding School*, London: Allen Lane

Wolcott, H. (1973) *The Man in the Principal's Office*, New York: Holt, Rinehart and Winston

Wolpe, A.M. (1974) 'The official ideology of education for girls', in M.Flude and J.Ahier (eds) *Educability, Schools and Ideology*, London: Croom Helm

Woods, L.R. (1904) *The Girls' High School, Boston 1852-1982*, Boston: Riverside Press

Woody, T. (1929) *A History of Women's Education in the United States*, 2 vols (reprinted 1966), New York: Octagon Books

Wynne, Brian (1979) 'Barkla's Ph.D students and the J – phenomenon', in R.Wallis (ed.) *On the Margins of Science*

Young, M.F.D. (ed.) (1971) *Knowledge and Control*, London: Collier-Macmillan

Zimmerman, J.G. (1979) 'Daughters of Main Street', in M.Kelley (ed.) *Woman's Being, Woman's Place*

Zimmern, Alice (1898) *The Renaissance of Girls Education in England*, London: Innes

Zouche, Dorothy E. de (1955) *Roedean School 1885-1955*, Brighton: Dolphin Press

Zuckerman, Harriet (1977) *Scientific Elite: Nobel Laureates in the United States*, New York: The Free Press

# Author Index

# Subject Index

# Subject Index

free love, vs celibacy as liberation for women 149
French sociology, perceived difficulty of 11–12
Freudianism, and the educated spinster 148–9, 151–3
friendship groups, among adult men 223; at 'St Luke's' school 49–60; of male and female adolescents 16–17
functionalism, Leach on sexual division of labour 136–9; theory of professions 241–2, 243–4, 245

Georgia, University of 123–4
Germany, doctorates refused to women 125
Girls into Science and Technology (GIST) 206, 210
Girls' Public Day School Company 99
Girls' Public Day School Trust 91, 92, 94, 120
girls' schools, chaperonage 75–6, 79, 179–80; curricula 105–108; dress rules 80–89, 177–81; financing of 70–71; friendship groups 49–60; in post-war era 165–8; lesbianism 158–9; rules 53, 55, 73–101, 177–81; science education 115–23, 188–90 see also boarding schools for girls, day schools for girls, private girls' schools, religious schools for girls
Girton College, Cambridge 77, 82, 85, 88, 108, 109–10, 144, 157, 163
Glasgow, Laurel Bank School 116; Park School 117
governesses 66–7, 68–9, 92, 143
graduates, women, marriages of 144–5, 147
Grant, Zilpath 111
Graves, Z.C. 111
Greek and Latin see classics
grid/group see group/grid analysis
Grimké sisters 139, 140
Grinnell College 125–6
Groucher College 79
group/grid analysis 37–45; applied to classics/science in curriculum 129; applied to old and new middle class 267; applied to social stratification researchers 216–19, 230
Guy Mannering Middle School 179
gymnastics, dress rules for schoolgirls 82–5, 178

habitus 29–32; of professions 112, 212, 247, 251–3; of scientific research 256, 261; of university teaching 197
Hadow report (1926) 166, 190, 191
Hall, G. Stanley 152
Hammond, Barbara and J.L. 145
Harvard University 127, 157
Haslett, Caroline 128
headteachers, women 173–4
Hearst, Phoebe 127

hedonism, post World War I, and the educated spinster 148
higher education, histories of institutions 290; see also teacher training colleges, universities
history of education, research on 281–4
Hollingworth, Leta Stetter 152
Holtby, Winifred 46, 154, 166, 181, 184
Homerton College 174
honorific capital 25–6
Howard University 126
Hunter College High School 126

indeterminate knowledge, of occupations and professions 244, 247, 251–3, 256; of professional education 29–30
Industrial Fund for the Advancement of Scientific Education in Schools (IFASES) 121, 187, 188–90, 192, 293–5
Institute of Community Studies 223
Institute of Mechanical Engineers 188
institutions, classified by group/grid 37–41
intelligentsia see new middle class
invisible pedagogy 34–6
Ipswich, Northgate Grammar School for Girls 71
Ireland, Republic of, girls' school histories 285

Kenealy, Arabella 132, 134
King Edward VI High School for Girls, Birmingham 75, 118
King's College, London 258

laboratories, in girls' schools 115–16, 191–2
Lady Margaret Hall, Oxford 77, 81, 87–8, 108, 110, 146
Latin and Greek see classics
lawyers, women 212–13
Leach, Edmund 10, 13, 136–9
learned disciplines, group/grid concept applied to 39–40
learned scientific societies, women's participation in 125, 127–8
lecturers, women, in teacher training colleges 174–6; in universities 196–202
legal profession, women in 212–13
lesbianism 148–9, 151, 158–9
Lewes, George Henry 157
literature, post-1945, neglect of education of women 182–5
London University, examinations 108–109; see also Bedford College, King's College, Queen's College, Royal Holloway College
Lumsden, Louisa 150
Lyon, Mary 90, 111

McClintock, Barbara 256
Macdonald, Evelyn 119–20
McKeen, Philena and Phebe 107, 122
Manchester University 77–8
marital mobility 231–5

# Subject Index

professions, feminization of 266; group/grid concept applied to 38; sociology of 207–208, 238–47; women within (1945-55) 195–215 *see also* architects, doctors, lawyers, lecturers, scientists

Project on Occupational Cognition (POOC) 221, 225–7, 230

prostitutes 77, 78

Pryde, David 95

public schools, boys', teacher training for 30–31

publications, academic, by women lecturers 198–201; by women scientists 254, 255, 258–60

Quakers 70, 100–101

Queen's College, London 91, 118

radical movements, and women's education pioneers 156–8

Ramsey, Agnata Frances 144–5

Redland High School for Girls, Bristol 69, 117–18

religious organizations, classification of 37–8

religious schools for girls 98–101

Richards, Ellen Swallow 124, 125

Ritter, Mary Bennett 127

Robbins report 166

Roedean School 91, 146

Roman Catholics *see* Catholics

Royal Holloway College, London 78

Royal School for Daughters of the Army 99–100, 120–21

Rugby Girls' High School 116

rules, school, attitudes of schoolgirls to 53, 55; in girls' schools 73–101, 177–81

Russell, Dora 153, 154

Sacred Heart convents 159

St Anne's College, Oxford 80, 110

St Leonard's School 91

'St Luke's' school 6, 7, 41–2, 47–61

'Saturn's rings' 212, 252–61

Sayers, Dorothy L. 46, 153, 154, 185

school honours, won by elite schoolgirls 56–7

schools *see* co-education, comprehensive schools, girls' schools, public schools, secondary modern schools

science, public/private faces of 246–7; universality and disinterestedness of 241–2

science education, for girls and women 115–31, 186–92, 266; neglected by sociology of science 208–209

Science Masters' Association (SMA) 187, 188

Science research and employment, women in 124–8, 202–12

science teaching in universities, by women 202

scientists, dispute with clergy in 19th century 130; group/grid analysis applied to 43–4 women 249–50, 252–61

Scotland, co-education 168, 169; girls' school histories 284

Scottish Mental Survey 221, 222, 224

Scottish Mobility Study (SMS) 221, 222, 224, 234

secondary modern schools 168–9

'semi-professions' 195, 212, 233, 239, 240

'separatist' pioneers of women's education 105–14, 139–41, 250

Sex Discrimination Act (1975) 192, 251

Sex Disqualification (Removal) Act (1919) 212, 251

sex inequalities, neglected in sociology of education textbooks 273–6

sex roles, separation of 136–9

sexual attitudes, of male and female adolescents 17–18, 44–5

sexual relations, and pollution beliefs 23

sexuality, female, and women's education 148–55, 151, 158–9

Sherborne School for Girls 159

Shrewsbury High School for Girls 83, 86, 118

Sidgwick, Henry 106, 109

single men and women, social mobility 232–5

single-parent households 229

Smith College 81, 84, 111, 112, 123, 157

smoking, by women 127–8, 155

Snow, C.P. 202–205

social capital 46–7

social class, cultural capital and 26–8; curriculum debate and 104–105; distinctions at girls' schools 89–98

Social Class I, professions of 238–47; recruitment to 235–7

social mobility, of women 231–7

social scientists, neglect of women 192–4

social stratification 216–37

social systems, classified by group/grid 37–41

Society of Friends 70, 100–101

sociology of education 163–4; and social stratification 217–18, 228, 237; and sociology of professions 238, 240; and structuralism 266–8; impact of feminism on 269–76; textbooks analysed 273–6

sociology of science 206–11

Somerville College, Oxford 108, 110, 156

Southwold, St Felix School 83

spinsters, social mobility 232–5

sports, dress rules for schoolgirls 82–5, 178; honours won by schoolgirls 57

'status professions' 248

stratification, social 216–37

Streatham Hill School 92

Streatham Secondary School for Girls 171

structuralism, applied to sociology of education 1–4, 8–9, 10–12, 32, 266–8